NEIL M. GUNN

SELECTED LETTERS

NEIL M. GUNN

SELECTED LETTERS

Edited by J. B. Pick

POLYGON
Edinburgh

First published in Great Britain in 1987 by Polygon
48, Pleasance, Edinburgh EH8 9TJ

The publisher acknowledges subsidy from the
Scottish Arts Council towards the publication of
this volume.

Typeset by Hewer Text Composition Services, Edinburgh.
Printed and bound by Billings, Worcester.

ISBN 0 948 27544 8

CONTENTS

CONTENTS

CONTENTS

such uncertain conditions. Pity. But there it is. It's now a year since my operation & I had hoped to be picking up strength a bit more. But enough of these disgusting topics. Meanwhile I'm scheming how to start a bed of cress in greenhouse, but Daisy always seems to know my inner intentions & move ahead. When I sort of drift away, I'm followed. It's a hard life. A week ago two BBC youths arrived with recording car. They were doing a programme on Edwin Muir. I hadn't two ideas in my head & they weren't on speaking terms — the ideas. They — at least the

FOREWORD

This selection was made from something like 1,000 letters; even so there are gaps in the record: We have no letters to Neil's brother John, perhaps his closest friend over a lifetime; Keith Henderson burned all his papers on the death of his wife; George Malcolm Thomson destroyed his when moving house; I could not trace letters to John Macnair Reid or Dr Peter John Macleod; and so on. But we are left with riches enough. Some letters are included for their biographical information; some for the ideas they contain; some for their literary advice or comment; some for the light they shed on Gunn's own books; some because they reveal character or situation; some for their political interest; some for their stories; some for their human warmth; some for the sheer fun of it. Letters addressed to the editor have occasionally been used as bridging passages to supply news of events when no others were available for the purpose.

All are printed in chronological order; they are dated exactly as Neil Gunn dated them, and if undated a guessed-at date is shown in brackets. I would have preferred to give the whole letter in every case, but space is so limited that it seemed best to reduce length and ensure as much variety as possible. Editorial excisions are indicated by dots contained in brackets (. . .). Dots without brackets are Gunn's own. Some of his spelling and syntax were eccentric in letters written in haste. I have retained the eccentricities, "sic" in the text indicating that the inaccuracy or eccentricity was Gunn's own. I have, however, tidied up small inconsistencies – in the same letter Neil might at one time indicate a book title with quotations marks and at another type it in capitals. I have placed them all in italics.

If the collection is read through from start to finish it both paints a picture and tells a story with a beginning, a middle and an end. Each letter also has a value of its own.

I am deeply grateful to the National Library of Scotland for permission to publish material in their possession, and to Stanley Simpson, Assistant Keeper of Manuscripts, for his unfailing courtesy and helpfulness. Many letters are drawn from the Neil Gunn Deposit 209, with its thirty-two boxes; and from the following Accessions: George Blake (Acc.4989); George Bruce (Acc.6154); Geoffrey Faber (Acc.5412); Andrew Dewar Gibb (Deposit 217, Box 1); Lewis Grassic Gibbon (Acc.7900, Boxes 8–9); Ian Grimble (Acc.5416); Francis Russell Hart (Acc.7231); David MacEwen (Acc.6117); Agnes Mure Mackenzie (MSS.9222); F. Marian McNeill (Accs.5453, 5804); Duncan McNeill (Acc.6489); Naomi Mitchison (Accs.5813, 5869); Alexander Reid (Acc.8348, Box 19); Nan Shepherd (Accs.5449, 6118); Douglas Young (Acc.6419).

There are letters to C. M. Grieve in Edinburgh University Library; to Ian Grimble in the Library of Balliol Gollege, Oxford; and many of those to the following are in the possession of the recipient or his or her executors: George Blake, James Bridie, P. H. Butter, Stewart Conn, William McCance, John MacCormick, Margaret MacEwen, Joseph Macleod, Ronald Mavor, William Montgomerie, Douglas Muhr, J. B. Pick. I am indebted, therefore, to Sheila Clouston (Nan Shepherd); Mrs. Ellie Blake (George Blake); George Bruce; P. H. Butter; Messrs. Jonathan Cape; Stewart Conn; Messrs. Faber & Faber; Michael Grieve (C. M. Grieve); Ian Grimble; Messrs. Hodder and Stoughton; Long John International (John Mackie); H.M. Customs and Excise; Margaret McCance (William McCance); Margaret MacCormick (John MacCormick); David MacEwen; Gertrude McKillop (Ian McKillop); Joseph Macleod; Elizabeth R. McNeill (Marian and Duncan McNeill); Elspeth McWilliam (Andrew Dewar Gibb); Rhea Martin (Lewis Grassic Gibbon); Ronald Mavor (James Bridie); Naomi Mitchison; William Montgomerie; the Duke of Montrose; Mary Muhr (Douglas Muhr); Genevieve Reid (Alexander Reid); G. Ross Roy; R. B. Simpson (Agnes Mure Mackenzie); George Malcolm Thomson; Maurice Walsh; and Hella Young (Douglas Young), for their co-operation.

The book could not have been produced without the permission and support of the Gunn Estate, and I would like to thank Dairmid Gunn for every kind of assistance and advice. Every kind of assistance and advice was also given generously by Margaret MacEwen and Francis Russell Hart. John Burns kindly read through the text and made valuable suggestions.

J. B. Pick

INTRODUCTION

Literary men often write dull letters: either they have exhausted their creative impulse in books and have no life left for their friends, or they are too conscious of style, effect and the opinions of others (including an imagined posterity) to be spontaneous. Neil Gunn is an exception.

Some of his letters he typed and of some he kept copies. In these he is defending himself against the world. They are letters to publishers responding to criticism or fighting his business corner; letters persuading political colleagues to a particular course of action; letters replying to attacks on himself or his books; letters written with a formal purpose; or letters arguing against a view he thought false, unjust or dangerous.

But for the most part his correspondence was written swiftly and spontaneously in a flowing, cursive hand, the words twining in Celtic fashion round the margins of the page and ending with a modest signature in a corner when space ran out. In these letters you do not look for carefully modulated periods, syntactical precision or thoughts protected against misunderstanding by definitions and caveats. They are rich in eloquence, humour and warmth, like the conversation for which they were an inadequate substitute – inadequate because as a rule he held himself back in letters from fully developing an argument or following a hare wherever it led him, breaking off with a "But enough", or "We'll leave that till we meet", for he preferred to discuss a question in depth when face to face, with evening running into night and a dram at his elbow (and at yours). Then he could judge your reactions with generous detachment and feel the temper of your mind. Books too were in the final analysis a substitute for companionship – as he said once, "Perhaps all literature does is give you a few friends". It certainly gave him a great many.

To these friends he was easy, helpful and courteous, writing with full attention to their personal needs and peculiarities of taste and vision. It is because of this attention that the word "spontaneous" needs qualification and explanation. Certainly he wrote his letters swiftly and fluently without concern for their status as "literature", and he trusted you to respond in the same way, with honesty and goodwill. But he was acutely aware of what it was necessary in the circumstances to say, of what it would be wise not to say, and how what must be said should be phrased in order to avoid inaccurate movements of the receiving mind. He wrote as a skilled player plays his game, moving with speed and grace to the right place at the right time. The mature Neil Gunn was never clumsy.

The mature Gunn, too, like the boy before him, was careful to retain within his mind a secret place to which no one was allowed to penetrate. As he writes in *The Atom of Delight*, "there is always the inner self that is not going to be touched." He guarded his emotions because he knew their strength and violence. His youthful moods of depression and bitterness – reflected in his early novels and short stories – taught him to conceal his sensitivities and at last to detach himself from them until he could accept with apparent equanimity the unpleasant manifestations of others.

The achievement was not easy. An example of his difficulties is the 1932 letter to William McCance, the painter, about the reception given to *The Lost Glen*: "I have just had a new novel published which the English reviewers . . . have damned to the point of farce. I was feeling pretty sick of the whole rotten writing business and fled for a few final days to the wilds where I fished in some of the loneliest glens in our wild north. . . ." This was his second book, written immediately after *The Grey Coast* but rejected by six publishers between 1926 and 1929; after serialisation in *The Scots Magazine* it lay in a drawer until the success of *Morning Tide*. George Blake, a director of Porpoise Press, wrote to warn him: "Whatever you write and publish now is of vast importance. You will be judged by a large and rather jealous public . . . and they will not be content with less than your best." But Gunn went forward with the book. It in fact received balanced appraisals in *The Spectator*, *The New Statesman*, and *The Times Literary Supplement*, but the adverse comments were the ones he remembered.

Not only did he feel criticism of *The Lost Glen* to be criticism of the Highland people, their situation and their history, but he may have suspected (although he would not admit it) that the book was deeply flawed, and that the flaws were due to unresolved turmoil in his own nature. Frank Morley of Faber and Faber wrote to Blake with acute, uneasy perception: "*The Lost Glen* is big with meaning and a blasted harassing book. I can tell you this right now that if Gunn isn't haunted and harassed and touchy as hell about it he's not human. I think it came from right under his heart, so you be careful. . . . The book bears signs of secret perturbations. When you're not quite sure you try all the harder to seem sure, and that's happening in this book. *The Lost Glen* is Gunn's *Hamlet*."

To reveal these secret perturbations in the market place was to put his pride in jeopardy, and Gunn's sense of intrusion was intolerable to him.

In fact he usually reacted adversely to criticism, and would not admit failure. The early letters to publishers Jonathan Cape and Hodder and Stoughton show his immediate response to disapproval: an effort at refutation, followed by a pragmatic offer of concessions. Throughout his life he complained about reviewers, mainly on the grounds that they dealt in surface praise or blame without concerning themselves with a book's spiritual essence and meaning.

Again, when the faults of his play, *Second Sight* were identified with helpful acuteness by James Bridie, he converted play into novel with the faults unpurged; when another play proved a failure he persisted with plans for its revival long after success with novels made plays unnecessary. He responded strongly whenever Faber had doubts about a book, meeting their difficulties with patience but always insisting on publication with only minor adjustments.

He was in the habit of sending a typescript to one or two friends before its submission to a publisher, but this was not to invite criticism so much as to obtain a sense of how their minds responded; if he altered anything it was as an act of courtesy. He was quite sure of his "rightness" because, as he wrote to Francis Hart, he "never had to wonder where next to go or what was to happen, for I was 'told', if you can follow. And often the telling astonished me." In the same letter he refers to the operations of "Mr. Balance", ". . . this internal thing that did the telling would stand no nonsense. It kept a continuous rein as it were on my *way*wardness, in the interest of what I could see it believed in as balance." Neil Gunn eventually developed in himself, by following this inner guidance, an ability to avoid in life the display of negative emotion and to balance light with darkness in literature.

There is more self-revelation about this movement of the spirit in his fiction than there is in the letters, for the writer of fiction often has the curious delusion that since he does his work in private, it somehow remains so; the sudden intrusion of a reader comes as a shock. In May 1940 Nan Shepherd wrote this uncomfortably perceptive letter about *Wild Geese Overhead* and *Second Sight*: "To apprehend things – walking on a hill, seeing the light change, the mist, the dark, being aware, using the whole of one's body to instruct the spirit – yes, that is a secret life one has and knows that others have. But to be able to share it, in and through words – that is what frightens me. . . . It dissolves one's being, I am no longer myself but a part of a life beyond myself when I read pages which are so much an expression of myself. You can take processes of being – no, that's too formal a word – states is too static, this is something that moves – *movements* I suppose is best – you take movements of being and translate them out of themselves into words; that seems to me a gift of a very high order."

Gunn responded: "You came uncannily at the heart of the matter and . . . when you hesitated at the word *movements* . . . then it is as if you were surprising me in my very lair. Where, to put it mildly, I hardly expected to see you – or anyone else." The words "uncannily" and "lair" are sharply revealing.

As well as charting the darknesses and difficulties of Gunn's young manhood the books chart the growth into mature balance of a writer who came to deal with the most profound questions of his time. It was the exploration through fiction of his problems and turmoils which enabled him to ensure that pride ceased to be the rider and became the horse. And this was done by concentrating not on himself but on the world outside.

Neil Miller Gunn was born in Caithness in 1891, the son of a well-respected fishing skipper in Dunbeath. At the age of thirteen he was sent to stay with a married sister in Galloway and from there passed the Civil Service entrance examination and found himself a clerk first in London and then in Edinburgh. At nineteen he was appointed an officer of Customs and Excise and spent some fruitful years travelling throughout the Highlands "on supply". In 1921 he married Jessie Frew (known as Daisy) and after some vicissitudes and the still-birth of a child, they attained gradually to a relationship of remarkable depth and fullness. The importance of Daisy's influence in his life is shown by the fact that she is referred to in almost every letter he wrote to his closest friends. From 1923 until 1937 – when he resigned to write full time – Gunn was "officer attached" to an

Inverness distillery. It is not surprising that we have few letters from that early period. (The first one in this book is dated 1925.) Human vanity makes it inevitable that letters from the famous are kept when others are lost, and it was 1926 before Gunn published his first book, and 1930 before he gained notable success.

His closest friends in the Excise service were Stanley Hill and Maurice Walsh; but there was no need to correspond with Maurice – until he returned to his native Ireland in 1922 – for he was a constant companion, while Stanley Hill lived just down the road. The correspondence with Maurice after 1922 shows as well as warm comradeship Gunn's willingness to supply plots and advice and to accept some payment as reward.

As his writing career developed he came to know most Scottish writers of his day – C. M. Grieve (Hugh MacDiarmid), Compton Mackenzie, James Bridie, Edwin Muir, Eric Linklater, George Blake, Naomi Mitchison, Nan Shepherd and others. The relationship with Grieve was a checkered one. In the 1920s when virtually the only "Highland" novelist of literary reputation was Neil Munro, *The Grey Coast* came as a portent. Grieve, who was producing a series of short-lived literary periodicals, greeted the book with enthusiasm and the relationship progressed through mutual encouragement. Grieve has written: "In those days of the twenties, when the ideas of the Scottish Literary Renaissance were first being canvassed, there was no one in Scotland with whom I was in closer touch." Differences began when Grieve championed Fionn MacColla as *the* Highland novelist, and then insisted that "no fiction whatever matters a damn in relation to Scotland while any poem whatever above a very low plane matters a great deal," and went on to imply that personal loyalties must be subordinated to his own over-riding sense of mission. Gunn was annoyed and bewildered: to him personal loyalties were paramount. He wrote in 1932: "You say your remark does not involve 'personal considerations of any kind'. Finally, as you know, it does not matter a damn whether it does involve such considerations or not (and such direct statements written deliberately for *public* consumption are hardly as impersonal as moonshine); but it does matter whether what you say is true or not." Letters containing a fair amount of controversy continued for a number of years, but a drifting apart was inevitable. It is worth noting, however, that Gunn had a hand in obtaining Grieve's Civil List pension, and contributed to the fund used to modernise Grieve's cottage in the early sixties, and that Grieve was one of those who wrote to Neil commiserating with him on the death of his wife Daisy in 1963.

During the thirties Gunn was among the leaders of Scottish Nationalist politics, and much in demand as a negotiator arguing the case for a responsible pragmatism and trying to bring warring factions into balance if not unity. The series of letters to John MacCormick, Professor Andrew Dewar Gibb and T. H. Gibson show his approach and method. He insisted that nationalists should work together on the basis of a shared overall aim rather than spend their time and energy in disputes about details of policy.

But by 1936, as the letter to MacCormick dated 2 July makes clear, he was no longer sanguine about electoral success and had come to realise that Trade Unionists and Labour sympathisers regarded jobs and bread-and-butter as more important than Scottish independence. "In short, we are driven back upon . . . an economic programme. And I am convinced that any patchwork programme . . . is not of the slightest use." He is facing the classic dilemma that nationalists may be entirely diverse in political background and principle yet at some point argument about policy differences becomes unavoidable. He even goes on to consider the possibility of working through the Westminster parties – which he had always repudiated – or turning the organisation into an educational or propagandist body.

The National Party of Scotland had been formed in 1928 as the result of an amalgamation between two other groups. In 1932 the Duke of Montrose, Sir Alexander MacEwen and Andrew Dewar Gibb were involved in setting up the more conservative Scottish Party, and in 1933 the Scottish Party decided to contest the Kilmarnock by-election despite the fact that the National Party had already announced a similar intention. Gunn argued the National Party case cogently and forcefully in a number of letters to Dewar Gibb and there seems little doubt that it was his intervention, based on a close association with Sir Alexander MacEwen on the one side and John MacCormick at National Party Headquarters on the other, which proved instrumental in resolving the Kilmarnock dispute, and then in bringing the two organisations together to form the Scottish National Party.

But by the late thirties Gunn was too busy ensuring his livelihood as a professional writer to continue a close involvement with the day-to-day working of the SNP. The 1942 schism between the backers of Douglas Young and those of John MacCormick over support for the war effort brought further disillusionment. Gunn states his position in a letter to Douglas Young dated 10 June: "You must understand that it's difficult for me to follow remarks you have made about MacCormick and those who may now think with him, because for years we worked together in the north . . . where the fine and tireless work MacCormick put in was very clear to me. In my view, the amount the whole movement owes to him can hardly be exceeded, indeed equalled. . . ." He makes plain his attitude to the War in a letter to MacCormick dated 4 December, 1939: "The forces of the world seem to be slowly aligning themselves into two groups: those who wish to retain man's freedom to express whatever integrity may be in him and those who don't. This freedom of expression is to me supremely important, and I am prepared to align myself and fight, accordingly . . . On this issue I am prepared to take a stand for or against any country, my own included." He refused, however, to join the all-party Scottish Convention, remained on good terms with Young himself, and subscribed until the end to Party funds.

This, of course, is only half the story. Even while strongly advocating the Nationalist case he was at one time telling Margaret MacEwen that he was an individualist, and at another an anarchist of the Kropotkin school. Yet in a 1933 letter to C. M. Grieve he sounds for a sentence or two oddly like a scientific authoritarian. During the 1940s he was engaged in a long-running epistolary argument with Naomi Mitchison in which he claimed to be a socialist while repudiating her collectivist position.

In one letter to Margaret (1938) he writes: "I was always an anarchist; and so far as politics are concerned, I am consistently haunted by the hard Scots feeling that they must be kept in their place, their real concern being the providing of the animal necessities of food, shelter and clothing. After that, three cheers for the intensest form of individualism." But of course politics will not consent to remain "in their place" – they seek constantly to dominate the whole of life. For several years they certainly dominated his own, and not to his benefit. His reflections on the growth of totalitarianism, with its emphasis on mind-control and control of the human spirit led him to write *The Green Isle of the Great Deep* (1944).

In a 1943 letter to Joseph Macleod, Gunn says: "At the time of the Stalin-Trotsky schism, I naturally supported Stalin (in argument, at least!) for the perhaps naive reason that I also supported Scotland as a country which had shown the power to order her own affairs. I do indeed think that Stalin, in his national stand . . . was dead right . . ." But "the amazing trial and execution of the Old Guard, the attack on

Finland, and so on, had a sort of hopeless air from a distance. A book like Louis Fischer's *Men and Politics* was not exactly reassuring. And the cry that the party is everything, the individual nothing was tending even here to become suspiciously like one of the slogans of a religious crusade – after the 'Jesus and no quarter' of our own Covenanters."

Whether Gunn could have resolved all these ambiguities and contradictions is not demonstrated in the letters. But it may be helpful to point to two of his basic beliefs: a belief in the natural goodness of man, and a belief in the democratic, classless structure of the old Highland community, which although close-knit produced people of marked individuality. To decide whether this is an accurate or an idealised version of the old Highland community would involve too long a discussion, but it is a view based on Gunn's recollections of his childhood, and carefully formulated in *The Serpent* – the book which began his argument with Naomi Mitchison. In a letter to Gene Pick (dated 24 June, 1952) about *Bloodhunt* he writes: "I was very interested, too, in your query about the possible Christian infiltration into Sandy's make-up . . . Sandy was for me *the* character and if he fails the whole book is a bit futile. I suppose I must have been trying, however unconsciously – or half – to get a glimpse of that peculiar quality that we have . . . called "goodness" . . . It seemed to me finally that it is not a specially Christian quality, not of any particular creed, but, rather literally, primordial. It probably had a very long innings in paleolithic times, the age of the hunters. It is at the root of the myth or archaic heritage (forgotten memory, so to speak!) that makes even respectable anthropologists babble o' the Golden Age." (Keith Henderson reports arguing frequently with Neil on the subject of the Golden Age, pointing out to him that it had "no possible date".) In essence what Gunn wanted was an independent Scotland wherein each individual would have responsibility and influence but no one would have the power to impose his concepts on others. But he also prided himself on being "a simple realist", aware that energy must be expended only where something practical can be achieved.

His intuitive belief in the primordial goodness of man led him to philosophies which can accommodate this view, particularly the illuminations of Lao Tze, Chwang Tzu, Mencius, and of Zen, with its insistence that enlightenment is each man's realisation of his essential and permanent nature. He first encountered Zen in 1953, not as something new but as something familiar which he recognised. As he

says in a letter (1964) to Francis Hart: "When I began reading about
Zen, I seemed to know a lot about it and to have used it in my writings
from the beginning!" And indeed there is as much of it in *Highland
River* (1937) as there is in his last book, *The Atom of Delight* (1956),
where it is specifically mentioned.

As years went by other writers turned to him for help and advice,
and he sought out those who had written perceptively about his
books. An extract from a 1944 letter to Margaret MacEwen about a
play of Douglas Muhr's shows his approach and the nature of his
concern: "It's extremely difficult and all I can do is encourage him.
Others send me their stuff and blunt criticism (which is not
necessarily a good kind) affects the recipient. So there you are! We
pretend to like criticism, but do we? There is, however, a way of it
that may help a fellow to another shot – but only if one thinks he's
capable of it. I am prepared to give Douglas the benefit of the doubt."
The character, intentions and foibles of each individual addressed are
taken scrupulously into account until such time as Gunn decides the
recipient is capable of concentrating on the task in hand rather than
upon his own feelings.

My own case is probably the best documented in this respect. Neil
gives a great deal of practical advice, but I have not included passages
of detailed criticism – "I ringed one sentence. Read the sentence
before it and then the sentence after it, and you'll find the tension
mounts; put back the ringed sentence and the tension slackens" –
because these are meaningless without the text. I have tried, however,
to show his indefatigable helpfulness. He writes in 1949: "Before I
may have been conscious of encouraging you, but now I throw you
over, and if you sink, it's your own dam fault . . ." He did not do so,
all the same, and in 1959 settles down to deal with the problems at the
deepest level of seriousness: "Now if you were really prepared to
work in that mood, taking time, no haste, at something you deeply
cared to do, something big and difficult because it would stretch your
faculties to the utmost in intellectual and emotional range, I am
prepared to tell you what you should do." And a few weeks later:
"You must take it from me that in your working life the opportunity
has now come. This is *it* . . . true realisation lies in your next book, so I
must talk to you not about the book itself at the moment but your
approach to it." He goes on to state the "chief fault" which blocks
achievement. "It's impatience", the effects of which "worm their
way down through upper frustrations to chill the vital warmth in
which creation takes place." This is more than practical criticism,

it is the experience of a lifetime applied to the development of an individual. In 1962 he writes: "I do wish you would get a full novel on the go. It would help *me* somehow if you pulled it off and became famous . . ." That this did not happen was a disappointment which he accepted philosophically.

Towards the end of his writing career Gunn grew increasingly aware that his efforts to search out the source of spiritual light were regarded by his critics as mystification, that his publishers were less enthusiastic about his work the more exploratory it became, and, in short, that he was no longer fashionable. After *The Atom of Delight*, which was virtually ignored, he wrote no more books and his letters reflect his dissatisfaction with the literary trends of the day. This influenced his attitude to the work of his friends. He writes to Naomi Mitchison: "If I were to do another book it would be even noticed less and might embarrass my publishers, so why do it. So I'm doing naught. And I don't say this in any critical or bitter spirit. That's the way things are. If one's work is running counter to the prevailing current, one mustn't expect much." He tells Alexander Reid: "*The Atom of Delight* was a flop . . . Even novels like *The Well at the World's End* and *The Other Landscape* didn't fare much better. And here I find you at the same kind of well! So forgive my uncertainty." Finally, he says to Pick: "They (articles in *The Saltire Review*) would never have been published of course if it weren't for my name in the Scottish field and the editor's belief that I had written some novels . . . So when your imagination boggles at the publication of this work of yours – well, I understand. We are both bogglers."

But the revival of interest in his books among academic critics overseas gave him renewed hope and vigour. He was delighted with the understanding of his work shown by Kurt Wittig. He wrote to Francis Hart with painstaking helpfulness about the genesis and meaning of his novels, and explained to Professor Nakamura of Tokyo the intricacies of Highland culture. The warm perceptiveness of Hart's concern with the books did more than concentrate his mind; it gave him a new lease of life at a time when he was ill and lonely after the death of his wife: "I suddenly had the feeling I'd like to . . . tell Rus about magic. Now the feeling was like that which I used to get sometimes when writing a book, long long ago – an eager pleasant feeling, at a little distance (and yet of the inner essence) in a magical light but which I had completely forgotten, so that I suddenly realised: yes, that's what made me engage in this queer writing traffic. . . ."

And all the time he was maintaining a correspondence with old friends like Maurice Walsh, Nan Shepherd, Keith Henderson and Naomi Mitchison. He had a marvellous intuitive sense of how and when to say "Goodbye". He wrote to Maurice in 1964 just a few weeks before his friend's death: "Whatever you may privately think about the Fates and the bitterness they can inflict upon us, still and on, and in their teeth if you like, man has created a golden time of his own. You and I had a share of such a time and those who were near us helped to sustain it, bless them for ever more." To Nan Shepherd he wrote in 1970: "In my search I came across some of your old letters. Marvellous . . . You're like a lovely day on the hills." To Naomi Mitchison in 1971: "How pleasant to get your distinguished card, and inevitably to come on two lines that summed me up:

> Do not care, do not be anxious,
> Life goes as it must";

and finally to the Harts on 14 September, 1972: "Dear me, that I should have to be silent. Fare thee both well. Neil."

What all these letters have in common is a quality of mind it is hard to describe but obvious to everyone who reads with sympathy. Its chief ingredient is a subtle, playful and joyous humour which becomes in the later letters all-pervasive. Indeed I would suggest that in any difficulty a reader may have with interpretation, a good rule might be: when in doubt assume the intention to be humorous. Humour is combined with courtesy, penetration and awareness – above all, awareness. Gunn is aware of everything – of the recipient of his letter, of his own motives and intentions, of the grace and beauty and power of the world beyond his window, and of the balance between darkness and light, so that despite the sadness and pain often seen at the end, we are left with a feeling of hope and confidence, with the sense that if a man is true to his own insights and has the courage to follow them he won't go far wrong. And the measure of Gunn's wisdom is that his awareness becomes a play of immediate perception, a form of spontaneity; even when sapped by illness and grief (he wrote in one letter about Daisy, "I'd destroy all I ever made for one glimpse of her sitting out on the patio in front of me, weeding"), there is always a gaiety and gallantry which bring with them a feeling like that engendered by one of those Highland days when light chases shadow over hills and water and a golden mystery moves in the mind.

ONE

THE BEGINNING WRITER

1925 to 1937

Neil Gunn began writing short stories in the early twenties. His first novel, *The Grey Coast*, was written upon his return to Caithness in 1922 after an absence of sixteen years. He was then thirty. The letter from Jonathan Cape accepting the book (1925) put some critical points, to which he objected. Yet it is worth noting that he made a deliberate effort to write *Morning Tide* (1931) in the "simple, direct English" which Edward Garnett of Cape had advised.

TO JONATHAN CAPE LTD.
MOYNESS, BRUCE GARDENS, INVERNESS   14 DEC., 1925

Many thanks for your kind letter accepting my first novel, *The Grey Coast*. It is certainly a study from life in the sense that the material conditions touched upon have a reality in fact (. . .)
I note your remarks about "fine writing" and shall very carefully study what Mr. Garnett has to say, particularly if the offending passages are indicated. I cannot altogether agree with you. (. . .) Believe me, I can appreciate how "fine writing" offends the sincere modern nostril. It certainly does my own! The implication, however, is affectation in the exquisite sense, and there's the snag! For such affectation in such a study as mine would not merely be unpardonable: it would damn. You may reckon, therefore, that I would not willingly be guilty, and that a consciousness of a certain quite ruthless sincerity (plus a fair amount, I suppose, of writer's sensitivity) would hardly have permitted a complete lack of acumen and self-criticism so far as "fine writing" was concerned. Yet presumably I have failed in my own particular intention and accordingly I shall await Mr. Garnett's remarks with much interest. (. . .)
(. . .) After all, the trick of "stark" prose can be as much a convention as "fine writing" – and, if insincere, much more repellent. There can be grace in an arabesque. (. . .)
Believe me,
Yours sincerely,
Neil M. Gunn

3

MAURICE WALSH was born in County Kerry in 1879 and in 1901 entered the Excise Service. He met Neil Gunn about 1912. They became close friends and Gunn was a frequent visitor to Forres where Walsh lived with his Scottish wife Toshon. When Maurice returned to Ireland in 1922 they challenged one another to write. Both first novels were issued in 1926: *The Grey Coast* (Gunn) and *The Key Above the Door* (Walsh); both last books were issued in 1956: *The Atom of Delight* (Gunn) and *Danger Under the Moon* (Walsh). During most of their writing careers Gunn helped Maurice with plots. Walsh died in 1964.

TO MAURICE WALSH
CUSTOMS AND EXCISE   11/4/27

My dear Maurice,
  There is no question about your rapid gain in the mastery of technique necessary for this type of work.[1] You now get ahead with a swing. If this part had been more definitely the solution to an earlier problem or plot, I'd have been waiting comfortably on my percentage! – more definitely, I say. As it is, I have distinct hopes of it. You go ahead. You know my ideas and I'm not going to reiterate. When the completed whole is seen in typewritten Ms there may be a surprise for us. Get down to it now with a will. Keep your eye on that sense of proportion you are so marvellously developing. If you bring off this novel you're made. And you'll have done enough at it and suffered enough from me, to keep you right ever after! And, beheavens, it's a plot you'll get next time! I'm as keen about bringing it off as you are yourself. This last part goes in holus bolus – though I ask you respectfully to consider my brackets and odd remarks. You'll have noticed how one wrong adverb kills a page when maybe a couple of dozen in the right key wouldn't be noticed. But mistrust me like the very devil. I have a tendency towards subtle restraint which is often quite needless. Moreover, the poaching novel[2] was returned by the publishers today. They simply won't have it. So all of a year's work has gone west. And the publishers are quite right. I see it clearly. I was chancing my arm; and having lost I take it in good part. The publishers are disappointed. They imply that my promise has petered out! I think the implication unkind but consider it, inter alia! Anyway, I'm interested in the car at the moment and what with

our holidays next week I'm looking forward to a month or two of carefree, bookless, writingless pleasure. So you needn't say anything about it. I never tell anyone but yourself what I'm doing, simply because I cannot discuss books and stuff easily. More subtle restraint! I suppose actually my writing, and what I care for in writing, has gone off the rails a bit and according when anyone tells me about the marvellousness of John Buchan or Arnold Bennett, not to speak of Warwick Deeping or Elinor Glyn, I realise my incompetence and murmur, Yes, really rather good, isn't he (or she, as the case may be!). My use of incompetence is in no way superior and springs out of genuine – even humble – sanity. There is one thing that I do realise now tho' very clearly, and that is that the publisher must find a market for his wares. Some fine things have been said in reviews about *The Grey Coast* (and one able fellow – one-time reviewer, he, on *Scotsman* – whose opinion I have hitherto respected, told me the other night that he had read it twice. His opinion was too flattering for sober repetition) – but in my account of sales recently received from publisher – how many copies do you think they've sold? Not 700. Interesting, isn't it? Now a novel by Warwick Deeping, which my wife got from library, is in its 59th,000. I read most of it. In other words, anything that ever I may get published is not going to keep the car in petrol. And anything that I may like to write is not going to get into print and I simply have no grouse about it. Yet next winter I shall very probably tackle another novel. And I've given that first-personal detail with the object of your chewing it. You should find it an interesting and helpful story. (. . .)

Neil

J. B. SALMOND became editor of *The Scots Magazine* in 1927. He published many of Gunn's short stories, and serialised *The Lost Glen* from April to November, 1928.

TO J. B. SALMOND, EDITOR, *The Scots Magazine*
LARACHAN, DOCHFOUR DRIVE, INVERNESS   30.11.27.

Dear Mr. Salmond,
    With what you say about these opening instalments of *The Lost Glen*, I agree. For serial purposes the reader is not put in

possession of any story. Actually the treatment of the theme is rather curious, being somewhat in the nature of a mosaic which doesn't quite give the picture until you stand back a bit (in other words, until you have read a chapter or two more than even what you saw). As you know, it was nearly all written before your idea of a serial reached me. However, the alteration of the first part of the book to meet your serial needs might not be an impossible task, for what you require, I take it, is the sense of dramatic "situation" between the characters indicated at an early stage (and at least implied in the first instalment) so that a reader may be tempted to see how it's worked out. But what really is important is whether the conception of the novel as a whole, with (to me) its underlying significance, would appeal to you. The theme is really rather a big one, and at this particular crisis in Scottish affairs I think at least provocative. Whether I have handled it well is entirely another matter! But you would get some idea of the scope of it from a perusal of the second half, which I am prepared to send on to you, and which will pretty well have to stand as it is. Seeing you are still considering the matter, would it therefore be the simplest way towards a decision if I sent you on the second half so that you may know whether the subject matter is suitable for your Magazine. If it isn't, that would end the matter; if it is then we might discuss it. And in that connection, permit me to thank you very much for your offer of hospitality. Unfortunately I don't get my winter leave until February. But if you would come to Inverness I should be delighted to put you up, and should enjoy a yarn about the ways of modern Scots letters for its own sake. Up here one gets out of touch, and, I fear, lazy. There is such a lot waiting to be written about auld Scotia at the moment, too; rather vital, modern stuff, it seems to me.

I am pleased that the short stories had not to cross the border. But I wonder if you could oblige me with a galley proof? Not that I'd make any alteration to annoy the compositor, but I do like to see my short stories (which I mostly write with some care) correct to the comma.

Trusting to hear from you soon, and with kind regards.

Yours sincerely,

Neil M. Gunn

I have a yarn of about 10,000 words which I believe might interest you – the Highlands in Glasgow (or rather, Gaeldom in the Gorbals!). But of that again.³

The Lost Glen, the second novel which Gunn wrote, was rejected by several publishers. Jonathan Cape, for example, made a comment calculated to fill him with frustrated anger: "We feel that you yourself are perhaps too Gaelic, too 'poetic', to write a strong novel." The letter to Hodder & Stoughton which follows is a copy, with no signature and no formal ending. Was the original ever sent? At any rate, it shows Gunn's feelings at the time.

TO HODDER AND STOUGHTON LIMITED, LONDON E.C.4
LARACHAN, DOCHFOUR DRIVE, INVERNESS   18 MAY, 1929

Dear Sirs,
    Against my better judgement I am prompted to thank you for your critical note accompanying the return of my Ms, *The Lost Glen*. I am sorry you could not see your way to accept the novel, but I assure you I appreciate your forecast that the work would not be likely to be a 'success', even if I do think that it might possibly pay its way. (The Editor of *The Scots Magazine*, for example, was very pleased with its reception as a serial both at home and abroad.)
    Those of us who are interested in what is sometimes called the Scottish Renaissance Movement must, I suppose, be sanguine enough to keep looking for the publisher who is prepared to take risks! Though why we should expect him to, heaven knows! for we are aware how comparatively easy – and acceptable – it would be to supply the staple fare of kilts, sporrans, and Romance, in island dawns and Celtic twilights – not omitting a helping of cabbage from the 'kailyard'! But, amusing as it may seem, we are sufficiently moved by the emergence of new forces in Scottish life to keep blasting away at the new claim. Possibly, after all, it is the only merit of *The Lost Glen* that it stands for the first honest attempt, as far as I know, at introducing the Highlands as they are today. Though honesty is not literature, I grant you, even if it's satire, or irony, or anguish.

Perhaps also I ought to have explained that this is not a first novel, that I am having a book of short stories published shortly, and that I am hopeful that a play of mine may be put on – not in London – this autumn. Finally, assuming that I decide on a complete recreation of this novel on a larger scale with a more direct concentration of purely human interest – for as it is it contains all the elements of the one novel I should like to see written against this background – would another view of it interest you? Or, frankly, is its whole tenour antipathetic?

NAN SHEPHERD was born in 1893, educated at Aberdeen High School and Aberdeen University. From 1915 to 1956 she was Lecturer in English Literature at the Aberdeen Training College for Teachers. She published three novels, *The Quarry Wood* (1928), *The Weatherhouse* (1930), and *A Pass in the Grampians* (1933), as well as a book of poems *In the Cairngorms* (1934), and a vivid account of the hills themselves, *The Living Mountain*, which was not issued until 1977. Her first letter to Gunn was written congratulating him on *Hidden Doors* in 1929. They met at a PEN dinner in 1930. Nan Shepherd died in 1981.

TO NAN SHEPHERD
LARACHAN, DOCHFOUR DRIVE, INVERNESS   26.8.29.

Dear Miss Shepherd,
    Your letter has today reached me from the Porpoise Press. Being so sensible of the value of your own work, I appreciate it very highly. Indeed, I have discussed *The Quarry Wood* with men like C. M. Grieve, *The Scots Magazine* editor etc., frequently, and would have written you personally were it not that I found more public ways of expression – as, for example, in a broadcast talk from Glasgow on modern Scottish letters, where I gave it as my opinion that your work is more significant than all the novels of 'the Glasgow School' put together. Had there been – there wasn't – a lingering doubt in my mind your first poem in *The Scots Magazine* would have dissipated it. For we have got to that stage where we need something more than a realism which is often little more than a species of reporting designed to attract at all costs – and none

the less when it is 'daring' reporting! I hope you are busy. If there is any chance of your being in Inverness at any time, please call round. My wife and I would be delighted to meet you. We could also have a quite useful little talk – even an amusing one – about literary affairs in Scotland today. Work of the quality you are doing will have to put up a pretty stiff fight. Interested forces should as far as possible continue – were it only to have the fun of it, for they are not likely to get their fun elsewhere – not, anyhow, out of second editions! I should be glad to hear that you are busy deploying your forces.

I'm afraid I'm rather lazy and haven't indeed written a word – beyond reviewing – for some months. *The Lost Glen* is still in my drawer – where it will lie for some time. Too political, I'm afraid; a trifle too concerned with the Highlands as they are; not enough romantic tartan. It is so easy to dish up precisely what is wanted!

Meantime, my interest has turned to drama. The Scottish Players are putting on a full-dress play of mine[4] in Glasgow in early October (I'm afraid it won't do them any good!). And the BBC, London, have just written requesting permission to broadcast my one-act play, *The Hawk's Feather* (in current *Scots Mag.*) from Aberdeen on September 24. Again, how they are to get it across, I don't know! But it all means that our forces are beginning to make a slight impression. But the real pleasure in the fight comes from the exquisite understanding of what Whitman would call a comrade.

Yours very sincerely,

Neil M. Gunn

GEORGE MALCOLM THOMSON (born 1899) founded the Porpoise Press with Roderick Watson Keir as an undergraduate spree in the mid-Twenties. When Thomson and Keir moved south the Press was carried on for a while by Norman Wilson, Lewis Spence and Charles Graves. In 1930 Thomson again took over Porpoise, this time in collaboration with George Blake, who was then working for Faber & Faber. *Morning Tide* was distributed by Faber although nominally issued by Porpoise Press and by 1937 when *Highland River* came out, Neil felt that the imprint was

"a fraud in a national sense". Thereafter his books appeared
directly under the imprint of Faber & Faber.

Thomson was for many years a leader-writer for the Beaver-
brook Press, and wrote a number of books, the first being the lively
and controversial *Caledonia*, in 1927.

TO GEORGE MALCOLM THOMSON
LARACHAN, DOCHFOUR DRIVE, INVERNESS   4 MAY 1930

My dear Thomson,
I am thoroughly disgusted with myself over this new effort
called *Under the Sun*.⁵ In fact, my impulse was not to send it to
you, but that would look silly, or so important that – here it is.
The only way I can explain it – or explain, at least, how I went
on writing it – is by reference to my experience of English
publishers. Edward Garnett, on behalf of Cape, always trotted
out his formula of "simple, direct English". They would have
published my short stories long ago if I'd have altered the style
of some of 'em. Now I maintain it's damned nonsense to
suggest that any writer of quality is going to use any style
unless it's going to express him. "Simple direct English" is only
one way – an excellent way – of getting certain things across.
It probably expresses all that Garnett has to express. So he's
lucky – Well, I thought I'd have a shot at it myself. And, oddly
enough, while writing had the complete illusion of warm
creation. I put this down to the actual truth of my picture. I had
also one or two other ideas in my mind possibly: the recreation
of this countryside and sea-board, of a family, without
melodrama, plot, murder, death, sex-appeal, or any of the
usual aids to "grip". These three days in a boy's life may have
been my try-out in slight fashion, of what would were it
inclusive, be an immense work! Anyway, I'm making no
theories here I'm too tired of 'em. And besides it's idiotic to
prejudice you, because I should like to get your frank idea. I
should also like your judgement *apart from* the commercial
aspect.

I also enclose the serial Ms we have spoken of. I think, when
filled out into the original mould, that it might "go". I know,
anyhow, that there's been a lot of enquiry as to when it is to
come out in book form. If you like it as it stands, send it back
and give me a couple of months to make it more shipshape.

There is in it the groundwork of a great novel about the modern Highlands. I should have tackled it on a large scale. I really must get down to something big in order to get a little peace from myself. I have in an exaggerated state at the moment that damned sensation – irritation of trifling!

My own suggestion (in this white-logic moment of reaction) is: 1) the last 40 pages (10,000 words) of *Under the Sun* as a pamphlet short story for you, and 2) *The Lost Glen* as an autumn novel!

But, as I said before, you need not consider my feelings in the matter at all. Sling 'em back – and I shall perfectly understand. (. . .)

I shall be glad to hear from you at your leisure.

Yours

Neil M. Gunn

Although I appear to be girding at this "simple English" business, I naturally chose a subject – boyhood – where at least it should apply. I had no sense of strain in its use or of a shadow of affectation. It did positively seem to meet the need!

GEORGE BLAKE, born in Greenock in 1893, became a journalist in London. He was acting editor first of *John O'London's Weekly*, then of *The Strand* magazine, and from 1930 to 32 a Director of Faber & Faber. In 1932 he returned to newspaper work in Scotland. During the period of his association with the Porpoise Press he was one of Neil's warmest supporters. Blake published over thirty books and died in 1961.

TELEGRAM FROM GEORGE BLAKE TO NEIL M. GUNN:
26 SEPTEMBER 1930

Congratulations Morning Tide Book Society Choice confidential meantime up the Porpoise writing Blake

F. MARIAN McNEILL (1895–1973) was born in Orkney and took her degree at Glasgow University. She worked for many years on the staff of the Scottish National Dictionary in Aberdeen, and was the author of a number of influential books on Scottish cooking and folklore. Like her brother Duncan she was an enthusiastic Nationalist.

TO F. MARIAN MCNEILL

LARACHAN, DOCHFOUR DRIVE   30/3/31

My dear Marian,
    (. . .) I read Catherine Carswell's *Open the Door*.[6] It's a splendid piece of work in every way. First class stuff in it. Why that woman did not go on writing novels, seeing she has taken writing as her job, heaven alone knows. One is almost tempted to wonder as to failure of inspiration or imagination or whatever it's called. Otherwise she was an ass. For it obviously is not laziness. Her energy, in detail, is remarkable. She has, however, two besetting sins: honesty and sincerity. That is a more damning charge than may appear. "Honesty is the best policy as the following story will tell." Ah these Scots Puritans – no wonder she loves Grieve! And no wonder the Highlander laughs within himself – and turns tender! But they mistrust tenderness these terrible people who love the truth and are honest! Yet they talk of being "continental" and gay and ever "free" – anything indeed but honest-sincere-calvinist! So we can forgive them a lot! (. . .)
    Yours,

    Neil M. Gunn

TO NAN SHEPHERD

LARACHAN, DOCHFOUR DRIVE, INVERNESS   15/4/31

Dear Nan Shepherd,
    I've delayed acknowledging your most interesting letter in the hope that I'd be definite about visiting Aberdeen. I should like a good talk with you, but I'm afraid to get anything said at all would require something more than the lunch hour my wife and I *may* be in your town – passing through by car. This is disappointing, as I think we might, given an evening, arrive at some remarkable estimate of the importance or value of literature! That two year old book of yours rather gets me.[7] I

could say so much on the issues you raise, for I have always a certain second view from the non-literary angle. For I am not really a literary man. I realise this with striking force when I meet many of my friends (e.g. C. M. Grieve). I play a little at it, but I laugh a little too. And I think out of the mixture there comes at odd moments a certain gaiety. For I don't know that one ever wants to have an understanding with anything so much as with life. A certain friendly relationship, mocking occasionally – a certain grimness too for the dumb spot, even the head bloody but unbowed, if without the gesture, even if not without the amusing knowledge of it. Which means that I'd be writing rubbish in another minute. Only – that book of yours. Good Lord. And your poetry – you make me a little afraid to enter in. Where of course no one can enter in. Which is not what matters. For the within would glow, if only the without could be made to sparkle. With a little belief, even a glass of wine. But I should certainly never be able to make anyone believe that art mattered supremely. Even if nothing else matters at all – beyond, that is, the sparkle, and, why not? the wine.

Which is the proper state of mind for starting a holiday. Well – if you don't mind – isn't it? Though who would sell his soul for a little gaiety? Who, indeed?

And when you say that the result of your poetry is "slight and small" you make my head buzz. What I once saw by way of sample had me staggering at a fourth reading. Steady a little, please, and have a thought for the lowly.

If by any chance we should be in your town next week, I may try to get in touch, but I cannot give myself much hope.

Yours sincerely

Neil M. Gunn

C. M. GRIEVE (Hugh MacDiarmid), born in Langholm in 1892, was from 1921 to 1929 a journalist on a Montrose paper, and edited a series of little reviews, publishing several of Gunn's first poems and stories. The two men met in 1924. Grieve's own early poetry was seminal and for a time he and Gunn championed and supported one another. Difficulties and disagreements began in the early thirties.

TO C. M. GRIEVE (HUGH MACDIARMID)
LARACHAN, DOCHFOUR DRIVE, INVERNESS   SUNDAY 6/9/31

My dear Grieve,
    Why the deuce didn't you approach me earlier? I would have
gone to London – for it was in my mind to go over another
small business – looked into the whole thing and set up ways
and means. A few weeks ago I got a good cheque for 'royalties',
but as I am myself bonded (big mortgage over house) at too big
a percentage, I set arrangements going for cancelling bond. The
advance I got earlier in the year I was tempted to invest in one
of these 'good things' that have proved anything but good.
Thus at the moment my affairs are in a sort of happy state of
equipoise! However, to come to business, I am enclosing a
cheque for £100, dated for Tuesday to give me time to see my
banker and arrange that it will be acknowledged. You seem to
require a further £50 to put you right by Wednesday. Well, if
you can't get hold of it anywhere, wire me Tuesday forenoon
and I'll fix it up somehow, I feel sure. This is the holy Scotch
Sabbath and I can't do much today, and am writing this to
catch the afternoon mail so that you should have it Monday
morning. If you are on to a good thing I should hate to think of
your missing it. You mustn't miss it. Now as to the good thing.
    I wish I could look into it entirely for your sake. Is it, for
example, an established and going concern? What sort of
balance sheet did they turn out last year? If, on the other hand,
it is entirely a new concern, what are the specific prospects at
this time of all times in our rotten financial history? If it is a
private company – and your note implies as much – what are
you letting yourself in for in the way of personal liabilities as a
director (quite apart from any partner fee of £500)? Please
don't misunderstand my asking questions like these. I know
lots about company affairs – often too much, for the civil
servant comes in contact with strange enough things. What I
am afraid of, to be quite frank, is that you[8]

(The rest of this letter is missing. Ed.)

WILLIAM McCANCE, born 1894 in Glasgow, was educated at
Hamilton Academy and Glasgow School of Art. From 1920–29

he was an illustrator with *Lloyd's Magazine* in London, and from 1922–26 Art critic for *The Spectator*. After running a private printing press in Wales he became in 1943 Lecturer in Typography and Book Production in the School of Art at Reading University. He died in Girvan, Ayrshire, in 1970.

TO WILLIAM MCCANCE

LARACHAN, DOCHFOUR DRIVE, INVERNESS   26/4/32

My dear McCance,

I have just returned from a holiday to be invigorated by your splendid letter. I was for a few days in London in the literary crush. I have just had a new novel published which the English reviewers (with one or two notable exceptions) have damned to the point of farce.[9] I was feeling pretty sick of the whole rotten writing business, and had fled for a final few days to the wilds where I fished in some of the loneliest glens in our wild north. It was nice to get your letter with its clear understanding of what finally matters when I came back. I may write again, but I'm hardly in the mood for it quite yet! I admit, of course, that in this new book (*The Lost Glen*), I was asking for it. It's one of these accursed things, I suppose, a Scotsman must get off his mind. And because I was dealing with my own people, and finding their conditions deplorable, and themselves – well, there was bred a certain repressed, perhaps fierce, reticence. The English naturally must misunderstand. I don't blame them – or anyone else for that matter. Though they might have made an effort to see what I was at, instead of damning me for my "bad writing." Yes, for those passages that appeal to you I was particularly damned. They call it "fine writing" or "jargon" – particularly again when it comes out of a sort of quintessential treatment of the white heat. A novelist should write "a simple direct English" and "say what he means." Maybe you can understand my relief therefore to see your talk of words that come "from finger-tips." The summing of a whole fastidious culture in a scarce perceptible gesture of fingers that are none the less strong for being sensitive. Indeed it is the tragedy in my book that a man with just such fingers strangles a man! But they consider that this was *not* inevitable. Naturally. Unless a man has stolen your money or kissed your sweetheart, why tragedy? From all of which you would think I was almost roused! But my rousing comes from you and is full of sound humour. Anyway, it is encouraging to me that you liked *Morning Tide* for the very reasons that gave me pleasure (forgetting the pain now!) in writing it. And I most sincerely thank you for the impulse that prompted so fine and generous a letter. I have a far, but clear, memory of trying to stand up to Grieve and yourself one night over Freudian interpretations! I was probably doing nothing more than balancing salmon fishing against the literary coterie! For I think, as you seem to suggest, that the city clique is a bad thing – and finally unhealthy – in the creative sense. Why we should be bothered with creation rather than sterility, I don't know. But once we have decided to bother about doing a thing, it does seem futile to rush about trying to accomplish its opposite. And getting your mind pinched into little pieces in the process and paying tribute to the man who is not a creator so much as a brilliant stylist of destruction – to flatter him in his many guises. Peace after that. The hills and loneliness. And an hour to gaze at nothing and think less, until the mind comes with benign amazement to its own surface and gazes round on a slow rich deep earth. I feel as if I won't get my bearings for weeks!

But more than enough. I did get your Prospectus and immediately thereafter by an accident it was destroyed. I should love to get another copy (my wife had designs of framing the etching). We are not in a position alas to buy such masterpieces – nor indeed to house them properly. But I am meantime deeply interested in the work you are doing. I remember very vividly some of your wife's work. It remains in my mind as something of an almost terrible flawlessness. And as for your own, I might desire the light on the top of the country road to the petrol pumps that embrace! But that's only the beginning of an argument! If ever you are this way, you will look us up. I should enjoy a night's talk with you. By the grace of God we might clear some cobwebs.

Scotland is in a most interesting condition at the moment with a strong Nationalist movement! But an end. Ever yours,

Neil M. Gunn

THE BEGINNING WRITER

JOHN MacCORMICK was a leading spirit in the Glasgow University Scottish Nationalist Association while a law student. He joined the National Party of Scotland at its formation in 1928, and became Secretary. In 1929 he spoke at a recruiting meeting in Inverness, when Neil Gunn enlisted. *The Flag in the Wind* (Gollancz, 1955) is MacCormick's own account of his involvement in political life.

TO JOHN MACCORMICK
LARACHAN, DOCHFOUR DRIVE, INVERNESS   22/5/32

Dear MacCormick,
  McNeill has handed me a copy of the half yearly agenda and I thought I might speed you on with a few private reflections. (. . .)
  The St. Rollox Res. on detailed Policy: I frankly think this an impossible resolution. Its all-inclusive terms could not be met by anything less than a weighty volume of analysis and instruction – I refer of course particuarly to ". . . state definitely the administrative measures that will be taken to deal with the reconstruction of *every* important section of Scottish *industrial, commercial*, and social life." My God! This is either a mouthful of words or the dream of a Mussolini! However, I cannot go into all its implications. The adoption of such a resolution with the consequent adoption of a full-blooded policy, would mean 1) the changing of the National Party into a political party in the ordinary sense and 2) the loss of the driving force of the national idea in internal and external squabbling over politico-economic points of trivial or no value . . . , . . . Now I know you feel that we should have a broad policy with certain large features defined, such as, for example, nationalised or nationally controlled transport. I think you're wrong, even there. (. . .) And why do it now? For what specific reasons? (. . .) What I'm trying to suggest is that whenever you come forward with a specific conception such as this you will tie yourself in knots and the major idea – the only idea – will be lost. Not to mention, of course, that every Nationalist close-questioned would give different replies (unless a full volume is forthcoming). Again, within the Nat. Party at present there are people with all sorts of fancy ideas

17

like Nationalisation, Free Trade, Tariffs, Individualism, Anti-nationalisation and so on. In short, you can't make us into a political party on the Westminster plan. What can you say, e.g., on what is considered a major political issue like Tariffs? You won't say Yes and you won't say No shortly and frankly. You'll be forced to take up with unimportant variations for the sake of being 'different', the attitude taken up by the present National govt. *when electioneering*, i.e. investigation by commission. You'll want to please. Quite. I agree with that because it means nothing – or, more correctly, represents our present policy which is perfectly sound and clear! You went through this election showing what was wrong with Scotland, why it was wrong, and *who* would put it right. For you to come along now and show the only way in detail to put it right *when* we do get control is – well, it will be considered a matter of arrogance by many! And for us who consider ourselves Nationalists to pledge ourselves to common "administrative measures . . ." is damned nonsense, apart from its insincerity. You and I should be arguing at once about these railways – not after we were in power at Edinburgh (which would be the only time) but *now*. I am prepared to fight with anybody – any Scot – *then*: but not *now*. (. . .). And in mentioning or instancing the railways I am mentioning a thing on which I would give way to you or any nationaliser. Transport should be national. But there are other things which it would be apalling folly administratively to outline and pledge ourselves to.

But I see I cannot go into this affair in a letter. And I know exactly why there is a need for a policy – or rather, why the need is felt. But basically the attitude is profoundly wrong and the need is the national weakling's mirage. You want to offer the people something: the bread and circuses once more. The politicians will consume you in the end, and when power comes and the difficult days of building are ahead, there will not be amongst the people the keen driving spirit of those who have fought and will jealously endure. It is not conceivable that folk would ever cry "we were better under Westminister." Never by gad, never by thunder!

Our policy at present is quite clear: a majority of members at Westminister; withdrawal; setting up machinery at

Edinburgh for calling a Parliament – with power to rule in interim, especially if there were trouble! – and calling of Parliament and completing of constitution. As regards economic matters meantime, any men of brains, like yourself, can meet any objections by simply pointing out that it is impossible that Scots would continue to endure what they would have power to redress. *Every Nationalist* can pledge himself to attend to *every* grievance when he's in power at Edinburgh. On each pertinent question of national status he can immediately outline various ways of attack. If he can't do that he shouldn't be let loose on a platform and certainly no "political program" such as the St. Rollox resolution suggests would do anything but smother both him and the national idea.

As for outlining the proposed Constitution, that's a merry thought, only don't appoint a sub-committee between drinks.

Wishing you the best of luck!

Yours,

Neil M. Gunn

TO C. M. GRIEVE

LARACHAN, DOCHFOUR DRIVE, INVERNESS   9/7/32

My dear Christopher,

(. . .) I wish you luck and an increasing fire. Which is perhaps different from a consuming one. For your violence, qua violence or anent that which you are violent against, may not enthuse me. And occasionally it leads you not merely astray but betrays you into the damnedest nonsense. Take your review of MacColla's book [10] (to which I am now looking forward as an epochal work; have just got it; Daisy is reading it). In the course of that review you say (haven't got the review by me as I'm writing this and other rectorial letters[11] under pressure) that MacColla has been kept back or denied outlet by "a horde of his intellectual inferiors" in the Scottish movement. After all, those who have any influence in the movement can be counted on your fingers. This is MacColla's first novel: it has been published: it has received longer reviews than any Scottish first novel (excepting *Hatter's Castle*[12]) within my knowledge; it has been praised: Compton Mackenzie boosted it in *The Daily Mail* (with a back thrust at such as I am!): The S.I.[13] praise it; and certainly *The Modern Scot* will laud it in comparison with the novel I now send you,[14] which was even denied in its facts (i.e. was misrepresented) in that organ. Nor have any of the "Horde" done anything but praise yourself. I still receive weekly abuse from the *John O' Groat Journal*.[15] Praise or abuse may not matter a damn, but at least recognise the facts. The only what might be called adverse review that MacColla's received, to my knowledge, appeared over Macnair Reid's[16] initials in *The Evening Times*. When I ran into Reid at Bannockburn he told me that a letter had been addressed by your – or MacColla's – publishers to his firm abusing Reid in a manner so scurrilous that the management had to take appropriate action. For any praise or abuse I don't give a damn, but I must admit that when Reid told me that, I felt pretty mad. (. . .)

However, I suppose these are dimensions incidental to the amusing pastime of writing. But don't, my dear fellow, come it over me with the inferior intellectual horde standing between MacColla – or anyone else – and his destiny. C'est tout. (. . .)

All the best. Ever yours,

N.M.G.

TO C. M. GRIEVE   20/7/32

My dear Chris,
   I'm glad you're doing the article on Macgillivray[17] and I am satisfied it will have an excellent effect. The middle of the month should do – but don't make it later if you can help it. I'll be away all September and want to see the boys fixed up more or less before I go. And it may be a bit of a job. I'll tell you how things go on.

Meantime about your come-back on my references to Rectorial tactics. I must say (completely impersonally, of course) that you achieve the splendid isolation of yourself as a fundamental thinker or poet over against those whose "radical psychological difference" (from you) doom them forever to the plane of strategy or tactics. All of which, forgive me for repeating, is sheer nonsense, so far as the Rectorial is concerned or my remarks upon it. I said, with regard to the Rectorial, that a certain strategy was necessary, having regard to P.M.'s own wishes and the laws of courtesy and custom governing a specific public affair. You yourself now agree to the need for such a strategy embodied (in the instance I gave) in not giving Colquhoun[18] hell in any article written for the purpose of praising Macgillivray or estimating his value as an artist and Scotsman for Rectorial honours. Yet in your *public* reference to this matter (on which we are agreed) you do contrive to make out a fundamental distinction which places you forever with the eternal verities and myself forever with the hole-and-corner of strategy. This is not an illustration of *personal* motive; it ignores even ethical values; but I do say that failing to perceive a frame of reference that was finite (and not infinite or pertaining to the realm of pure idea) you misjudged the whole issue and so wrote nonsense. You had no personal motive, I agree; but it might not be an uninteresting speculation to consider how far you have achieved for your readers an immediate *personal* reflection upon the mental processes of your object, myself! All that is elaborating a trivial point, but it happens to illustrate also your attitude to what I said about your review of MacColla's book. I never questioned the value of the book *or* your estimate of it (I hadn't read it, as explained); all I did was to state that your remarks about MacColla's having been kept from achieving his destiny by a horde of his intellectual inferiors in the Scottish movement was damned nonsense because, with all its implications, it was more than literally untrue. You say your remark does not involve "personal considerations of any kind." Finally, as you know, it does not matter a damn whether it does involve such considerations or not (and such direct statements written deliberately for *public* consumption are hardly as impersonal as moonshine); but it does matter whether what you say is true or not. If untrue, then your philosophic (or other) end would have been better served with different illustrations. To manufacture a non-existent attitude in others to illustrate your own Truth is to take yourself into the realm of fantasy. One can be as impersonal as one likes, as irrational as one likes, from day to day and theme to theme, but it is no use talking of fundamentally opposed conceptions of this or that and taking one's stand on *one* of them forever and damning the other fellow for a stand he has never taken at all.

Like you I am not concerned with the personal (though you have been personal enough in the public sense even to the extent of having tried to prejudice my chance of that invaluable £100), once it is clear that we are writing of, or discussing, ideas on a plane where "personalities" are not merely futile but irrelevant. What C.M.[19] said about my book, e.g., was of no personal concern to me, but it illustrated at least that MacColla could be boosted by one of the "horde" in the Scottish movement when one like myself was not. So with the Modern Scot (though there there are misrepresentations of facts). But enough.

When we leave these minor considerations and get on to the true plane of ideas, there's nothing for it, as you say, but talk, and someday, with luck, we'll have that talk. Meantime merely let me say that I admire fundamental integrity too much to be anything but dismayed at the thought that friendship or any other personal consideration should interfere with its pure drive. I realise what you mean by poetry being more potent than fiction because it can obviously get to grips at once and can treat ideas and attitudes quintessentially. But when you say fiction is futile, not worth a damn, then you raise interesting considerations all the way from Dostoevsky to Joyce and Proust. If Joyce is futile in his treatment of Dublin when any poems "above a very low level" would not have been then I am prepared to be shown the mysteries. (. . . .)

(Typed copy, unsigned Ed.)

In 1933 ANDREW DEWAR GIBB was Lecturer on the Law of Scotland at Cambridge University. In 1934 he became Regius Professor of Law at Glasgow. He was also the leading theoretician of the Scottish Party formed in 1932 by a group including the Duke of Montrose and Sir Alexander MacEwen. The pledge referred to was designed to commit members of all parties to devolution for Scotland. Since the National Party of Scotland, of which Gunn was a member, had been formed in 1928, the opportunities for misunderstanding and conflict were many.

TO ANDREW DEWAR GIBB
LARACHAN, DOCHFOUR DRIVE, INVERNESS   8 JANUARY 1933

My dear Gibb,
It was nice of you to write and I privately welcome the
expression of your opinions. Scotland has suffered so much
from unnecessary division in the past that we should have
learned our lesson and at least be able to correspond or talk
with intelligence lively enough to see a common End rather
than a common intrigue! But I know we are human – and Scots
– and I'm half afraid that this present period, when we might
have achieved some unity, is drawing to a close. Presently there
will have to be definitions, consequent divisions, and all that
follows inevitably therefrom. You say that at least you are glad
that we shan't cut each other's throats. But once division and
opposition are established what's going to protect the throat?
Take e.g. the present position in East Fife. I have just seen your
"pledge", and I cannot see how any Nationalist can give it. To
me it is not so much ambiguous, as purely devolutionist. Now
no nationalist can take the devolutionist pledge without
breaking through his party's policy and inviting expulsion.
Assuming for the moment that there is a correct interpretation
of the position (and of course at the moment I have no
knowledge of how any other Nationalist considers it), then it is
possible that the Labour candidate (assuming one) *will* take
your pledge, for he is committed to devolution. Accordingly
we may have the spectacle of the National Party and the
Scottish Party fighting each other at any election. Nor can I see
how in view of our clear policy and your pledge this can be
avoided. A monstrous state of affairs no doubt but one after all
brought about by our open eyes. It is not a case of laying
blame, but of seeing clearly. You may assert that your pledge
does not mean devolution pure and simple. What then does
"the maintenance of the Union, without separation of the two
Kingdoms of Scotland and England" mean? To me it is not
intrigue of any sort that we need to be afraid of: it is lack of
clear definition of our objective. With such definition there can
be no intrigue.
Now let me try to show how simply and clearly defined is
the Nationalist position. It can be put under three heads: 1) all
Scottish members at Edinburgh; 2) A joint council for certain

reserved mutual affairs; 3) decisions (or recommendations). In this way Scotland achieves sovereignty *and* at the same time recognises her joint obligations with England, not to mention natural mutual advantage. Anything less than this degree of sovereignty no Nationalist can accept. Any member of the Scottish Party must have known that he the Nationalist was committed to that end and has been so committed for years. A devolutionist pledge is therefore in the direct nature of a challenge to a Nationalist which he must accept. You have to this degree forced the issue, and it is just alas possible that the throat-cutting will follow. Our opponents will be happy and we shall both suffer!

Why then, will the Nationalist not accept the $\sqrt{2}x$ now in order to achieve the x later? (The question is implicit in your excellent analysis.) The proper way probably to answer it is simply that on a matter of private right there can only be the one dignified attitude for a nation as for an individual. This not only fulfils one's own self-respect but achieves respect in the minds of others and the form of respect called national responsibility is at the moment more essential for Scotland than possibly any other thing. Properly understood, properly grasped, this particular quality is not merely going to help us to attain or to achieve any particular end, but will sustain us through the difficult times *following* achievement and that particular grip or grit may be vastly necessary then. I see it, coolly, not as a matter of false dignity or facile sentiment, but rather as twin qualities of will and enthusiasm, without which neither a nation nor an individual can achieve very much. Pardon me if this sounds in any way doctrinaire. To me, it is quite vital. We recognise our joint obligations, our desire for friendly relations, for mutual advantage, for co-operation by contract and treaty. *But* Scotland must talk as an individual *in her own right*. And this must be stated now. Not to *speak* of it, to let it be implied that it's in this or that condition as if it were a furtive something that may not be mentioned outright, is bad for us all and for our country now and in the future.

But to depart from this Higher Criticism! – or rather, to apply it on the plain (sic) of practical politics. What is the outstanding thing about NPS? To me it is its success, felt throughout Scotland and at Westminster. In four years it has accomplished more than the Liberal Party in forty – incomparably more: and that not merely on the political plain (sic) but as you so well know, in arts and affairs generally. I am not here putting forward any plea for this party under any sort of personal usage, for in a very practical manner I am detached from it. I am merely trying to see results and assess them. Moreover I have had great opportunities of studying the reactions of the average Scot to the policy of the NPS, and I am finally convinced that, with sufficiently able leaders, we could achieve our complete end more quickly and definitely through the NPS than through any other policy-system or organisation whatsoever. You need only accept that as a personal statement, of course, though I'd be prepared to go into considerable justifying detail. Anyway, here is a Party with a policy, an organisation, hundreds of branches throughout the country, propagandist literature, a monthly organ established, a weekly one in prospect, and already with a name and such success as can no longer be ignored. And that name and that success based on work mostly of the unknown folk in Scotland. For the rich have not come in, nor big business, nor the lairds. In fact the only analogy is "the rising of the common people of Scotland in the War of Independence", as the historian writes, which is almost worth a cheer!

Can we, then, change or sacrifice our policy and organisation – for what? and with what certain result? It has been said that NPS has not got the leaders. Even if it were true, it provides no reason for supposing 1) it will never get them or 2) for preventing true leaders from coming in to lead. If one thing is more apparent than another it is positively almost indecent haste in which a good man has to take his share of control. There is no dog-in-the-manger attitude amongst those directing the NPS and if there is one thing more than another they desire it is men of breadth and brains.

But I must have exhausted your patience already. One final word. Devolution will come probably in spite of us – because of the Nationalists, not because of any other people or body of people. And the Nationalists will be sufficiently organised to deal with that, too, and to make certain that the final thing which you desire and we desire shall certainly come. I am prepared to uphold as a mere matter of argument (on tactics) that your Party is taking the long way round to obtain what

you desire: even if I could not swear to it what it is precisely that you do desire! But that for a smile at parting.
Yours sincerely,

Neil Gunn

It was T. H. GIBSON of the Scots National League who proposed the union between that body and Lewis Spence's Scottish National Movement to form the National Party of Scotland in 1928. He was for a time one of the joint editors of *The Scots Independent*, and in 1933, when this letter was written, a prominent member of the London branch of the party.

TO T. H. GIBSON
LARACHAN, DOCHFOUR DRIVE, INVERNESS   3 APRIL 1933

Dear Gibson
    MacCormick has sent me a copy of your letter to Angus Clark and I should like to compliment you on its logic and sanity. That extremism in general stands for purity and courage is a species of self-delusion practised by the ego on itself a' for its glory. Division has been Scotland's arch-fiend and has always stood upon "doctrinal purity". It may be that we are like that and therefore any hope of our ever misgoverning ourselves may mercifully never be realised.
    At any rate we should by this time have learned from our history that if ever we are going to achieve a national aim it can only be by a major harmony that refuses to be wrecked by a minority discord. Now I maintain that this harmony can be achieved in Scotland today, but it can be achieved only on a basis of broad principle and will inevitably be wrecked by over-early definition of detail or machinery underlying the principle. Inverness has learned that lesson! But has learned further that such a broad attitude has nothing to do with compromise – it has been deduced somewhere by those scientifically investigating psychology and is applied widely in school for perverts and defectives (hence particularly applicable to us!): first of all, then, *establish points of contact* and from that work out to the solution of disagreements.

Now that I've started on the subject let me ask your attention for views I have arrived at after close touch with all levels of feeling and thought in Scotland, particularly over the last year. Presumably our prime concern in this affair is to see Scotland get self-government. Anything that stands in the way of that realisation, whether doctrinal purity or canting heresy, must be damned. If, e.g., it could be proved that insistence on such words as "Republicanism" or "Sovereign Independence" would so result, then it strikes me that our duty is plain. It's rather disheartening to think of our efforts resulting in no more than giving satisfaction to extremists a century hence as they proceed, complete with sporran, to lay wreaths on Scotland's final Culloden. And in so saying I am not considering England at all. England has nothing to do with this affair. The idea of England's trying to prevent us realising a united aim is merely amusing. (. . .)

We need hardly look for luck in that direction! Accordingly our problem as I see it, is to present such a policy 1) as shall give us a nation's status and 2) have the maximum appeal *now* to our people through whom (and whom only) this status can be realised.

In national status there are two broad concepts – Republicanism and membership of Empire. I say straight away that Republicanism (or similar separatism) is antipathetic to the overwhelming majority of the Scottish people and cannot *today* be realised either by forceful or peaceful methods. Whether Republicanism is good or bad I'm not discussing. I merely know that Scotland will not have it now – and less and less as time goes on under anglicising influences (what she might ultimately do as individual member of Empire is another matter, for *then* her national consciousness would have been awakened, and if she thought Republicanism good, she'd simply adopt it.)

If we wish our present fight to be fruitful we must therefore recognise that Scotland today desires to remain within the Commonwealth (or, rather, Empire, as you define it). Our problem now, as I see it, is to present as simply and shortly as possible, yet with sufficient clarity on essentials, the broad principles that will cover our aims without raising defeatist divisions on machinery or details. Those broad principles are for me presented in the resolution we carried at Stirling[20] the other Sunday and I would beg of you, because of the amount of unanimity already achieved upon them, and because of the greater unanimity it is confidently hoped will be achieved throughout Scotland very soon, to give them your utmost consideration. I have a deep respect not only for the work you have done and are doing but for your savoir faire and judgement. With complete control of our own affairs and our own taxation (the first and second principles) as you know, we have complete control of everything. With those two principles assured we could control what we liked and *become what we liked*. To fight amongst ourselves now over some long-phrased definition of "independence" that the Scottish people could merely take in their stride if they found it a reality and desired it, is surely insanity – even traitorous insanity as its result now would be by internal division to destroy the chance of our final nationhood at all.

After control of affairs and cash, then membership of the British Group. And that's all. Like you, I think Dominion status damned nonsense (as I told Ian Gillies.) As the two creating nations, with joint responsibilities, (e.g. India), obviously some form of *joint machinery* is essential to meet our *unique case*. What Canada or Ireland or any other country may do is entirely its own concern. Your analysis of this point is exhaustive and final.

All that I say now is that we should make no immediate effort to define that machinery, but when we have achieved a fighting unity in Scotland, then it is for our experts in constitution making to get down to their work. If, however, we could get experts on to the thing soon, then well and good. But I merely say that time will clarify opinion, and the final result must not be a journalist's piece of propagandist "uplift" (. . .)

After all, we are spending our fairly valuable time on this business and occasionally the smile is more cynical that sees fellows growing heated about the niceties of "Dominion status" over against "Sovereign Independence", and filling columns in the press with their wrangles, while the vast bulk of Scotland is not merely amused but hardly even apathetic! Just as you achieved the National Party out of discussion, so again the National Party *on its basic principles* must achieve unity in Scotland. Every ounce of its strength should be directed to that goal. If we slip back too far, we're done. And the time has come for a new surge forward. Granted reason and work, I believe it is possible within the next twelve months. With unreason and division, we can merely dig ourselves in for good.

Robin MacEwen[21] will be in London in two or three weeks and hopes to call on you.

My wife sends Greetings to Mrs. Gibson, on whom many blessings.

Yours,

Neil M. Gunn

P.S. *The Freeman* has just come in with Clark's and MacColl's[22] attack on MacCormick and Executive. This is really damned bad. If the party has any guts at all surely it will hit out at this sort of thing. If we cannot support our own men – while admitting their weakness and errors in judgement and anything you like – from this sort of slander, then the game is a pretty miserable one.

TO C. M. GRIEVE

LARACHAN, DOCHFOUR DRIVE, INVERNESS   28/5/33

My dear Christopher,

I am delighted to send this packet to an address in the Shetlands – not for the pocket's sake! I have long felt that some such Retreat was what you needed in order to create whatever synthesis or final (more or less) harmony you may achieve – or perpetrate. Good! Let me know one of these days what you are thinking about, and in reply I'll tell you all the news of the inwardness of many things, including the doings of the Nat. Party, on which you may not have the right slant – in the doing or practical sense. I have been tremendously occupied for a long time on purely practical issues: possibly a hellish waste of time, but at least educational! I have tried to work out action on a rational basis, with as clear an application of psychological principles as I could encompass. But of that again.

I am more than delighted that you are working and finding your new self. Don't force things. In the beginning fertility throws a slow shoot. And the loss of what you call circulation is nothing but gain even if it has to be endured in dryness. In a definite sense, I envy your isolation. Indeed I have been thinking for some time that I'd like to get into a remote place myself but I'm afraid my writing is not the lucrative kind, and *Sun Circle* won't swell my bank balance. I'm afraid you won't be greatly taken by it and may indeed be anti-pathetic to the sort of spirit that informs it.

I found the old pagan circle idea very illuminating. (Such Druidic philosophy as there may be is my own, though the history otherwise is accurate.) One could have piled on shocking detail (what is sometimes called "naturalism") – bloody and sexual – and give an appearance of a challenging *tour de force*: but it was too easy and too like providing a circus for library readers. If I desire to strike a golden note, why shouldn't I? Anyway, the usual "realism" bores me; and even the best sort of daring intolerance grows tiresome unless it proceeds out of something profound and towards synthesis or harmony. Possibly you may find your harmony in transcending humanism (via anti-humanism). All I could see was the harmony of the circle a man in his ultimate loneliness puts about himself. There is a malignity and cruelty in nature (or God or the gods) that man has to keep at bay by an endless defiance and watchfulness, while also he can merge with such Forces in moments of timeless vision and delight. That harmony of poise or balance may be achieved: and in its perfect achievement should show towards man and nature a benign face (were it only in contrast to the Malign Forces!) And that is irrespective of critics or any of the disruptive "realists".

I did acknowledge *Scots Unbound* – at some little length, if I remember. Most of it had the sheer uniqueness of creation but odd parts (mostly the "rebellious" parts) hardly did you justice – by perhaps not being concerned with issues shown to be deep enough. But you can carry a lot of that ballast – perhaps wisely. But more again. (. . .)

Meantime my heartiest wishes for your sojourn.

Yours

(No signature. Ed.)

TO ANDREW DEWAR GIBB

LARACHAN, DOCHFOUR DRIVE, INVERNESS   28.7.33

My dear Gibb

I was on the point of writing you in order to try to fix a

meeting somewhere in Edinburgh then and hoped to lay certain matters before you in their final aspects, when the *Record* came in with its announcement of you as a Scottish party candidate for Kilmarnock. This has certainly given me a severe shock. The National Party decision to fight Kilmarnock is months old and weeks ago schemes were considered and drawn up. In view of recent troubles, never has it been so essential for the National Party to fight an election, and not merely for any tactical good to itself but for the advancement of the cause for which it has strenuously fought. The National Party has been accused by many of its followers in recent days of watering down its policies, of making overtures to the Scottish Party, in short of stultifying its essential being in order to achieve harmony in the fight for self-government. If it has done so, then manifestly it has not been very successful and those concerned must feel rather fools!

I am writing this to you in the frank friendly way we have talked and corresponded, and I feel therefore that I must tell you that I shall do my utmost in every possible way to support the National Party candidate and to oppose you or any other Scottish Party candidate that is put up against him. And I do this because I believe that it is essential, vitally essential, at this time of all times, that the National Party, with its wide-flung organisation, should close its forces and go ahead. The National Party, as you know, has been in existence for years; it has quickly been creating branches and laying solid foundations at a cost in work and cash by earnest men and women of whom nothing is heard in the press; that is my one great hope of ultimate success; it has done all the pioneer work, raising new parties and developing councils and what not in its wake; it has contested elections at great sacrifice to us all, and its creed has been to fight and fight again; it has given, in short, the whole Cause of Scotland a body and a name. If it has been attacked recently both from within and from without, it has come through that attack firmly and has these last few months been laying plans for a wide definite push for which in the near future Kilmarnock was to feature in this – as Kilmarnock shall.

If we did not foresee an early appearance of the Scottish Party in the field, it was because the constitution of that Party, particularly in so far as it dealt with action in the constituencies, where its first professed aim seemed to be to secure a satisfactory pledge from a candidate of one of the established parties. We appear to have been misled, and I trust you will understand us at least in our feeling that the Scottish Party is stepping in in an effort to take advantage of all the immense spadework the National Party has done, together with its propaganda against the Westminster Parties (by today's *Record*, one of your officials is using our very terms in this connection), and doing so, as I have already said, at a moment vitally important to us and to the Cause we have at heart.

I have done my best, as you may believe, in my effort to achieve the unity that is the only strength, to get all men of sincerity and ability in the one line. If I were to suggest that N.P. at this juncture were to stand aside in favour of the S.P. I should definitely be damning the N.P. for good. Of that there can be no doubt. The S.P. on the other hand, can stand aside, by virtue of its constitution – as I have already pointed out, for this direct action before even a bye-election has been announced is an infringement of it, and because the N.P. is the greater and older body. Further I understand your secretary has been told long enough ago that the N.P. was putting up a candidate.

All in all, then, we cannot but see that the interference of the S.P. is a deliberate and provocative challenge to the N.P., that it deliberately forestalls anything in the nature of unity of principle in the Scottish fight and that it annihilates the hopes of men of good will. Well, we accept it. The result will no doubt be ludicrous for all and certainly pretty tragical for Scotland.

Now please don't misunderstand my frankness. If it is the firm conviction of the S.P. that the N.P. is wrong, that its policy as summed up in its four points is wrong, and that it must therefore be fought, then I respect the S.P.'s decision to contest Kilmarnock. And in these circumstances you will respect, I hope, the need of the N.P. to fight the S.P. in a way that will, by inevitable force of circumstance, be bitter and to the end.

Perhaps as a people we are unfit to govern ourselves, incapable of rising above internal dissension. I have struggled to deny that conception. And I should not like yet to despair.

With all regards,
Yours

Neil M. Gunn

On 29 July, 1933, Gibb replied:
I think there must be some give and take, and assuming we were to stand down in Kilmarnock (I can *promise* nothing: it is for the party) you would, in equity, have to give us a run in other constituencies.

A meeting was arranged between representatives of the Scottish Party – the Duke of Montrose, Sir Alexander MacEwen, Andrew Dewar Gibb, P. Shiels Henderson, J. Keran McDowell; and representatives of the National Party of Scotland – T. H. Gibson, Neil M. Gunn, John MacCormick, J. M. McNicol, R. E. Muirhead, Dr. R. F. Muirhead, W. Murray.

The meeting was held on 5 September, with R. B. Cunninghame Graham in the Chair, and agreement was reached that there should be a joint statement of policy for the Kilmarnock election, the Scottish Party accepting the National Party's "Four Points":
1. A Parliament in Scotland with taxation and financial powers.
2. To share with England the rights and responsibilities within the Empire.
3. Joint machinery to be set up to administer these rights and responsibilities.
4. The Nationalists to be an independent political party having no connection with any English-controlled party.

On 29 September John MacCormick wrote to Gunn:
I am writing (. . .) to ask you to bring all your persuasive powers to bear on Sir Alexander MacEwen over the week-end to get him to press his Executive immediately to accept McNicol (as candidate).

In December, 1933, MacCormick drew up a Memorandum on the fusion of the two parties. There was provisional agreement on 22 December to combine the organisations into the Scottish National Party.

The candidate eventually decided upon for Kilmarnock was Sir Alexander MacEwen. He fought without a specific party label.

TO A. DEWAR GIBB
LARACHAN, DOCHFOUR DRIVE, INVERNESS   17/10/33

My dear Gibb,
    When I wrote to you last time you thought I was unduly pessimistic about the state of affairs, but you'll know now how near everything was to a bust up. I think we have saved the

situation: all depends on Sir A.M. If he sticks by his opening address and does not accept 1) dilution of his policy and 2) Party help from any Westminster lot, like the Liberals, we're right and there will be a mighty surge forward.

Towards that end I cannot impress sufficiently upon you now the need for immediate fusion – fusion certainly as soon as possible after the Kilmarnock fight. This would permit us 1) to obviate the inevitable recriminations and personal fights that too much time will produce; to get men appointed forthwith to their constituencies (such as yourself, e.g., to Univs) to give them a chance to organise; and to get ahead with *work*, comprising, 2) the Book of Scot. – upon which I have talked to you – a vitally important thing this; and 3) that weekly newspaper to which I have been giving much thought. These are huge tasks and properly fulfilled would produce immense results. May I depend on you on your side to drive ahead towards this fusion?

Already, e.g., there is a large measure of agreement. Take our four points. No. 1 (control of affairs and cash) the S.P. accept totally. No. 4 (independent political action) you are now really committed to. Sir A.M. finds it the only essential argument against a man like Barr. . . . That leaves 3 and 4. What about telescoping these two into a simple single Point that would include their essence. (Their essence really means joint machinery (without further definition) so that the Scots Parliament *would not be a subordinate Parliament*. Vital, that.) Do you feel like having a shot at it or what do you think? The ideal would be, of course, the acceptance of the 4 Points. But we're not going to be pig-headed over a sanctity of phrases. Let me know. My idea is – and MacCormick came up here from Kilmarnock and agrees with me – that *privately* one or two on your side (say, yourself, Sir A.M. and Duke) and one or two on ours should agree amongst themselves *beforehand* on statement of policy. That means friendly reason on the job. MacCormick is seeing Sir A.M. perhaps on Sunday and will, in right circs., mention the matter. Meantime you and I might thrash something out.

The boys were charmed with your generous Kilmarnock speech. Really they were. I was delighted to hear it. MacCormick and I went thoroughly into the Univs. seat. He thinks it pretty nearly hopeless for you – or any Nat.! As far as we are

concerned, it's yours. And I told Sir A.M. about that, too. But
you really must go into a place where you can fight – with
increasing hope. Cathcart you'll find no damned use either.
The ideal place at moment is probably Falkirk, which would
immediately surge ahead if fusion brought about. You'd better
have a talk with MacCormick. It's the *best* we want for you.

I must have a talk with you this year. Meantime, it's hardly
an exaggeration to say that everything depends on next
fortnight.

All the best,
Yours,

Neil M. Gunn

TO C. M. GRIEVE

LARACHAN, DOCHFOUR DRIVE, INVERNESS   14TH Nov. 1933

My dear Christopher,

(. . .) We were talking about you the other night when a car
load of tough guys, including T. S. Eliot, descended upon us. I
didn't get to bed until 5 a.m. Reminded me of some nights you
and I used to have in the old days! No chance of your coming
this way? If at all possible, make a night of it. The whole
Scottish situation requires review. We probably differ on many
points in tactical sphere and writing is too slow. I think from
above downwards there should be a certain ruthless organisation of all levels of action. You conceive that somewhere in this
there is compromise. I don't – or, rather, I recognise that where
you have a given psychology, like the Scottish, you must deal
with it as scientifically as possible in accordance with such rules
as advanced psychologists have formulated. To a profound
extent this is an educational matter. When an expert like A. S.
Neill is dealing with a perverted or sub-normal child he doesn't
slam educational facts into the child with the help of a rod, like
the old dominie: on the contrary, he apprehends the level of the
child mind and makes a point of contact. Neill achieves *his* end.

The lack of achievement in Scotland in past has been due not
to external but to internal warring elements.

The foregoing does not mean that A. S. Neill does not
express himself to his peers on his level. Quite the opposite.
If there are 3 or 4 levels of thought, each attempting to

achieve something sincerely, nothing can be more fatal to that achievement than internal warring.

But the application of general principles to specific ends through specific organisations is a matter not to be touched on in a letter. But I try to indicate where you and I possibly differ, and a good talk would be interesting. Let me know how you are placed.

And excuse the hurried note. I get damned little time to myself these days.

Ever yours,

Neil Gunn

TO A. DEWAR GIBB

LARACHAN, DOCHFOUR DRIVE, INVERNESS   20/12/33

My dear Gibb

I am just advised of the meeting on Friday which I most regretfully shall be unable to attend. Perhaps, however, I may let you know my thoughts, after the manner in which we have exchanged views in the past.

I consider that fusion is absolutely essential *now*; and any suggestions as to the continuance of both parties, I am dead against, and shall use all my influence to counter. Practically it is impossible to run two organisations without loss of drive and without that internal disharmony and those mutual recriminations which human nature cannot avoid. You know this. We all know it. Already speeches are taken up with explaining the two parties, assuring the country of their mutual esteem, and all that sort of trifling waste of time which leaves nothing but vagueness and doubt in minds of listeners. Meantime what is being done about those immensely important matters: failure of fishing, unemployment figures, transfer of industries, Glasgow rating under new Bill etc? Never have we been presented with such powerful material, yet clearly we are already beginning to suffer from lack of a single co-ordinating organisation. There is an immediate danger of the whole movement losing its prestige and force in the people's minds. Rather than that should happen, I am definitely out for immediate complete fusion *or no working arrangement between the parties whatsoever*. The S.P. has now had every opportunity of seeing the N.P. in action. There can no longer in the minds of S.P. be any doubt as to what N.P. stands for. Very well. Either there is a fundamental difference in the parties upon which fusion is impossible, or there is none. If there is none, why mutually destroy by keeping apart? *If there is a fundamental difference, what is it?* Above all things let us be clear and honest in this matter.

I wrote you last about the Four Points. Now you know – as Sir Alex knows – that these 4 points sum up the mutual policy. You know how they were designed and you gave me the impression of your approval (a private matter, of course). Why not, in these circumstances, let us stick to them? The benefit to you would be this: that you would take control in a party that would be all the stronger for having no further mere verbal changes in its oft-changed policy. This would be an incalculable gain. And, anyhow, anything *less* than the 4 Points, the N.P. cannot accept as a whole. And I certainly shall not. Do please believe me, Gibb, when I say that I am making no mere Party point. I am, as you know, detached. In the personal sense, it can never mean anything to me. But dammit I am anxious to see some result for Scotland out of all the vast anonymous work so many of us have done for that cause.

My program, suggested to our boys as that which should follow Kilmarnock:

1) Fusion.

2) Appointment of candidates immediately to constituencies, as all our experience has shown that our greatest weakness has been lack of organisation;

3) Preparation of Economic Policy (Book on Scotland in say two parts: 1, Survey; 2, application). How obviously this requires a central single organisation, dominated by a single policy!

4) A weekly paper.

It is abundantly clear to me that if we came out into the open as a single party with some such broad progressive program, we would make the country take notice. And *then* things would begin to get busy.

Do work it out. Unless some fair-minded fellow like yourself can pull the strands together in a leader's way, I despair. It *can* be done.

Anyway, good luck to you!

And the season's greetings and blessings on Mrs. Gibb and the children.

Yours,

Neil Gunn

TO MAURICE WALSH   INS. WED. (1934)

My dear Maurice,

I've just got your letter and as my brother [23] is arriving this evening in order that we may both proceed to Caithness for a few days' salmon fishing, I'm writing you at once. Brandt's[24] letter is very interesting, and I think it bears out my earlier suggestion to you definitely. You should get in touch not for a commission but wisely to see whether what you are going to give your time to is "up their alley" (gorgeous!). This business of trying to think out a single short story is not enough for you in your attained position. It's too much of a struggle in the void and in itself does not tend automatically to produce others. You want a background and a set of individuals that would be a sort of breeding ground – in the vague way that your Small Dark Man and Co. did become. Very well, I suggest Dublin and a new set of characters. Once you have got these lodged in your head, *I know* that they would go on doing things until I'd have to use physical force to stop you and them! You hate the thought of that just now. It's like a great mountain that you'd have to sweat blood to move. But *whatever* is suggested will be like that. You know all this just as well as I do. What you really want to do is to shirk it. I know you to your last lazy atom – knowing a little of myself.

I have now got to get you to commit yourself to a first step. What I therefore suggest you should do is to write Brandt somewhat in these terms:

I am very interested in what you say about the S.E.P.[25] and I certainly should like to send over some short stories. Perhaps it would be wise therefore if I took advantage of the suggestion to submit what ideas I have in mind so that we may get the editors' reactions. Well, I'll tell you what has been biting me for some time. I should like to deal fairly comprehensively with Dublin's Fair City. Into it I should introduce a young adventurous American who in a series of adventures – each a complete short story in itself – would penetrate all sections of its life – social, governmental, gambling, artistic, etc. – in a way that would be realist and romantic. The style would be easy and if written in the first person (by myself, as one of a group) not without its occasional humours. I have not thought the thing out in detail, but I should like to know first of all whether such a background (and the descriptive work would be firsthand and occasionally somewhat novel) would appeal to the S.E.P. – and, if it does, whether the S.E.P. has any particular suggestions to make. (My mind is still in a state of flux and open to any suggestion.) I perfectly realise that if the S.E.P. considers such material up their alley, and asks me to go ahead, that does not tie them to acceptance of the product . . .

Something like that – quite simple and innocent, Maurice! If the S.E.P. should show keenness – then it's up to us. I'm prepared to do my part. I should ask for leave in June and go to you for a fortnight – during which time we should certainly be able to draft 4 or 5 plots for you to work with – while I drafted the remainder here.

Think it over. I know it sounds big. But the bigger the better and be damned. Together we are capable of any iniquity. I haven't an idea in my head at the moment. Neither have you. Which makes everything nice and tidy. Except that we introduce the chap at Jammet's.[26] I admit I have some wicked notions in my head. We'd do it allright. So send off that letter. Think of me signing an agreement to write 40,000 words on whisky![27] That should give you courage. You couldn't write worse than I have done.

If I had a story for Brandt, I'd send it you. But I haven't. I have one – but it's one of these exquisite psychological things – bloody hopeless. But I will try to do one – and let you have it some time soon. I get so little time to myself. Did you recently see a short story of mine in *Scots Mag.* about the sea? But that, too, would not be their style. It's hard luck on me! (. . .)

Love to you all

Neil

A final word to dear Toshon.[28]

TO NAN SHEPHERD

LARACHAN, DOCHFOUR DRIVE, INVERNESS   26/12/34

My dear Nan,

I felt like acknowledging your note by return, it was so charming and wise. At least, I hope it was wise, because it was so clairvoyant and, by such deft implications, so congratulatory! Which means no more than that I was delighted you said what you said about certain evocative paragraphs. For if even one other sees them, then they are there, though all the rest of the world be blind. Isn't that right – even mathematically? Cheers. It's odd to have written something that you like and in the same instant to know that you should cut it out 1) if you wish the critics for once to refrain from the word obscure 2) if you want to sell. Whereas the something is not obscure to you at all, but on the contrary the only clear thing in a waste of pages!

It's different in poetry. It's no doubt the fashion to expect it there. So *you* get off with it. Though of course you don't do it in the way I try to. I'm earthy. You have real light: sometimes all light (as I do maybe sometimes be all dark.) I am left with that impression of light: sunlight, icelight, clear water. Have you ever known a coldness so perfect that it took the skin off you, like heat? Then you've never touched the iron of a cartwheel in winter ice. Crying: O cold and cold and wild! With all the red cry behind that. The lapwing cry. The running wheel.

In the Cairngorms was an ambitious title.[29] You move in it like air and light and running water. What pleasure it gives me to say without politest shadow of reservation what fine poetry this is. It's distilled – and I know all about distilling of spirit – which spirit is, come to think of it, always crystal clear!

My congratulations.

Yours,

Neil Gunn

TO THE DUKE OF MONTROSE

LARACHAN, DOCHFOUR DRIVE, INVERNESS   10/7/35

My dear Lord Duke,

I have been having a talk with Sir Alexander MacEwen and Mr. John MacCormick about the general position of the Scottish National Party over against the forthcoming General

Election and I hope you will forgive me for intruding a moment, as I do not willingly trouble anyone unless I am sincerely moved myself. Your present attitude towards the Party and towards Liberalism has been indicated to me and perhaps because of the years of service I have given the Cause, you may be willing to consider for what it is worth my dispassionate opinion.

There is no question of my presuming for a moment to discuss or argue against any belief or judgement at which you have arrived. All I should like to do is to indicate what I feel would be the results on the fortunes of our Party of the taking of any decisive or disruptive step by one at once so eminent in our Party and in the affairs of the country. There is no doubt in my mind at all that if, before the impending General Election, your Grace publicly joined up with the Westminster-controlled Liberal Party, the effect on the SNP would be very nearly disastrous. I am just back from a fortnight in the Irish Free State, where I was questioned about the recent break-up of the SNP. This was a reference to the recent McDowal secession.[30] In short the idea has got about that we are disintegrating through repeated internal disruptions, and if you were now to be made to appear in the press publicly to sever your connection – and you know too well how the press would use the occasion – with the SNP the effect on the fortunes of those who continued to fight in the Nationalist ranks would be one of bewildered depression. The adverse effect on the candidature of MacCormick in Inverness and Sir Alexander MacEwen in the Isles would, to my certain knowledge, be dishearteningly severe.

May I ask you, therefore, not to modify your judgement or opinion in any way, but to refrain from taking any step to express it or give it form until after the General Election which now at the most can be only a matter of months hence. It is with the utmost diffidence that I write you thus, but I am helped, too, by the belief, if I may be allowed so to express it, that you may not have fully realised your own consequence and power among us. It is in the name of the Nationalist candidates who are pledged to fight and will fight in the forthcoming election and of the great number of active workers who are now doing their utmost to organise the constituencies, that I make my appeal to you.

If you like, when the Election is over, we could meet and discuss the whole position of our affairs afresh and consider what new departure or policies may be necessary. To raise any new or disruptive issue at this hour would be, I am certain, unsound in wisdom and fatal in practical issue.

Again with my regrets for this intrusion,
Yours very sincerely,

Neil M. Gunn

In his reply the Duke of Montrose suggested that as a member of the Liberal Party he would be able to exercise influence to obtain agreement between the two Parties to support each others' candidates.

JAMES LESLIE MITCHELL (Lewis Grassic Gibbon) was born in 1901 and spent his boyhood in the Mearns of Kincardineshire. After a period as a journalist and several years in the Services he settled down in the south of England to write. He organised the *Voice of Scotland* series for Routledge and it was for this series that Gunn was asked to produce a volume on whisky. Mitchell himself wrote a remarkable number of books, uneven in quality, between 1928 and his death in 1935.

TO LEWIS GRASSIC GIBBON
LARACHAN, DOCHFOUR DRIVE, INVERNESS   11/11/35

My dear Gibbon,

Your book has moved me deeply. You are yourself so moved by the suffering poor that your relation of what will be dubbed their coarsest thought or feeling achieves another truth and even a certain moral fervour. There is an integrity in this trilogy of yours[31] that brings relief to the written word. And I understand so well the relentlessness of an attitude – as in Ewan – that forswears charity and becomes the granite wedge, cleaving forward, though the heavens come down in small bits. I might criticise *your* attitude here, but in my charity (as you call it) I can't. Ahead with it, and let all the cant of "literature" look after itself. This is History, and history like life is born in pain and not in sweet imaginings!

I salute you (holding my balance). And Grieve will claim you because of the wallops right and left. But you're doing something far bigger than that. Any fool can blast and condemn. You blast and condemn your parson in a way that does not move me at all. But you have got inside your Spartacus. And inside the real Spartacus (as you have shown elsewhere) was humanity and a charity more terrible than any granite wedge. If I had any criticism at all, it'd be that I'd commend you to the humanity of your own Spartacus. Ever more power to you. Great stuff.

And thank you for your kind remarks about *Butcher's Broom*. The poor seem to obsess us both! And in my locality, as I tried to show, there did exist traces of the ancient kindness and interest of the Simple Folk. It goes far beyond the Gaelic – though our records are in Gaelic only.

I've been away for some days, and have not been able to get down to thinking about that book.[32] But let me say at a blind venture that I'll take it on, on the understanding that if I cannot do it I will let you know no later than one month hence. My official position, with official access to fact, may hamper me. Sort of know too much about the actual business! And I am possibly a trifle diffident about tackling the personal essay business – and particularly on such a subject. And possibly that is what attracts! Let me know the terms some time. I have to get a new car.

Yours with the haste of keen admiration.

Neil M. Gunn
(No mention would have to be made by publishers in *any* way of my Revenue position.)[33]

TO JOHN MACCORMICK
LARACHAN   2ND JULY 1936

My dear John
(. . .) For a great number of years the workers of Scotland have been putting up a strenuous, self-sacrificing and often bitter fight for better social conditions. Whatever our economic faith, we have to recognise this. I have talked to Trade Union and Socialist leaders in the North here, and their position is simply that in no circumstances will they allow

43

what they consider any extraneous issue to interfere with this fight. Many of them are frankly favourable to self-government, but they are not prepared, they say, to consider the matter as a living issue until first of all they have ensured the workers' economic position.

In short, we are driven back upon (. . .) an economic programme. Of course the Party has pinned its faith already to an economic programme. We are committed to it. But the frank truth is that we have no economic programme. And I am convinced that any patchwork programme – partly Socialist, partly Tory etc. such as we have now and then framed up – is not of the slightest use, quite apart from the all-important consideration that it would take years to get it across to the people.

Now if this be the real position, then, it seems to me, it logically forces us to one of two alternatives: either the Party adopts one of the existing economic faiths, such as Socialism or Liberalism, and goes all out on it on a nationalist basis, *or* it follows the suggestions of your Memorandum and acts through all other parties, remaining itself the rallying ground and inspiration of the self-government movement.

The inherent danger of your plan is a subtle dissipation of Nationalist energies and a transference of personal loyalty to another Party. Would it be possible adequately to guard against these possibilities? If it were possible, then undoubtedly we could open out the fight on a much wider front. It might be possible, as you suggest, to work within the Labour Party for example in a manner that might tend to swing the whole Scottish Labour movement round towards creative work for self-government. It might; but have we any grounds at all for supposing such a happy issue? A realist answer to that question would weigh heavily with me. And such an answer should not be impossible to get. We know the public declarations of men like Maxton and Johnston. What are they worth? Could not the real possibilities be explored in a private way and the results conveyed to members of Council?

I ask these questions with regard to one single point because what is now before the Party challenges in a fundamental way the past tactics of the Party. The moment is grave, and personally I feel I should like to explore more closely all possibilities behind the suggestions and proposals you make before coming to a definite decision. Your proposals are concrete and do definitely provide the basis for such an exploration.

(Typed copy, unsigned. Ed.)

TO ANDREW DEWAR GIBB
LARACHAN   29/9/36

My dear Gibb,
I'm afraid the Mod and nights without sleep have kept serious correspondence at bay. (. . .) The question of an organiser raises an immediate concrete issue (. . .) for what specific purpose would he or she be employed? Take Inverness. We have worked for a long time here. I have driven a speaker in my car 130 miles in a night to address one meeting. We bore the expense ourselves (. . .) But the fact is I cannot guarantee an increase in McCormick's vote. There might even be a drop in the vote (not in Nationalism) because folk are not disposed to go on casting a vote for a cause they don't believe will succeed, when they have behind their Nationalism a very definite economic attitude. If such a position is general, what are we going to do in the next general election? Would standing in many constituencies and coming croppers endanger the undoubted rising growth of interest in Nationalism itself?
(. . .) Again, assume that political contests are not to be the main immediate aim, how about our political attack? I can see, for example, a National Party more closely knit than the present body, less tolerant of anything but the pure doctrine, the head and fount of Nationalism, and devoted to propaganda of an undeviating and, if necessary, extreme type. Outside that body dependable Nationalists might carry on the work right into the camps of the existing Parties. I can see John MacCormick is a Socialist. Assuming a man of that kind entered the Labour Party, I should say he ought to do so not in any Macchiavellian way but frankly as a socialist who is also a Nationalist. In my opinion we must, if we are to succeed, fearlessly attack existing bodies. We must, by whatever means, make them *see* our position. That was my whole aim, for example, when I first approached you when you were in the Scottish Party. I have been damned for that approach to the Scottish Party (. . .) but I know I was right. (. . .) The kind of

organiser the Party is going to have becomes very important because above all things that organiser must be an enthusiastic Nationalist. If the Party for a time is to become a propagandist educational body, the ordinary electioneering organiser would, it seems to me, be of little use. (. . .)
With all regards,

Yours sincerely,
(Typed copy, unsigned. Ed.)

TO MAURICE WALSH
LARACHAN, DOCHFOUR DRIVE, INVERNESS   5/2/37

My dear Maurice,
(. . .) You'll be hearing from your pal Carl[34] about *And No Quarter*. Good news it'll be whatever it is. It'll be your best work besides. The only respect in which you are like poetry and wine is in the slow inevitable cumulative certainty of the maturing process. I'm longing to see the thing in print. I'll look for a certain quality which may not be there. If it isn't I'll tell you with great frankness. That it'll be moving in many parts I have no doubt. That's not what I mean. But you are becoming an artist, there's no doubt also. Also a money-mongerer on a large scale. The two sides do now and then have a friendly tussle. But I offer no comment. How can I? – who am glad to get £2-2s for an article and it well thought out and carefully written.
Highland River is due on April 1st – all fools' day. Just about right, I think. I'll send you a copy – but without any compulsion upon Mrs Walsh to read it. You'll be writing now and then so movingly, you great bloody twister of a play-actor, that I can imagine your wife jumpin' up, fair overcome, and kissin' ye on the nose. Alas my nose'll be in no danger o' sic daft delights as she falls asleep, like a water lily at night, on the Highland River's monotone. It's a good thing for me that I have achieved the disinterested detachment that perceives beauty in a' its phases. Though how far such detachment is the result of inward growth or of outward defeat, who can say? I'll leave it to Toshon. For the rest, I'll carry a hankie, so that there will be nothing wrong with my nose anyway. (. . .)
I am clean off writing – have been for a long time – and now

begin to perceive that a critical time has arrived. If I stay on
here, I'll do nothing. I feel as if I'd finished a certain phase of
writing. If I turn to writing again, it could only be as a result of
thought and long periods of time to myself. The snatching of
an odd hour to do a bit of scribbling has no longer the slightest
interest. Neither has the picking up of a few guineas, because
while I'm working we have now all the money we need. Daisy
is keen to clear out. I'm not caring much either way. (. . .)
Greetings to Ardnaglaise,

Neil

They did indeed "clear out." Neil resigned his job in the
following letter. He and Daisy went "off in a boat" to the West
Coast and the Isles, and then set up house near Dingwall. Gunn
was for the first time entirely dependent on writing for a living.

TO MAURICE WALSH
INVERNESS   23/2/37

My dear Maurice,
I read it all in one long dithering wallop and me in bed
recovering from a temperature, and Daisy beside me with one
growing. The doctor had examd. us both and found all vital
organs hale and hearty. Daisy had never kept warm in bed long
enough – like myself last winter – but she'll stay put now for a
few days. The good maid is back, so we'll be flourishing soon
again. I think we're getting tired of Inverness.
However, to this yarn of yours,[35] which has its faults, being
slow maybe in the beginning as they say, and with expressions
of romance at long odd moments that my thin-bloodedness
might not have courage for, and so on and what not here and
there, but what do they all amount to but the just, personal
mannerisms of the traditional story-teller? Who the hell are
Chambers or anyone else to ask you to be slick here or there?
You tell a great story in your own way, and it is your very own
way, and when it is a good way it is grand. Which is all the great
poets have been able to do ever. Tippermuir[36] got me where I
thought there was nothing of me left, and it moved me, by
God, like the war pipes. Cheers to you, boy! The atmosphere
of that Gaelic camp is thick with easy life. And if you give the

Covenant folk hell, they deserved most of it. And if you have historic warrant for your treatment of Rose, alter nothing. And if you haven't, never mind the thin-skinned susceptibilities of your Scots publishers, for when all is said and done a Rose is your second heroine and you have married her. And, further, it is a duty, I maintain, for all folk like ourselves when writing of the old clan chaps to curse them as land grabbers and in the end as betrayers of the folk.

Your movement of masses, of armies, is grand. The whole historic treatment is excellent. And I can see your whole self shaping up every now and then to assessment and judgement – a thing that is new to you but which you carry off nobly.

It will be objected by the realists that your romance is a little too pure, your characters too chivalrous, your dark Rose more romantic type than living female. There is an answer to that, too, but I'm not bothering now.

My advice then is to send it back to Chambers with only one sentence struck out and that *the very last in the book*. Say to them that you feel the action of the book depends on a creation of atmosphere which can be created only in your leisurely style, but that you'll be able better to assess this when you get the galley proofs. Then should there be an odd paragraph here or there that you could dispense with, why you might do so. *Don't* let *them* do it. The suggestion as to cutting part about releasing Margaret from stocks is *bad*. A good scene.

Which is all at the moment.

My congratulations on your best work. And a very special word of praise for your historic detail. It's hard work on my part, but, goad man, I'm surely guiding you to the Great Work.

Love to Toshon.

Yours ever,

Neil

TO H.M. CUSTOMS AND EXCISE

LARACHAN, DOCHFOUR DRIVE, INVERNESS   5 JUNE 1937

In recent years I have felt called upon to pursue certain literary work which has resulted in books that have been publicly discussed as of some small value to the literary tradition of my country, and I feel that as this new work might interfere, without my always perceiving it, with the proper prosecution of my official duties, the only honourable course open to me is to resign. This decision has been made the more imperative through eye-trouble[37] which has gradually but cumulatively affected my sight.

In these circumstances, and in view of my record of service in this Department of over twenty-five years, I should be glad to know if your Honours could possibly contemplate the grant of a pension, however small. Literary work, when not of a popular or commercial kind, can be uncertain of issue and unremunerative in result, and though I am prepared to take this risk, I would yet ask your Honours to consider my case as a special one based on a long period of faithful service.

I am, Honourable Sirs, your obedient servant,

N. M. Gunn[38]

TWO

THE FULL-TIME WRITER

1937 to 1956

My dear Christopher

Your letter has just come in and evokes ancient and pleasant days, so that my morning's work on the travel book[1] can go hang while I address you. In a sense we both represent aspects of things Scottish (inter alia!) and it mightn't be a bad idea if we carried on our debate to see what comes of it, or – more realistically – for the fun of it. Though, as you say, the only way is by random talk, taking things up to look at them, let them drop, and look at them again. You see in my work evidence of the sentimental. I, in yours, evidence of the romantic-sentimental. So there may be some points of common vision! While a touch of dry humour now and then may mercifully be perceived.

However, let's clear this mercenary business out of the way first. I am particularly interested in your remark that but for certain elements in my work, I should not only have had a greater commercial but also a greater artistic success. Here you align yourself both with popular opinion and with the opinion of critics like Day Lewis and Sean O'Faolain. Let me say further that but for these elements, I should probably have been *chosen* by the English Book Society (in the case of *Highland River*). As it was the latter postponed decision for three months and then finally *recommended*. Had they *chosen*, their first order would have been 75,000 copies, and my fortune would have been assured! Now I know these elements were against me. And should I ever write another novel, they will almost certainly be more pronounced. So in heaven's name don't pull my leg over mercenary motive, for the poor damned leg has every reason to feel sore and every reason to curse the idiotic thrawn brain by which it is animated. As you know, most writers who damn others for being a commercial success would gladly avail themselves of that success if they could. I am not deceived in this matter nor, on the other hand, merely purist.

Why then do I humbug myself with these elements? Sean

O'Faolain, in his critique, says that when he started HR he thought it was going to be a "masterpiece", but then it got lost (I forget his words) in the bog of Celtic mysticism. Day Lewis runs much on the same lines, except that he takes exception also to the preachings and moralisings of Lowland writers (thereby making sure that Scots frae a' the airts get it in the neck.) I imagine that you (apart from the preachings and moralisings possibly!) take the same line. Yet I am sure you will have your own definition or exposition of these elements and until you care to define them with some precision I might merely waste time in first assuming and then analysing. So get down to it! For of course they present merely a text or fixed point – and we must have something like that or otherwise the confounded lack of a sense of reality in these critics and in yourself would have us arguing, old-Russian-fashion, about vague nothing.

Well, now, out of that general clearance for foot room, let us pick up a thing here and there and have a look at it. Take this Celtic mysticism of yours (and the critics). You all detest it. Not only a bog but a drowning bog; its "vagueness" completely antipathetic; and a real danger because inclined to cling to and smother the up-and-coming. May I be permitted to appreciate your point of view? Even to know a little of this history and to what extent it is an imposition from without upon the hard factual Gaelic mind? Anyway, take it that such intelligence as I possess has tested the hull of this curious bark, with a knife fore and aft, and that O'Faolain's shake of the head was not unforeseen nor my own attitude altered thereby (however more clearly as a result I now see the limitations of O'Faolain). The first simple test I should put to that Irishman (as indeed I should put it to you, though it is not important enough for your own purpose, unless as factual illustration) is this: pick out any paragraph in HR and discover for me in it this "vagueness" of Celtic mysticism. I know it cannot be done. Because any paragraph there I can analyse to elements real to the psyche and designed by me for some artistic – or other – purpose – precisely as you design your poems. My final design may be a different one from yours – you may not like it – but that does not affect the reality of the process in each mind. (. . .) Again, Edwin Muir quoted me to show that I was merely elusive (I wish I could show you this review, for Muir always handles the apparatus of clear thinking at least). But then I cannot help that. There are thoughts which are devilish elusive. And that elusiveness of the mind is a reality, and every writer with a mind has to do something with it or about it on paper. (...) But this elusiveness is the very antithesis of vagueness. It is indeed a deliberate and difficult effort to get and hold in that region where thought tends to get lost in the rarefied. (...)

(Typed copy, unsigned. Ed.)

MARGARET MacEWEN, born in 1913, was the younger daughter of Sir Alexander MacEwen. Her father was involved with the founding of the Scottish Party and later in its merger with the National Party of Scotland, and Neil was in close touch with him in the thirties about political matters. Margaret, who acted as her father's secretary from 1934–38, was a frequent visitor to Larachan and became a life-long friend. In 1938 she joined the Communist Party and remained an active member until about 1947 when she drifted away from politics. After the war she worked as a medical secretary, first in Kent and later in Edinburgh, where she settled in 1952.

TO MARGARET MACEWEN
BRAEFARM HOUSE, DINGWALL, ROSS-SHIRE
FRIDAY   (OCTOBER 1938)

My dear Margaret,
    I was glad to get your letter and find you had become happily placed in your new surroundings. Your news reads very interestingly and I try to visualise your busy office life – complete with 1d. cups of tea, and your life in your flat – complete with wall paper – though that's a trifle more difficult! I was amused, too, at your description of your first meeting with Douglas,[2] which was correctly in character! Not too easy for you, adventuring alone into a new life. Indeed, when we saw you off at Glasgow, the vision of you setting out alone had something rather heroic about it which stuck in my mind for quite a time. My blessings went with you. And I was glad to think you had enjoyed your last few days in Glasgow –

and even to learn that you were a trifle sad parting from your "bourgeois national" friends. Let us hope you won't forget them too soon – though I can quite understand how, in the living atmosphere of the *Daily Worker*, they must appear slightly unreal and as belonging to a dead age! I like your remark about the perfect antidote to depression and defeatism and the lack of time to cry over spilt milk. Good for you and the *Daily Worker*! When I feel more than usual, that I need reinvigorating, I'll know where to come. You could show me round as a specimen and as a warning. Not that I shouldn't have a few things to say for myself, I warn you. And clever as you may become in dialectics, I should still contrive to throw a few mental arabesques here and there.

I was very interested in your descriptions of office life, of how things are arranged, and of how from high to low folk call each other by the Xtian names. That's not exactly new to me. When I was a small boy in the far north, young and old called each other by their Xtian names and had done it for a thousand or two years. Which looks like the beginning of a nationalist argument. And what anyway could these primitive folk have known of the immense library of communism? True, true. I withdraw. Meantime.

And didn't Chamberlain do well?[3] I'm sure your office was relieved and should be glad to hear that if you did not lead the prayers you at least prompted them.

Which reminds me that I haven't sent *American Testament*[4] back yet. I'd like Daisy – who is half way through it – to finish it. I read it all with great interest, for his effort at describing the impact of the communist idea on the traditional literary mind had a particular appeal. I am not going to say anything about it meantime, or I should be writing for hours. I like its subtle persuasiveness. It's the real suasion of politics; and the Jewish mind is affected personally in ways that are not always obvious, but nonetheless affecting for all that, though perhaps not in a way finally to satisfy a mind that is not worried by the Jewish problem, profoundly nowadays becoming a psychological one. If there's sense in that. In short, there is a great amount of invisible special pleading, based on premises that are taken for granted. However, it's ungenerous to appear to criticise without first of all showing the tremendous merit. So enough. Meantime, again.

This is no more than a hurried note to give you cheers on a successful start to your new venture. Whiles when I am taking my solitary walk away up through the fields, I have a few words with you.

I am glad you enjoyed your last few days in Glasgow. So did I. Especially parts of 'em. Peter John and Ena and John and Joey Reid[5] landed on us here recently and stayed for several days. There wasn't much sleep and I am only now recovering.

Good luck, Margaret. And our thanks for your offer of hospitality – so generously put. That was a nice thought. I don't know when a visit may be made to London but I should certainly say it will be before your six months are up. You'll be reminded of your offer.

I trust you are behaving yourself very properly. You'll smile at that as being bourgeois. Ah well.

Yours

Neil

TO MARGARET MACEWEN

BRAEFARM HOUSE, DINGWALL, ROSS-SHIRE   28 NOV. 1938

My dear Margaret,
(. . .). About my going to London, there is a tentative arrangement at the moment, that we shall both be in London at the beginning of February. Daisy is then going on to see her sister somewhere about Exeter while I shall fly to Munich for a short holiday. I want to spend a day or two in London, either going or coming; and if you could spend an hour or two showing me around, how much I should be your debtor. Do you think you could manage that? At your present rate of progress into the fascinations of your new life, I begin to doubt it. Though, to be quite candid, I am delighted that your new life is giving you what you call self-confidence. And I was greatly struck by your Marxian symbolism on the wallpaper. That was pretty brilliant of you. But if you don't look out, you'll be held guilty of subjectivism. If you develop your individuality, or rather your individualism, in this way, you may find yourself some fine day doubting the philosophic basis of your creed. And that would be a tragedy! Personally I shouldn't think so, of course, but then I was always an anarchist; and so far as politics are concerned, I am consistently haunted by the hard

Scots feeling that they should be kept in their place, their real concern being the providing of the animal necessities of food, shelter, and clothing. After that, three cheers for the intensest form of individualism. But someday I must have a real debate with you on Communism. Perhaps when I come to London? Unless, of course, you attack me before then. Though I have the awful weakness of being soft-hearted. You don't think so? Oh come! It's snowing here at the moment heavily and the whole valley is filled with flakes. I'm sitting looking out through it while I'm talking to you – and dashed the spiral can I see of any sort. Unless you're becoming a spiral yourself – for I can see you easily enough. No, you're not a spiral yet, thank heaven – just your fair hair with snow on it and you smiling in a way that is difficult for a simple fellow to fathom. Must be your new London ways.

For I can see, too, that you're getting a trifle superior – I refer to your description of the Glasgow impasse over ice cream v. tea. Good old Scotland. None of your slithering lack of individualism. I personally should be very deeply moved over whether I was to have ice cream *or* tea. There, now, was a real issue. But you English people, with your vague ideals, won't see it. I should hold up everything until I made sure that I was going to get my tea. All the rest could have ice-cream. And if I know a thing or two about you, you'd have put up a hefty fight for tea yourself.

(. . .) I am reading one or two strange books over again that have nothing to do with politics; and reading a little on anarchism, which I have always found so attractive, and which more than once made my concern for the Spanish problem very acute. How I should like to see a country like Spain attempt to put anarchism into practice. Abolish leadership (are we ever going to get rid of the tyrant: Are we seeing a bureaucracy being established in Russia – steadily increasing in power, rather than "withering away"?) and the State. But there, I'll be arguing in a moment. And I'm beginning to be afraid that the chances of anarchism being established in Spain are beginning to fade. (. . .)

All the best to you, Margaret,
Yours ever,

Neil

DOUGLAS MUHR (1912–1956) was a salesman visiting Inverness when he first met Neil Gunn. By the time Margaret MacEwen joined the Staff he was employed in a management capacity with *The Daily Worker*. Douglas wrote plays, some of which he sent to Neil for comment. He became a Sergeant Instructor in the Army during the War and a teacher after it.

TO DOUGLAS MUHR

BRAEFARM HOUSE, DINGWALL, ROSS-SHIRE   17/7/39

Dear Douglas,

(. . .) We are very sorry to hear you're off form. You were looking a bit tired when I saw you in London. It's wild nature you need and a suspension of thought *and* a harking back to the dear old instinctive life. The bloody world is killing the individual mind. Send the bloody world and all its robotisations and beehives and capitalistic greeds to hell from out your distinguished mind. Pity I hadn't a boat or I'd have engaged you as one of the crew at an utterly sweated wage. But in the West we're being with friends.

Cheers,

Neil

Neil Gunn withdrew from the Council of the Scottish National Party in June 1939.

TO JOHN MACCORMICK

4 DECEMBER 1939

Dear John,

My regret, formal and informal, that I can't attend the Conference on the 12th.

I am sorry that I have got out of touch with you and therefore with affairs inside the Party, for it leaves me unable to make a practical suggestion. But travelling to Glasgow is a three-day affair and in these desperate times rather expensive. I should imagine that the great majority of ordinary members firmly believe in prosecuting the war and the Council's position is accordingly a difficult one, particularly as opinion must be divided even there. I think myself it is very necessary to keep the Party in being and the effect of any step should be considered accordingly. Take these Aberdeen resolutions, for example: do they emanate from a large body of opinion or from a very small one? As old Lenin knew, you can't do anything effectual unless you have some power behind you.

Personally, my attitude to this war business includes motives beyond the immediate issues of self-government. For a long time I have been troubled and uncertain about Russia, but recent events have satisfied me that Stalin and Company have got bitten by the lust for power. Communists in this country seem still to confuse Stalin with communism as many a simple wife does an errant Moderator of the Wee Free Kirk with Christianity. The forces of the world seem slowly to be aligning themselves into two groups: those who wish to retain man's freedom to express whatever integrity may be in him and those who don't. This freedom of expression is to me supremely important, and I am prepared to align myself and fight, accordingly. Scotland's national historic attitude, before and after the Declaration of Arbroath, shows her as one of the earliest and finest champions of this freedom and it is inconceivable to me that she adopt any other attitude now. On this issue I am prepared to take a stand for or against any country, my own included.

And meantime my belief in the need for realising our Party's aim is, if that were possible, growing stronger.

The position therefore to me is that we must press as strongly as possible and by all means to realise our aims, but not in such a manner as to dissociate ourselves implicitly or explicitly, from such forces as may be fighting to retain individual expression of opinion. There is no division here, for this very freedom is, as I say, implicit in the Scottish tradition, and any declaration by the Party should make this grand old historical fact clear.

(. . .) members may think this an imperialistic war all round. But the fact remains (. . .) we can express our opinions about the Westminster Government, and if we are not in a stronger position the main blame lies at the door at the Scots themselves.

To illustrate, my difficulty with the Aberdeen motion is this. Take Resolution 1). What is a just international settlement? Would it include freedom for Czechoslovakia and Poland? (. . .) Accordingly, how is such a settlement to be achieved without fighting Germany? If Proposer is not going to fight Germany how is he going to get his just settlement? In short, the logic of his own resolution compels him to support the very war that in Resolution 3) he calls us to oppose! This is unfortunate for it would be very nice to indulge ourselves in the luxury of demanding a just settlement without doing anything more about it.

(. . .) I shall be glad to hear from you.

With all good wishes,

Yours

(A typed copy, unsigned Ed)

TO MAURICE WALSH

BRAEFARM HOUSE, DINGWALL   22/3/40

My dear Maurice,

We were delighted to hear that Toshon has got over the worst of her bad time, and pray that progress may continue even if she has to forego bowling into Dublin for a while. She bowled pretty well and consistently while the going was good. Once or twice to me it was a fair substitute for big-game hunting in Africa, and I never failed to admire the way you cowered and endured with a fortitude that saw every approaching car within ten miles and was never voiceless. Begod, we were game. But at our best our *sangfroid*, our nonchallance (sic), was a pale affair beside the full-blooded darlin gaiety of the girl herself's. Wagner should have seen her before he did his stuff about the Valkyries – or whatever. Though I have the awful feeling in me that she'll be at the bowling again. Very well so. Keep your jar full. You and meself took a lot of beating most ways with our minds made up.

And your book[6] as ever was arrived yesterday afternoon, and I looked at it fore and aft and muttered belles lettres, and went out and planted my early potatoes and cabbage, my lettuce, leeks, beetroot, carrots, radishes, and so on, for we are digging not only for victory but for subsistence. And then I came in. And when I was half way through your volume, a man came in. And after a long time he went out. And I finished it at midnight. I give you three more cheers than Barrie. The whole thing was a delight to me. The sonorous tone of your bellowing poet's voice was solemn with laughter. And I don't know anyone else who could have brought it off. You brought it off in a way you didn't bring off *Sons of the Swordmaker*, which, however good the writing, could not be finally brought off, because its whole ethos belonged to another age, different in spirit and outlook. For the same reason no one can write a ballad today, however fine the poetry they put intilt. The king sat in Dunfermline toun drinking the blood-red wine once and forever. You cannot get him sitting in Dunfermline toun making linoleum. And a bottle of Bass. *Son of Apple* cheered me to chuckles as all good drink should. It was like coming on yourself and you knowing you have more than the price of one drink behind you. Begod, it was grand. For you could have come such a helluva cropper. The delight I get when you do something passing well makes me feel you owe me four drinks and if I were anywhere within reach at this minute I would haul you out so that at the heel of the hunt I would still be able to remind you that our only purpose was to buy a little present for Toshon. And we would drive safely home in a bus.

Pity it is that worlds divide us and a waste of seas. About coming over – we'll be saying nothing meantime until that red-haired woman is thinking of cricket again, of bowling like the son of Apple with his duck egg.

Cheers for *The Hill is Mine*. A gorgeous title. And I'm glad Chambers like it. I'm thinking of taking out the licence for my car now! If the S. E. Post take it – we'll enquire about flying over to Dublin.

I'm writing articles myself for a pittance, but I was never one for ambition, and thank God we are easily contented. (. . .)

And to Toshon herself my fond greetings.

Neil

TO NAN SHEPHERD
BRAEFARM HOUSE, DINGWALL   17 MAY 1940

My dear Nan
(. . .) You come uncannily at the heart of the matter and I feel, well, there's one person anyway! One either sees a thing as you do or one doesn't. That's the sort of conclusion I've come to. Some of the reviews of my book[7] admit of no intermediate conclusion. And it is natural that without a certain eye many a scene would be unspeakably bleak and boring. As you can understand, no one but the writer knows when a critic puts

his finger on a sore or an important point – no one knows so infallibly. When you hesitate before arriving at the word *movements* (movements of being), then it is as if you were surprising me in my very lair where, to put it mildly, I hardly expected to see you or anyone else. You evoke life in its movement of transition, to arrest for an instant the movement and glance of its body and eye, to do something of the same kind to what we call inanimate nature; but somehow it has in it a rare delight. I don't mean here the Walter Pater or Renaissance attitude, the refining of the senses to a gem-like etc. etc. Not that at all. Something, in a sense, quite other. A momentary apprehension of the primordial sense of life, alert, quick-eyed, arrested in a grey rock-face rather than in a gem... and at the same time a curious half-consciousness of an extra dimension of apprehension, with its momentary thrill. I am not at all sure... that we have not here the beginning to an extra dimension of being. But enough.

How I relished your thrawing my neck over the cliché. Delicious of you. And what a cliché it was. I mean, how few will see it. It was pretty well done. More and more you'll find me – gin I go on writing – using cliché and slang and swear. A perversity, this, but done, damitall, with a manner. Isn't that what's wrong with these pleasant English characters whom you don't care much for? How many of us are clichés? And in a shooting lodge, on sporting holiday, well, I mean to say, what? Think it out. I actually delight in George. I had nothing to do with writing him at all. At any moment I could repeat him like a medium. (. . .)

Yours,

Neil

ENA MacLEOD at one time acted as governess to the children of Sir Alexander and Lady MacEwen. She married Dr. Peter John Macleod, who was first a General Practitioner in Lewis and then in 1940 became Medical Superintendent of the Miners' Rehabilitation Centre, Gleneagles. He and Gunn met at the Inverness Mod. in 1936. After her husband's death Ena lived in Perth and the Gunns often stayed with her on their way south.

BRAE   24/8 (1940?)

My dear Ena,
    Many thanks for your salutations and enclosures. I read
Peter's[8] opus straight off in the lamplight and paused to read
bits to Daisy – fancy Peter laying in to the poor miner who is
having his hand stroked by the masseuse! – and she laughed.
He fair lays about him, not without a notable exercise of ironic
wit. Hardly the phraseology of departmental custom whiles! But
really a capital bit of work. And we thought the head blokes
were reticent over some political implication. Land, that's not
it at all. It's that he swings a claymore at the medical windmills,
psychiatrists, sweet masseuse an' all, and tells you the miner's
psychology as if no trade unions existed in order to maintain
the high and splendid dignity of man. I chuckle and shake. Not
to mention the Press, which might accordingly have things to
say about it to embarass a gentle and innocent Department ...
But I'll read it again and perhaps even suggest parenthetic
additions, such as "(not that I grudge any miner having his
hand stroked, even while lying on a couch, strange as such a
procedure may seem)". Peter must be more objective. Just
because he himself does not like having his hand stroked, he
should not deduce etc. I think I may place it on record (...) that
this is the first Report I have ever consumed with pleasure. (...)
    Yours,

    Neil

AGNES MURE MACKENZIE was born in Lewis in 1891. She
worked as a lecturer at Birbeck College, London, and wrote
several novels as well as many historical studies and text-books. In
1942 she became President of the Saltire Society. Neil met her in
Edinburgh during that year.

BRAEFARM HOUSE, DINGWALL, ROSS-SHIRE   13 MARCH, 1942

Dear Dr. Agnes Mure Mackenzie,
    Though I had an order in for your Saltire pamphlet[9] when
first I heard it was to be published, my local bookseller only

managed to get it for me today. I have now read it and yield to the impulse to salute your grace, though writing is about the poorest way of doing that yet invented, remembering as I do, in those matters, the hand of reality. To pay you back, as we say in the North, I have a good mind to tell you (to pay you back, I mean, for your references to myself) just how extraordinarily charming you were that evening and how clear the picture that remains of the Scottish tradition attaining its flower. Life is more than letters at the end of the day, particularly when it is life like that. As your pamphlet makes out, it is the sort of life we need more abundantly. But even in Scotland we have our glimpses of it under the visiting moon. Though it's tough, as you say, that London should have such command of the moon. Those Gaelic-minded arabesques! But you were charming.

I have been chuckling, too, over your articles in *The Scots Ind.* You see, in Inverness when the movement first got going, the lads brought to me all the tough cases, the fellows who could explode the whole notion as dangerous parochialism. Sometimes the results were embarrassing, as in the case of the working engineer who said he didn't want any of this Wallace and Bruce business: he wanted facts and figures. So facts and figures he got. After a month he said he was ready to do his bit. So the wise secretary tried him out at a small country hall. Contemplate the secretary's surprise when the bold engineer said he did not give a hoot for facts and figures, what really mattered was the spirit of Wallace and Bruce, and proceeded on that basis to tell his audience where they got off.

Blessings with you, and my deep acknowledgements,
Yours very sincerely,

Neil M. Gunn

TO AGNES MURE MACKENZIE
BRAEFARM HOUSE, DINGWALL   7-4-42

Dear Agnes Mure Mackenzie,
Your letter arrived as I'd just got your *Scotland in Modern Times*, after long delay, from the library, and now, wae's me, I'll have to think of buying. Which is tough on a poor fellow. But it's broad and sure and sets off immense research with the gallant air of a feather in your bonnet. While I confess to an

abysmal ignorance of most scholarly things, including history, I must say that I have found the reading of Scots history at any time difficult. It was either dead uninteresting with no space at all given to real social conditions, the life of the folk, or if really concerned with the truth about Scotland then – it was difficult to read because of the mental complications engendered in the process.) I once wrote a novel on the Clearances, called *Butcher's Broom*. I had rather to screw myself up to the Gloomy Memories (more traditional lore was in me for some of the "cleared" came to our coast), though I did find a certain sardonic interest in the case put forward by Loch[10] and others on behalf of Sutherland. After a bath of Scots history of that kind, I tend to sheer off more reading about it and about for a time. We have our limits of endurance!

Also, too, I suppose I have really given a lot of time to modern Scots affairs – and when you add a day's work in Civil Service (now finished), not to mention the odd hours in which I did a bit of writing, – well, you'll really have to excuse me if, in a country place, far from libraries and affairs literary, I have not yet read your main volumes. But I'll come at them. For I do think this is noble work. You make me feel that what moves you is what moves myself – not any particular desire for public acknowledgement but something simply in the nature of tribute to a land that gave us much. And if I could take off my bonnet with half the grace with which you stick a feather in yours, I'd be prepared to call it a day to the Shades of the past and the bens and glens of the present, with a thocht for the industrial areas, woe is us.

You talk about my not getting too involved in public affairs. How wise the kindly thought, but alas! I'm now on one of these Committees of Enquiry appointed by our Sec. of State – post-war hospital policy for Scotland. When I'm not travelling to Edinburgh I seem to be receiving piles of evidence. They are good enough, however, to pay our railway fares! Then there are local affairs – home defence etc. Bread and butter haven't had a word written to them for a month! However, they're not objecting. And here's the Saltire Society asking me for a pamphlet on whisky distilling. Well, well. It wouldn't be so bad if one could buy a drop itself, but here in the home of the ancient art and industry, there's none to be had. Needed for export to America, for profits (up to E.P.T.), for army messes

THE FULL-TIME WRITER

and wealthy clubs, but for the crofters and fishermen and myself, not a drop. Even our history in process of being made is sometimes difficult to contemplate with a sufficiently serene objectivity. Whiles it may even seem that something more explosive than a pamphlet is needed. Perhaps the real explanation of the Highlander's good manners is that he had to have them or bust. Let us smile anyway.

I could give you a lot of amusing information about the inner history of, e.g., how the original National Party and the Scottish Party came to combine. I found Cunninghame Graham very reasonable and helpful. It was often a sair fecht all the same. Our capacity for schism is truly remarkable – but can only be understood, I feel, in terms of our history. Individualism was bound to run amok when any central cohering body for the common good did not exist. Some of us had a private meeting in Perth recently. I am glad you are hopeful about the future. And things are certainly moving. But a lot of sound broad sense will be needed to guide the uncertain stream. More about that in the not distant future.

I am glad you enjoyed *The Silver Darlings*. I am not so sure about *Young Art and Old Hector*, should it come your way. *The Times Lit. Supp.* reacted adversely, as I expected. To me there's here a very difficult matter of literary assessment – one on which I could give you my views but on which I am open to any opinion. It's perhaps concerned with a fundamental difference in our (Eng and Scots) social beginnings. If you like, a difference between the feudal and the primitive communal. But a real and possibly important (consider "proletarian" and myth), difference. I should be glad to hear from you – though indeed you'd be much better engaged on that really necessary school series – on which my blessing. And thank you for your letter anyhow. It was an enlivening salute amid much dreary public work. We get so little so long of the living quality of life.

Yours very sincerely,

Neil M. Gunn

DOUGLAS YOUNG, born in 1913, was a lecturer in Classics at Aberdeen University, and later at St. Andrews and in Canada. He published several books of poems and some translations of

Aristophanes into Scots. In 1942, at a time when Young was resisting conscription on the grounds that, by the terms of the Treaty of Union, no Government of the United Kingdom had the right to impose it on him, he defeated William Power in the election for the Chairmanship of the SNP. As a result John MacCormick resigned his position as National Secretary. (See Notes 11 & 12)

TO DOUGLAS YOUNG

BRAEFARM HOUSE, DINGWALL, ROSS-SHIRE   10 JUNE 1942

Dear Mr. Young,
    I shall be in the Outer Isles on 27 June. In any case I never have spoken at public meetings of any kind, so please never consider my name in that connection.
    Thank you for your copy of the *Trial and Defence*,[11] which I read with great interest. It does away with all ambiguity. When the Glasgow Herald report of conference came out with a heavy headline: "Conscientious Objector as Party Chairman" – it certainly contrived to mislead the public, more particularly those wanting to be misled. It also put a person like myself in an equivocal position, for I happen to be on one of those Government Commissions of Enquiry (appointed by Secretary of State for Scotland) and part of our duty is to meet and hear representatives of the Scottish public.
    Personally I am grieved that there has been any split in the party. I have always done my utmost to keep the effort united. Scotland has been badly cursed by this fatal tendency to schism – a natural result, no doubt, of the lack of a central cohering body or government – but it's sad that we cannot consciously overcome it.
    You must understand that it's difficult for me to follow remarks you have made about MacCormick and those who may now think with him, because for years we worked together in the north, particularly in organising Inverness-shire where the fine and tireless work MacCormick put in was very clear to me.[12] In my view, the amount the whole movement owes to him can hardly be exceeded, if indeed equalled, by any other individual, and partly in that aspect which brought the whole issue as a united and live one before the Scots public. Accordingly you may realise that I should

68

meantime wish to look into this matter and consult those with whom I previously worked both on the practical side and in considering questions of policy.

I have resigned the Vice-presidency simply because I have long held the opinion – and expressed it to many Council members that those in office should be active Party workers. Living in the far north, and often away from home I naturally got out of touch with internal Party affairs. In my personal circumstances the best I feel I can do, at least meantime, is to assist the common cause by my writings – the article on the essence of Nationalism in the current *Scots Magazine* to which you have referred, being an instance; as well, of course, as by personal contacts with those in literature and public positions.

Yours sincerely,

Neil M. Gunn

JOSEPH MACLEOD was born in London of Scottish parents in 1903, and educated at Rugby and Balliol College, Oxford. He published with Faber and Faber in 1930 the well-received poem, *Ecliptic*. Director and Lessee of the Festival Theatre, Cambridge, from 1933 to 1936, he began to study drama in Soviet Russia.

During the war he was one of the best known BBC newsreaders, and published several books of poems under the pseudonym "Adam Drinan." He died in Florence in 1984.

TO JOSEPH MACLEOD

BRAEFARM HOUSE, DINGWALL   15/4/43

Dear Joseph Macleod,

I have just read *The New Soviet Theatre* with the deepest interest and must offer a word of thanks, because it does manage to put across the *spirit* of the great adventure, and this most books dealing with its economic aspects have rather failed to do. Not but that I have been impressed and heartened by them, particularly the last I read on Red Medicine (I am on a Government Committee at the moment concerned with a certain aspect of public health, post-war, in Scotland).

However, what I have missed in all these is just the point that you bring out, namely that this intense planning is designed not to regiment the individual but rather to free him. And of that I was beginning to be a bit doubtful. One can stand a fair amount of suppression and cruelty and bumping-off, realising the need for force in a transition period, but the purgings of 1937 began to make some of us think. The amazing trial and execution of the Old Guard, the attack on Finland, and so on, had a sort of hopeless air from a distance. A book like Louis Fischer's *Men and Politics* was not exactly reassuring. And the cry that the "Party is everything, the individual nothing" was tending even here to become suspiciously like one of the slogans of a religious crusade – after the "Jesus and no quarter" of our own Covenanters!

At the time of the Stalin-Trotsky schism, I naturally supported Stalin (in argument at least!), for the perhaps naive reason that I also supported Scotland as a country which should have the power to order her own affairs. And I do indeed think that Stalin in his national stand (with his attitude to other nationalities, minorities, power of secession, etc.) was dead right from every point of view, including the international. The awful business is this of the power that corrupts – the one or the ruling few. It is easy to write of the "withering away" but so apallingly difficult in human history to achieve. And when you say (p.166) of three great producers: "They have not yet discovered that Communism means not the submission of the individual human's understanding to the community, but his liberation through it" – well, I begin to wonder!

It is, then, on so fundamental an issue that your book comes alive for me, and the evidence you put up is grand (not that you need expect any ignorant layman like myself to hang on to your multitudinous names though they do give the telling detail to the picture.)

I gave a cheer for all your apt references to the Highlands – except perhaps the last, for I am not sure that your Russian critic has got the right historic slant on the Macbeth period so far as the folk were concerned, and your own Nazi equation is just too temptingly apt to be intuitively sound. But that would need a few words, not of historic learning (where any of your Russian readers or students on Scotland would beat me hands down), but of another kind of knowledge or common sense. Though I might even have a shot at historic records – out of, say, the charter chest at Dunvegan. In short, what I gather from your almost intuitive searching for individual freedom within the concept of Socialist realism may derive, via the blood, from an ancient Gaelic commune! Which is certainly worth a cheer all to itself. After which, off with the bonnet to these Russian lads.

Yours sincerely,

Neil M. Gunn

NAOMI MITCHISON was born in Edinburgh in 1897, the daughter of J. S. Haldane, and married Gilbert Mitchison, who served as a Labour M.P. from 1945 to 1964. She published her first novel, *The Conquered*, in 1923, and has been a prolific writer ever since. After settling near Campbeltown in Argyll she wrote to Neil Gunn about his book *Second Sight*, and a lively correspondence followed.

TO NAOMI MITCHISON

BRAEFARM HOUSE, DINGWALL, ROSS-SHIRE   18-4-1943

Dear Naomi,

(. . .) As to your three ways to change things profoundly – cheers. There are probably a dozen methods of attack. And we should be beyond revolution in the bloody sense. We have had about enough blood for our lifetimes. At least that's the way I feel. But then I have always been a little repelled by the materialist interpretation of history and all the rest when it becomes the new religion. Religion and ideals and what not. Fine! But oh God, they do manage to prosecute them to the nth in cruelty. A drunk man with a revolver is a happy child compared with the fellow who has power to convert you. Anyway, if history is to have any meaning at all, surely hundreds of years of understanding of the democratic concept as we have had it in Scotland must count for something. If not – if we have to copy Russia or somebody else – then don't expect us to be impressed. After all, take the organisation of the Scottish church, from Kirk session or local soviet up to the General Assembly and you might say it gave Russia its governmental pattern. What a wealth of belief and enthusiasm and shedding of blood went to that foundation! And what do you enlightened revolutionaries think and say of it today? At least we have something to go on. Which is my whole case for Scotland. I know what you mean when you say that it's no good just altering things so that folk can go twice a week to the films instead of once. But that's precisely what they'll do however you alter things. What could be altered for the better is the community spirit and the kind of flicks. Though here again I am not sure that the highbrows should have it all their own way. Before you came to Carradale and found what country living really meant, would you have been a sound person to have been placed in charge of their entertainment? And could we have relied on you to have shown generally the model behaviour pattern for such a reformed community? Of course we can now, I know, and your poem "The house and myself" proves it! An extra cheer for that! Verily a capital and most wicked poem. When you ask me if you are talking through your hat – I just remember the hat. Any talk through it would be fascinating – in contradistinction, that is, to ideal talk, at any time. (. . .)

Yours,

Neil

TO NAOMI MITCHISON

BRAEFARM HOUSE, DINGWALL, ROSS-SHIRE   29-6-43

Dear Naomi,

Here's in answer to your last, for if these film folk descend on me I may not do much letter-writing for a month or two. Nothing definite yet about beginning,[13] but then they live on telegrams. The BBC have asked me to do a fisherman Portrait – a 45 min. affair – and I've just been putting them off by telephone – until later in the year. And these days are so lovely anyhow that the thought of work fair goes agin me. Lord, how nice it would be laying a course on, say, Carradale![14] I liked your remarks about discipline and not dithering in a recent letter, but I could do with a lot more of the dithering myself. And I must say, besides, that talk of discipline and all that comes very well from you. If I put a fellow in a novel who may have any sense of discipline at all, you sicken at the sight of him as a galahad. You accuse me of "purity" and what not. So where are you? You'll have discipline just where and when you want it, and that is generally in some idealist affair, disguised under the name of practical politics. Fine day! If discipline, selection, consistent and sustained action are necessary to achieve anything, perhaps they are necessary even in a novelist's character if he wants to bring out summat! Living may not be so high an art as politics, but if you are going to import drama into any of its parts such part must be something other than an easy-going splurge. They may be an easy-going lot in Carradale, but you don't know the total story, presumably. It is a happy thought that you have to regret the lapse of the *droit de seigneur*. So please just step off it and lower somewhat the elevation of your nose as you glance along it at the poor old Philosopher.[15] He has no doubt had his day and his generation in a communal pattern that wasn't bad as patterns go, any time and anywhere, so let us at least salute him as we go on to regard the general deliquescence of your Gael. I am beginning to believe that there may be something lacking in the historic sense of the story that you say Agnes Mackenzie criticised, but if you send it on to me I shall be delighted to confirm that learned and charming lady. In any case, in the *Serpent*, I had the minister's son who "deceived" the lassie, another young fellow who had to get married soon after Halloween, and the simple lad who thought he would just get married in the usual way. A fair cross-section, even for Carradale: No? All right. But you feel you would far rather I had followed the fortunes of the minister's son, or the Halloween lad. And very nice, too, but leaving dammall to write about, and just for the very reasons that prompted your admirable disquisition to me on discipline. And if this has the sound of a boomerang, how happy the sound! I'm afraid I'm having a chuckle as I write this, but a chuckle sounds dreadfully heavy on a typewriter, so I had better stop this and go on to your eloquence about my joining Convention.[16]

Well, I'm not joining yet, not joining anything for a while. And you must give me credit for many long years of consistent service. I was at the beginning of the National Party, and years afterwards fought the Scottish Party in its beginnings and duly absorbed them. Just before the Convention break with the SNP I had got some Edinburgh folk to come into the SNP and they are now among its best workers. They don't want me, they say, to "desert" them. And in Inverness – and so on. And the students of the University SNP Associations keep on asking me to be an Hon. President. Now I am not putting much stress on all that. I know what it's worth. But I do feel that for a little while yet I should go on working for the common cause, and perhaps some time be able to use what little influence I have in bringing about a natural healthy cohesion. Please give me a little time. And I can work all round, even if you think that a somewhat self-important statement. For instance, here's a copy of John MacCormick's pamphlet on Convention. In sending it to me, Dr. Macdonald hopes that I'll be able to make it the subject of a full article in the *Daily Record*. Well, that's somewhat naive! For how can I in the capitalist anti-nationalist press boost a pamphlet written to further the aims of a nationalist group? But I will try. I'll certainly write that article – and in such a way that they will have to hesitate before daring to refuse it. It will seem from the article that I am giving Convention my blessing.

And you making me write all this on a day of such sunshine that it's off after the dead philosopher I am, fair on to the moors, where there is a lost burn, where whiles I fish, and other whiles dip in a pool and sit on a rock to dry. By God, it's good. Peewits, grouse and the individualism that takes the wandering air on its skin. I never enter that world but I can look back on other worlds with a certain eye; and if such a picture raises no more than a troubled pity in your attractive eyes, well that's not an unattractive picture either.

Yours,

Neil

TO NAN SHEPHERD
BRAEFARM HOUSE DINGWALL 7/8/43

My dear Nan,
To expect that you will get 7 for your book is extravagant. If I got 3 like yourself I'd lift an ear for the bugles of the millennium. And that sudden thought makes me laugh as if I'd heard a new poem. But it's the sort of air that surrounds your understanding, and the unheard sound that is not Keats's but hangs between your ear and all the Grampian mountains into one mountain. And the sound is less sweet than what Keats heard, though perhaps he could find no other word but sweet

for it. For words, as you say, are gross enough at best. Anyway, it's no good saying anything about the reviewer in your Aberdeen paper. Apart from Edwin Muir, they have nearly all said the same. And there is just this compensation – they'll call it "escape": O God, their labels – that there is a sort of rare freedom in being unnoticed among the damned. It cleanses the mind of ambitions and brings what true delights there may be to the act of catching the unheard melody all for its own sweet sake. Or words to that effect. So you have one at least who will be waiting to know if you have caught it. Though that is going too far. For what can the best of us know or see or hear beyond the set of the body and it listening? What is communicated, one might say, is communicated by a rare chance. But that is not true. For there is an inevitability in the business beyond time or chance. And you are fair set by the nature of you in the midst of that inevitability. So forward you go. Having a mountain, too, puts you fair in luck's way. It might have been a reviewer whom you felt it in your intellectual need to analyse (not the spirit's need, O Lord: – and therein lies all the distinction by which literature finally knows itself) like any ordinary novelist like myself. But I'll leave the reviewer alone for awhile, too, at least so long as there are ordinary folk who have a few true responses left like old croft women an' sichlike. Don't you agree? It's full of fun the whole business is, as one tries to catch the tail of it glimmering out of sight! But it's fine and rare to catch the smile on another face. So I salute you yourself.

I got thinking the other day of that last short story of yours. Even apart from what it was all about, it leaves its haunting behind, so that it takes precedence (. . .) over all other readings in the same kind which have come across me in recent times, and there have been a few Russians in the haphazard crowd. It came on the tip of my mind that you and I might have made some money in the distilling industry. But at once I doubt it. It's not the money we would have been thinking of.

The film-making hasn't yet started. Many difficulties in the way – but the script is now finished, so I'm just sitting waiting, and doing nothing, with not an idea in my head. Though I have a continuation of the adventures of *Young Art and Old Hector*[17] – possibly out of a sort of perversity for the English could make nothing of them. But that is as yet confidential, for

I'll have to make up my mind whether it's worth publishing. By the way, Joseph Macleod (BBC announcer and an authority on Russian Theatre and Literature) wrote me out of the blue in enthusiasm over *Young Art*; calls it unique in English literature and babbles o' Tolstoi!

And – to give you more of my news – the *Highland River* you speak of now and then was recently published in a 2/- edition. When I heard my publishers were printing 25,000 copies I thought they were clean mad, but faith they told me shortly after that the whole lot were gone! It fair wandered me. Even *The Serpent* is out of print. But I am assured it's because folk don't know what to spend their money on.

So I enjoyed your letter and invoke God's blessing on you. Sure and it's the sweet girl you are.

Your,

Neil

TO GEORGE BLAKE
BRAEFARM HOUSE, DINGWALL, ROSS-SHIRE   3 OCT., 1943

My dear George,

It was nice hearing from you again. I was beginning to wonder what had come over you. I was down south in connection with that post-war hospitals Committee, but all our meetings were in St. Andrew's House and I never got a real chance of visiting Glasgow. These meetings are over, our Report completed, so here I am, back in my Highland hole and preparing to haul the hole in after me for the winter. Though as a fully-fledged private in the Home Guard, I whiles indulge in mock battles, though my main job is what is called "Intelligence". I get lessons in the compass – and try to keep my mind from wandering to a very unstable compass on a more unstable boat in western seas and Daisy's mouth dry with excitement. I admit that the only job – alas, this too too human flesh – that I should have cared for in this mortal hunting would have been command of one of those small swift seacraft that go at the rate of countless knots with their engines roaring like the hammers of Hell. Man, George, that would have been pretty exciting with a nice bit of sea running.

So the lad has gone into the Navy on you. Well, well, I don't blame him. The sea is a great element. Though it's shame it should be on our pows that his adventure on that element should be so terrible. By the holy God, we evolve pretty slowly. The mechanistic man has done it on us, and the artist – the only bloke who could have done it on him – is once more of slight consequence in the world of affairs. But he'll come into his own. It's the only faith left. He has a job to do, and then a few more. So buckle your belt.

I heard you had left the newspaper. And I'm glad to know that you have more freedom. You can't grow without some of that odd element. I have just been turning down one or two literary requests – at least business o' that ilk – because at present we have enough to live on. Marvellous to say, some of my books have been selling modestly. Remember that book you were good enough to praise when it came out, *Highland River?* They produced it in a 2/- paper edition, 25,000 copies of it, and sold the whole lot in a week or two. I suppose we're having an odd kind of revenge on the reading public in the sense that they haven't anything much but books to spend their luxury cash on!

The Serpent sold out its first printing, too, straight off. Our real difficulty now is getting a dram to buy!

And I am glad you liked *The Serpent.* It does raise a practical issue, George. Frankly, I naturally felt it was quite the wrong time for work of that kind, with its seeming old-fashioned divorce from time and place and mood. But then again I wanted to put over certain values, which I think are for all time, and if we are going to be governed in these matters by what is no more than a passing public aptitude in such matters, how are these values going to survive? In these matters it is surely up to us to choose the field of action! If I can't have my own racing craft on a western sea, I'm going to create what craft I like on my own sea! How's that by you?

You must tell me more about what you're doing in novel ways sometime. I write political articles, too, and get well paid – what a lovely revengeful joke! – for dealing with what amounts to Scottish nationalism. You've been tasting that dubious pleasure for long enough.

How's Ellie? Whenever this war is over, and if God is kind, she'll hear us giving a shout at her Lodge gate.

I was glad to get your news about Barke and others. Nary a

word reaches me up here. Don't be so long in writing again.
And what about this Theatre of yours?

Daisy is cultivating her garden and sends greetings. I also toil
there, but as a navvy, a spade-digger. Steady monotonous toil
suits me!

Yours ever,

Neil

TO NAOMI MITCHISON

BRAE, DINGWALL   5/4/44

Dear Naomi

(. . .) I do appreciate your difficulties, in running your farm
and with your neighbours. You *should* have more time for
writing. And I say that not out of sympathy (how could I?) but
because you do happen to have a way of making *authentic* what
you are writing or talking about. That is so excellent and
refreshing. And you cannot blame the women for not feeling
all at once at home in your world of thought and action. You
have just got to accept that. You won't, of course! Any more
than you accept the sort of stuff I put in a novel. You feel it
should be more vital, with more kick in it for the times! I do
understand. I have done years of work behind the scenes in
politics. We could argue about all that. What is not arguable is
your particular power and personality. It would infuriate you
if I suggested that the dead ewe and the stolid women (they're
anything but in their own way) are of the conflicts that deepen.
All right. Let us leave all that. But for heaven's sake do attend
to your writing. I read your *Blood of the Martyrs* some time
ago. I was greatly taken with its catholicity of understanding as
distinct from its intellectual appreciation of folk and events.
The propaganda (parallel with our times) could so easily have
been pushed. This appalling modern tendency to live – and
fight – and destroy – in our heads. And it can't just be offset by
trying to live in our bowels. We must get somehow a living
authentic balance . . .

Cheers.

Neil.

THE FULL-TIME WRITER

Dear Naomi,
    (. . .) If I'm a queer devil, Naomi, you're an incalculably
charming woman. And that's it in a nutshell, in this literary
business anyway. Unless we are concerned with life in its vivid,
living moments we should take to pamphlets. Incalculably
living, aware that it should be beneath everything, the reason
for everything and its last meaning. Hellsbells, woman, I've
just been listening to the news, and have been told with
triumph that we shall soon be able to get dehydrated potato
which we can mix with a little water and find indistinguishable
from normal mash. And you – even you – acted upon
unconsciously by psychoanalytic news, suggest that I – me –
thinking eating wicked, somewhere far ben! Really apalling.
When I consider the number of women who don't know how
to boil a potato. When I think of the food we have in the
Highlands and how it isn't cooked. Lord, the flavour of a
Golden Wonder, steamed in its jacket, until it bursts its coat in
laughter. An oatcake that is really crisp. Butter, real butter on
that oatcake. Heather honey. Our berries. Our game. Our
prime herring. Hill mutton . . . I refuse to talk to you about it.
You will be calling me a gourmet next. Go away.
    How delightful of you to utter the ultimate compliment by
saying you think *The Green Isle* was written for you. That sort
of response would make anyone write a book. In fact, I wrote
The Green Isle right off, just because an old friend of mine in
Ireland, who has mostly for company now his little grandson,
was so affected by what he considered the inner truth of *Young
Art* that he said I mustn't leave them at the River. So I didn't.
Can you think of a better reason for writing a book?[18]
    And when you accuse me of anarchism, do you mean the
anarchism of Kropotkin or just individual chaos? There is a
mighty difference. That the herring fishermen should be in a
co-operative is anarchism. That they should be run by a State
herring industry Board is – what? I have been a socialist all my
life, and still am, but I have always been aware of the servile state.
I have been supporting Tom Johnston[19] in all his planning
schemes. I now hear he is about to bring in a Bill on Herring
Report lines, with a strong Herring Board. I am genuinely dis-

appointed at appearing to go against him here. But there's a limit. That doesn't mean that I don't know what such a board could do. Nor does it mean that I have any hope that the fishermen would themselves ever do anything in the way of organising a co-op or union. But certain things have got to be said sometime. There's a point where a thing takes the wrong turning. We must have an elementary time sense and look ahead.

Think of what your criticism amounts to. My book is against fascism. You take it as being against Communism. Now isn't that a thought! In analysis, what does it amount to? If we take dialectical materialism as the unity of theory and practice, that practice having primacy, isn't it odd that when I leave the theory out and describe only the practice, the actual practice, you assume communism? Yet I described fascism, using its proper word "corporate" in the Italian fashion, and even describing the salute, which is so different from the Russian one! (. . .)

Yours

Neil

Dear Naomi

(. . .) In my support of the electric Scheme, I also met a lot of opposition from the perfervid Scots southrons. Afraid it might spoil the Highlands and be a sell-out to big business. That sort of attitude is costive, deadly. Nothing is ever done without difficulties and dangers. We have forgotten how to take a chance. But now that the Scheme has made a start – if I'm any good as a prophet, you'll find Highland communities beginning to quarrel because this one or that hasn't got in first or is being left out. Fine! Let us quarrel like blazes – so long as it's over a matter of life and growth. This idea that we should never have anything unless first of all it's perfect on paper . . . But I'm not going into that either. Yes, I can imagine a few having a quarrel with the *Green Isle* because here I have been and will be supporting planning and a' thing o' that kind and yet. . . . But it's all of a piece.

My Left friends – did I tell you that I have been a Socialist since the age of fifteen – won't like the book in their bones. But let me put a very simple aspect like this: The trouble with my communist friends is that they can't see that any sort of revolution necessary for this country should not be of the Russian kind in its execution or practice. For example, we have freedom of expression about political personalities and affairs. Why not let us keep it? Hell, surely we are civilised enough to make a fight to carry through a new dispensation without first handing our liberty of expression to the kind of folk which a mass movement shoves into power. (. . .)

Yours,

Neil

TO MARGARET MACEWEN

BRAE. TUES. (JULY 1944)

My dear Margaret,

(. . .) Your remarks on the play[20] completely sound and I understand them fully. If you read between all my lines, you may find them there! Only there is this extra point. Douglas is not doing a "realistic" play. It's a sort of blank verse affair, intended to "translate" onto planes of art. His crucial mistake is not that he has not drawn on experience (actually he has in a true sense) but that he has written in terms of the head, of explanation, instead of in terms of the spirit, with the spirit's emotional power. *Murder in the Cathedral* is just as divorced from "realism", but it's moving. It's extremely difficult and all I can do is encourage him. Others send me their stuff and sometimes I find it difficult to help just because I know a certain kind of blunt criticism (which is not necessarily a good kind) affects the recipient. So there you are! We pretend we like criticism, but do we? There is, however, a way of it that may help a fellow to another shot – but only if one thinks he's capable of it. I am prepared to give Douglas the benefit of the doubt! You are perfectly right in saying that the subject matter could be made good drama. One or two Russians have done it, as I suggest to Douglas. So we must leave Douglas to his fight, which is primarily always an individual and not a social one! The social comes in of course.

But enough of that. You can practice your critical faculties on my new book, which, I'm afraid, no one will like. It should be out under a fortnight and I'll send you a copy. It's about your old friends Young Art and Old Hector anyhow. In

Paradise – just for a change! So we keep going, with a cheerful
spirit against all adversity. The critics can say what they like.
Doleful people are only a nuisance. And some like cutting folk
up. Why worry?
We'll keep you aware of our movements.
All the best, Margaret, and a smile for the world. You're
doing grand work.
Yours,

Neil

TO NAOMI MITCHISON
BRAEFARM HOUSE   16 JULY (1944)

Dear Naomi,
Your letter gave me great delight. I roared with laughter at
parts, and certainly regretted that I wasn't at the Highlander's
Institute. I could have done with a few tunes myself. The truth
is I don't know the Highland parts of Glasgow – apart from
Mod. ceilidhs in strange places. I somehow get caught up by
certain journalists and others and go to their pubs. There is also
a Highlandness that I tend to shy clear of, especially on the
official side – and other sides too. I cannot even begin to talk
about it – at least talking is the only way. Writing is necessarily
dull and, in explanation, rather pretentious. If I saw the man to
whom you gave the rose and the buttermilk (and you grew
angry because PEN saw you as a Dresden shepherdess!) for
five minutes, I'd tell you all about it – nine times out of ten. But
this business of the salmon poaching[21] – you see, Naomi,
fundamentally, anthropologically, or as you like, it's a matter
of the laws of the tribe. In our tribe we would never sell a
salmon we poached. Again, we would not poach a river which
we got permission to fish. Mostly it was adventure for
youngsters – and there were two ardent keepers – and many an
old wife or widow got a tasty cut for the good of her heart. The
laird was pure dog-in-the-manger, inasmuch as he did not fish
the river himself. Indeed it was only fishable for a day or two in
spate. So the code worked. Often this adventure for the one or
two boys who liked it was pure bliss. I'm just dead certain that
they could never have complexes after it! And the boys came
in contact inevitably with one or two old men who were

integrated in themselves because they carried forward the old communalism of the tribe in a completely unselfconscious way. There really was a social pattern underlying all. I suspect it is this that fascinates you, but when you search for it, it disintegrates – as the pattern itself is disintegrating – under your hands. Not, to tell the truth, that you are a good searcher. You have too many of the irresponsible moods in yourself, as ye ken fine! But there it is, and the "example" you should be after setting is not too obvious and so the hurt and the malice and the tough ones have an innings. Some of them need the fear of God or the fear of the tribe put into them – a difficult operation now that they don't believe in either. Another thing – once a community begins breaking up, it is really remarkable how the negative or vicious aspects come out. Without the broad view, this sounds alarming, and when a writer draws a character like Old Hector he seems to be romancing. Again, and in somewhat similar way, the city sophisticates mistrust old H. He irritates them for a far more subtle reason than that he is a "provincial". Once disintegration of the psyche sets in – particularly on the sexual perversion side – normality or wholeness becomes anathema or at least something to avoid and jeer at. It's a long argument and not for a letter, as I said. And as you said at the PEN, the basic trouble is economic. But it's more than that, and that's where writers should come in. And that, I suspect, is why certain writers hesitate over joining the CP. I was talking to a Communist of some importance on the organisation side of the Party the other day and he said he would wipe out the whole of Eire if this would help to defeat the Nazis. Some of us have to keep our heads. It's not easy because we lose the communal warmth. It's grand being in on a side and fighting like hell, even if it's only fighting to keep hell in its place. But I'll be preaching next! And my publishers tell me that the 1st printing (8,000) copies of *The Green Isle* disappeared quickly – preaching enough! So I can't help you with your salmon. Though in yourself you draw the quick of life out of it which is more than salmon any day. And your capable hands will never be too good on the curb!

Cheers for you. (. . .)

Yours,

Neil

O. H. MAVOR (James Bridie) (1888–1951) was born and educated in Glasgow, practising as a doctor there until 1938. He was also a prolific writer of plays and a founder of the Glasgow Citizens' Theatre. Gunn and Bridie met in the late Twenties, and Bridie gave Gunn good advice (which he did not take) about his play *Second Sight*. They remained in close touch until Bridie's death, and Gunn had a deep regard for his humour and honesty.

TO O. H. MAVOR (JAMES BRIDIE)
BRAEFARM HOUSE, DINGWALL, ROSS-SHIRE   25/11/44

My dear O. H.,

I must say thanks to you both for your kindness to me in Glasgow. Now that I know you can eat in some place other than your famous Arts Club, perhaps you will lunch with me on a future occasion. I'll look forward to that.

If I'm writing you rather than your wife (life has its less pleasant twists), it's because I have a sort of feeling of guilt over that meeting in the Literary Club.[22] My only hope is that nobody will know I was there as your guest! You see, I didn't expect that kind of gathering, and when I ran into Christopher Grieve, the fun was bound to start. When Grieve was talking his hot stuff, twenty years came back in a rush and I could not help chuckling. I just wanted to roar with laughter (and the day's drams didn't reduce the desire.) Not, I mean, that I particularly disagreed with him. But I just knew all about it, and wanted to cut through the inevitably vague and destructive stuff, in order to get at the ultimate intention of Grieve and Maclellan.[23] So I talked. It was afterwards when Fergusson, the painter,[24] said to me, "All this is very serious to me," that I felt I had been somewhat light-hearted! Perhaps you'll forgive me. A jaunt from the country makes a savage feel pleasantly adventurous.

I did enjoy some talk I had with your wife at lunch. Good sense in charming guise is so rare a commodity.

Again with my deep thanks.

Yours,

Neil M. Gunn

Don't quite know where I am with the film folk, but I expect to be done down anyhow, so it's fine.

TO JAMES BRIDIE
BRAE, DINGWALL   14/3/45

My dear O. H.,
  Your book arrived last night, and I sat up reading *Lancelot* to
its wonderful end. Really a grand bit of work. Some time I shall
tell you why I think so. Though the language could hardly be
plainer, as talk, there is an after impression, like a kind of
overtone, of essential verse. Debunking and being clever can
become terribly tiresome. The thought of having to endure a
bout of it can draw a groan. You take the analysis of chivalry in
your stride, and then go for that ultimate distilling of the spirit
which is, I suppose, literature's ultimate aim. Anyway, a salute
in the passing – and my best thanks for the book – which I shall
peruse play by play.
  I was interested in your news of the "Academy" meeting.
Pity things go like that with us. Always such a hell of an
amount of Ego and self-boost about. But we've never really
had a chance of becoming civilised, so it's no good being upset.
You must often have wondered at my interest in nationalism,
but what was behind it has always been the kind of thing that
prompted you recently (if I may judge by *Glas. Herd.* report)
to give what journalist blokes would call a drama blueprint for
Scotland. I was really delighted to see it. I was delighted to see a
fellow like you showing the practical boys just how a job of
organising should be done, with the full plan given, and all
detail allowed for. I have been doing this kind of thing outside
the press for many years. I have no illusions. Nor, for that
matter, any ruddy ambition. (I have recently been approached
by two constituencies to stand as M.P. and, no doubt like
yourself, have refused my name for Lord Rector contest at
Universities several times.) I really hate making a public fuss.
And I say as much to try to show you how convinced I am, by
sheer hard experience, that we have to take a part in creating
the practical plan. Not many can have stewed up so much
economic facts about Scotland as myself. But I know that
what's needed is the reviving of the spirit. But you can't revive
the spirit in the air. Dammit, you've got to bottle it, so you've
got to know how to make the bottle. You had a fair shot at
making the dramatic bottle.
  Now the annoying thing is that when you've done that, you

get blokes like C. M. G. (who knows better) writing silly little crabbing letters about your efforts to the press. I perfectly understand your reaction. Whether you're right on this small detail or the next doesn't matter a tuppenny toss. At least you've made a theatre. The bottle is in being, and talent is given the chance to fill it.

But you've got to expect that. One thing the "Academy" (we're not *nearly* ready for it without the inverted commas) would have done – given a chance for analysing this very position. What a joy I should have taken in ruthless analysis before C.M.G. an all! But constructively. Keeping grip and guiding to an end. We all need this kind of critical analysis –

But my pen will really get going if I don't watch it!

My wife goes to Inverness on Tuesday and hopes to get *Tedious and Brief*, so I'll be at you in and out!

That cinema lad has been asking me to meet him again. So if I do come south soon I hope we'll have one or two.

All the best and a thousand thanks.

Neil Gunn

TO NAOMI MITCHISON

BRAEFARM HOUSE, DINGWALL, ROSS-SHIRE   4-2-46

My dear Naomi,

Life always comes walking out of your letters on her own two feet. And very attractive feet too. However, this is but a salute to your kind words about my book. You raise one or two interesting points moreover. That about analysis and defeat at the end, for instance. No, it's not because I grow tired of the business exactly. Actually I'm sick of defeatism, and would send it to the devil if I could. But we can hardly distort to suit our propagandist fancy. All the same, my next one,[25] now with Faber for production probably about the end of the year, does not give in to defeat and is full of constructive suggestions. It deals with hill sheep farming and is over 170,000 words long! I had a real fight with myself over the end and found how remarkable a hold a theory – socialist theory – can get on one. This was my difficulty: A young fellow wants to follow his father as a sheep farmer. In the end, he has to clear out. Normally that would be the end of him. Another emigrant. But I don't want that to happen so – as there is no one else with the money – I have to introduce a sound landlord who is prepared to do things to the land by way of reclamation etc. The inter-war period. In the end you see a young fellow with plenty of guts and ideas and knowledge prepared to put up a fight, backed by a dear old landlord! And me who knows what our landlords did to the Highlands! How easy to arrange for young fellows forming a kind of glen soviet and all that kind of sweet unreality. But I'm afraid, Naomi, whatever my writing may look like, I'm just a hard bitten realist. . . . Peace and constructiveness be with you, on the County Council and in your writing, now and ever more. I gather from a painter who was up here[26] that the poets and literary highbrows of Glasgow look upon me as one who might have done something in literature if I hadn't turned my back to follow the primrose path of success! The *Green Isle* rather shook some of my communist friends (think of me introducing GOD), but now, trafficking with a landlord in order to find a way out of defeatism! . . . Sure and it will be the finish of me . . . Never mind, it's a good old fight – and I'm not done yet. And if they get obstreperous I might even do a pyscho-analytic novel on coteries and things. (. . .) It's at least charming of you to see my work falling into a sort of pattern. There is such a lot of clearing work to be done so that writers coming after us may take a lot for granted and get on with what may be spiritually exciting. (. . .)

Yours,

Neil

IAN McKILLOP shared Inverness digs with Neil in 1913. He married Mabel Mackay, a schoolfriend of Daisy's. Ian's parents had a sheep-farm at Crathie, near Laggan Bridge in Inverness-shire.

TO IAN MCKILLOP

BRAEFARM HOUSE, DINGWALL, ROSS-SHIRE   29 AUG., 1946

My dear Ian,

I am a careless fellow. I meant to call in to see you in the Spring about a small matter touching the use of your name, but somehow – well, you know how, with the very best intentions, a lad can get waylaid, or met by someone at the wrong time beside the right place? Ay, ay. But I was up over your old countryside the other week and was charmed by places like Crathie. And that reminded me of a novel I have written on and around hill sheep farming; and that again recalled your old folk, and even the little black diary that your father kept. I quote from the diary in the book, but alter names and so on so that the originals are impossible to trace. It is absolutely and entirely an imaginary story, and the incidents never happened in any house that you or I ever knew. But I did want to do for hill sheep farming what I tried to do for sea-fishing in *The Silver Darlings*. And a film company have bought an option on the new book. Perhaps you heard that a film bloke was staying at Kingussie in the Mains Hotel? He had a great time there. He had of course read my book and was trying to find out something about hill sheep farming before he got down to preparing a script. Whether the company will actually do the film is still undecided, so I'm saying nothing about it mean-time. However, what I wanted to say to you was that you had got so mixed up in my mind in old talks about hill sheep farming that I felt I should dedicate the book to you. So I did, in a tentative way, intending to make any alteration in proof and hoping that I might see you sometime before it was too late. I'm afraid now it is too late, as the book is due out in November (perhaps December) and so must be all ready and fixed on the printing side. I know it is – and is now at the binders. Anway, here's the legend that appears on it:

To my
OLD FRIEND IAN
and the sheep farm on the Grampians,
not forgetting the little black diary.

It was my way of paying a compliment to you and your old folk of whom I have the happiest memories. The situation of the story itself is not given as the Grampians; it could be anywhere in hill sheep farming country in the Highlands. I want to give it a sort of universal air. In short, this is a sort of private matter between us. I'll send you along a copy when it comes out.

Our best regards to you all,

Neil M. Gunn

THE FULL-TIME WRITER

J. B. PICK was born in 1921. In 1945 he wrote an article on Gunn's work in a little review (*Gangrel*) and sent it to him. Gunn replied courteously. In 1946 Pick published his first book, and he and his wife Gene moved to Wester Ross, where he settled down to write full-time. Gunn called on them in the Spring of that year.

TO J. B. PICK

BRAE   22 OCT., 1946

Dear John,

That was a good letter,[27] with all the *innate* generosity coming through! Up Freud! Perhaps I had wondered whether all the self-consciousness and introspection might not be too much for you, but as you wisely say: that's the way it is. Your apperception is so marvellously acute that it makes me laugh; induces the natural gaiety that the girl Nan was after; which is how and when and what. These parentheses – I know. I haven't the heart to cut any more out. Like a mannerism, a pathetic effort at being playfully normal, but, hang it, with courage too. What's being perfect anyway? If a few more flaws would make it easier for her, wouldn't you shove 'em in? Not to mention making it easier for the chap in the *Times Lit. Supp.*

Ranald and Adam are a bit difficult. They move as it were objectively, males across the feminine field of vision. And don't confuse Ranald with the nihilist. He represents the theorist in action. I have met many Communists like him, for instance; and other theorists, too. The novel could have assumed Dostoevskian bulk. The point for us is: can we assume so much now that we can dispense with the bulk? I could have shown Ranald in London, an occasional vision of him on the brink of nihilism, glimpsing the annihilating futility of action, with a swift movement away towards the personal salvation of logical action; and so on, with numberless characters around; but that's not quite the intention of the book. And you see all that. I leave *you* to deal with the nihilist.

Adam is a little more difficult. More blanks to fill up. You wonder why Adam cleared out to London. That kind of chap always clears out when he finds that circumstances are enmeshing him. The need to be "free" is always overpowering. The antithesis of the "responsible" social theorist. He might adorn the perfect anarchical state, which is perhaps why Aunt

Phemie is surprised to find that she rather likes him some-where. There is perversion here, in Adam. The balance – sanity – is in the eye of the woman. Getting at the source of life is natural in a woman: Adam hunts it perversely, because our male has become a perverse social animal.

No book should need explanations. That's where the writer of it is flawed. Yet I'm not too sure about filling in the blanks. So I'll let it go. Life does move with a certain amount of mystery, and no ego is ever wholly logical. There is no end to analysis, as you know. We can but select significantly. I admit Shakespeare might have saved scholars a lot of trouble had he filled in the blanks in *Hamlet*. But perhaps they like the worry! Life is very strange! And I make no comment on literary comparisons.

But all this would need talk. (. . .)

My dear Jean,[28] for heaven's sake don't feel that you have to write a letter about that book of mine. Writing is such a bore that I am giving it up myself and going in for sheep, as I told you. Though I am not promising absolutely – yet.

Yours,

Neil

TO GENE PICK
BRAE   24-10-46

My dear Jean,

Daisy was just leaving with *The Shadow* to post it to Faber when in your letter came, like yourself, and even the old typewriter was interested – after the business of writing to a publisher, though to give Geoffrey Faber his due he did produce a volume of verse – and says this is more like the thing. I agree. What a charming and thoughtful letter all in one! Daisy even went further and suggested that I should try to tell what did happen in London when Nan went back, but I suspect that her motive is complicated by the notion that it would be a good thing to see me working again! I know you. And what then is going to happen to the sheep? Daisy doesn't give a hoot about the sheep. Or perhaps, being able to see further, she suspects that it is herself who would have to be looking after them mostly, and if they were there, she just would. It's very complicated. Meantime there is no more word of houses, but

I am writing agents and may advertise. At the moment, it looks as if we may not be disturbed until May. It's a long time!

You wonder if Nan can help Ranald in London. The way it struck me is that she would help by *being* rather than by *doing*, whatever she might actually do. That's about all that can be said. Ranald will go his own way, quite remorselessly, but Nan's *being* will affect him in the deep places, until at last he will question what is missing in his theory (Nan and Aunt Phemie discussed it), and this will lead him to doubt, and perhaps ultimately to sacrifice. The revelation of this would have to be pretty profound. It's the kind of thing that John will do one day. And he will do it all right, in whatever form. It cannot be forced. It comes; but comes inevitably. That's as sure as that the sun is shining on me just now through the window. It is perhaps more important primarily to *be* than to *do* (what heresy to Ranald and his Marxist friends!) but – the doing has to be done, and a wise woman always knows this. John may rightly object to the word "knows". But sure I always let him have his own way. Though you and I did rather put him on his back over mathematical values. Though there again he was, of course, right, but don't tell him that.

Your remarks about Adam are very interesting, especially when you talk about his being concerned with life but for Nan surrounded by death. He is to me a real character. A real person. He has a life of his own. That must make him appear incalculable, when shown in snatches particularly. But I'll tell you what has often or ofn struck me about what we call "modern" art. The pictures themselves – think of some surrealist ones – have an air about them of death. Now we know that art "translates" from one plane to another; and in an age that was dynamic with life, where the life urge itself was strong as a song, then the translation of it to a static "immortal" plane might add profundity to the vision of life. But our age (consider nihilism) is sapping the life-source itself. It may be for this reason that I almost unconsciously surrounded Adam, the modern artist, with the actual aura of death. Or am I just analysing now? If I'm not, then the creative urge is indeed oddly incalculable.

Or does this sound more like 3 a.m.? We enjoyed your visit very much, and it will not be the last one, butlers or no butlers.

There is no hurry for the MS. It's a copy, though I have to keep it by me for reference.

Once more my thanks for your letter and our fond greetings to you both.

Neil

TO GEOFFREY FABER OF FABER & FABER, ABOUT *The Shadow*
BRAEFARM HOUSE   29 NOV. 1946

Dear Geoffrey

(. . .) To me the first part is the best, but perhaps I had a sort of intuition that you might not think so. Amid the increasing trend in these days towards ideologies and violence or cynicism or nihilism, I was trying in that first part to get at the living positive source of life itself and tell the inner story of what was happening to it. Was it D. H. Lawrence who thought that the modern novel needed first a bomb and then philosophy? I am not sure that he was far wrong, even while I should be repelled by the idea of trying to do something "new" merely in order that it might be labelled original or unusual. There is, I feel, something far more in this than that the ordinary traditional way of spinning the yarn has become a trifle grooved and lifeless. I cannot help even wondering, if I may say so, whether you and your two readers while manifestly prepared to accept the "new" or unusual in poetry are not so prepared in the case of the novel . . .

(. . .) As for that "final meaning" to which you refer, I suppose I have been dealing with the living source of life as found in (I hope) an attractive young woman, placed somewhere between the political theorist and the too introverted artist, thus making a kind of allegory of our present world. . . . I'm afraid I can do no more to the book now, and shall quite understand if you would not care to publish it, though of course I should be sorry.

Yours sincerely,

Neil M. Gunn

TO NAN SHEPHERD
BRAE, DINGWALL, ROSS-SHIRE   14 APRIL '47

Dear Nan,

You can imagine the kind of reviews that reach me whiles, so a letter from you just about puts me right! "The kind of magic that obliterates itself, so that the words seem to vanish into the thing they have conjured up." I can quote from you too! And how exquisitely you can do it! Than that quotation, what more searching could be said on the use of words, of language? When I read a writer whose words call attention to *themselves*, I feel a self-consciousness in the air. And self-consciousness is our disease, everywhere. The cult of the Ego, the Self – how it is destroying (directly through violence) life itself! The world smells of it, the smell of death. Even to mention magic is to "escape". So it's nice to see the sun shining and the flowers growing and let words melt into the magic! You're good at it.

I'm afraid I have written another novel wherein there is a lassie who has notions of all this. Forbye yourself, I wonder how many will be able to read it? Geoffrey Faber was fair stumped himself, and fears for my public! But I was adamant. It won't be out till next spring – and is very different from *The Drinking Well*.

Which is about all my literary news.

Have you been doing anything yourself, and you didn't mention any more moves about your hill book?[29] Though I can see, Nan, that the world doesn't want the well water. It doesn't know that it needs it.

But this is a word of greeting and a cheer for the eyes that see. May you have lovely days and the sun coming.

Yours,

Neil

TO MORLEY KENNERLEY, FABER & FABER LIMITED
BRAEFARM HOUSE, DINGWALL, ROSS-SHIRE   25 JUNE 1947

Dear Kennerley,

It was thoughtful of you to hunt out these income figures of mine. As I got some cash for films, the total was even better, so the Income Tax authorities had a proper onslaught, against which the £132 for six months proved inadequate ammunition.

I should, of course, have seen the demand coming, but then you cannot blame me altogether as I had expected some cash from reprints. Away back a year last January when *The Key of The Chest* had been over-subscribed, you wrote saying that a reprint of 10,000 copies was ordered. Some months thereafter, I was told that reprint of 5000 was imminent. Nothing ever appeared, and now you do not even mention the book. A year last March, a secretary said that you were expecting a reprint of *The Silver Darlings* any moment. Since when, no word of it. *Young Art* was busily being reprinted over a period when he didn't even exist! And you wondered recently why I smiled when you said you were reprinting *The Drinking Well!* From which – and more of the same – I sort of conclude that news of anything reprinting really means nothing – until possibly some priority machinery is set in motion, like the marble in the gambling game, though I'm merely guessing now. Unfortunately, no Income Tax inspector works with marbles, as I know so well, having been a Civil Servant for 25 years and used to instructing the public in the inexorable ways of accountancy. The whole position is wonderfully complicated, too, as the result of a trip which I have just had to one or two of our Scottish cities. One Scots author[30] rather gloated over me by producing his Statement from which it was clear that his publisher had managed to get him nearly four times the amount of paper expended on me by mine – in each case, our last book. There seemed to be a sort of general feeling that the firm of Faber is not really interested in the novel and wants paper for other and more expanding business, what are considered important books. In which respect Faber may be quite right. The trouble with an author, whose first novel appeared over 20 years ago, is that he too may want to go in for more important business, like reading philosophy or contemplating his navel. And thank God anyhow that a blessed Labour Government has raised the Old Age Pension to 26/- a week, for by the time he is due to get it his navel, having shrunk, will have convolutions added to it which may assist in the esoteric search. It may be a subtly self-compensating universe, this of ours, even when everyone does his damnedest, including the idealist or totalitarian, if I may conveniently lump them as one. Then again, if an author did make something during the two or three years when the going is good – which means the sort of position at the moment, hence all the cerebration – he would probably spend it on the wrong things, like buying whisky or a washing machine for his wife, which, as we say in the North, are not in it anyway. I rather fancy that they intuitively feel it's now or never – and have it in their bones from history that they are fated to be on the wrong dog. Especially those of them who have been writing for a long time and think that they may have established a faint claim to some kind of priority, particularly when their books do actually sell when they are visible.

Yours,

Neil M. Gunn

Why do you always go in for *Morning Tide* and *Highland River* so confidently? I have never heard that you had any difficulty selling other reprints. The sight of something new sometime would at least be lightsome.

TO MARGARET MACEWEN

BRAEFARM HOUSE, DINGWALL, ROSS-SHIRE   TUES. (WINTER 1947)

Dear Margaret,

That was a nice letter and what you had to say about *The Silver Darlings* was pretty sound. The Director feels very bad about it. You see, they cut out all the simple human build-up, that gave depth and texture, leaving only the high spots of violence, which accordingly were strung together rather jerkily. For instance, they did rather a lovely sequence of the little Finn chasing a butterfly. We saw it on the screen after it had been made, in Wick. But the cutter cut it. And I'm disappointed myself, because the film as it stands still has a basic strength, a sort of real communal skeleton that could have carried a living flesh. And it would have been a change from the usual kind of personal plot from Hollywood. However, there it is; though there's a thing in it all that is disturbing at deeper levels, for it would seem that humanity, to be properly entertained today, must have violence. Protest as you like, and blame whom you like, but the evidence, whether on the screen or in the press, is almost overwhelming. Violence is box office. And the only folk who can give a half intelligent analysis of the situation are the psychoanalysts. And they're not too cheerful!

I'm afraid you won't like my next book,[31] due out in the Spring. But then most of my political friends probably think I'm in a bad way! Though I did get an enthusiastic letter from Douglas Muhr about *The Drinking Well*. He even understood about the landlord! It's going to be filmed next year, by the way.[32] Ealing Studios – and the Director is really good at his job. They've been asking if I'd be prepared to help, but No says I. Of what use is the mere author at any time?

We've had a busy year. I haven't written anything since the spring. So it's time I was settling down. We were up in Caithness and down in Edinburgh and have had a lot of folk for short visits. It gets sort of wearing in these days of rations and what not. Next week we are having an artist,[33] who paints in the abstract, for a week, and after that we're hoping to be alone for days and days and days!

I'm glad to hear you're finding your job interesting, Margaret. In these days I doubt if life has any more attractive gift to offer. I hope you've done your interviewing with high efficiency and satisfactory results and are already finding more time to breathe comfortably. At the moment we're certainly not in the mood to go anywhere for Xmas, so we should be seeing you, and that will be grand. Let us know in good time about your holiday dates. It seems a long time since I haven't seen you, as the folk say here. I've got petrol coupons, so there should be nothing in the way. Good luck, Margaret, and blessings on you.

Neil

TO GEOFFREY FABER
BRAEFARM HOUSE, DINGWALL   JAN.1948

Dear Geoffrey,

(. . .) I am pleased that you were taken with *The Silver Bough*. I almost enjoyed it myself, and I think the blurb should begin: "In this book the author has gone on holiday with an archaeologist who . . ."

Anyway, it's the kind of book about which I should be glad to get any helpful criticism or suggestion. I don't want an incident or character to be ambiguous or difficult, not even mysterious! But the critic on his part must make himself quite clear to me . . . and unfortunately I am not really sure what you mean by your chief criticism concerning an inadequate "tie-up between the cairn story and the Donald Martin story", particularly when you see "the more obvious tie-ups". I'm really sorry to appear dull about this, but the obvious tie-ups are probably the only ones. Yet I may quite well have missed putting in an explanatory paragraph. It's so easy for a novelist to assume he has made clear to others what is clear to himself. For example, when Grant first mentions to Donald Martin and his sister that he has discovered the skeleton of a young mother and child, discusses the possibility of their unnatural double death, and goes on to make the parallel between the living young mother and child and these skeletons, Donald's sister abruptly gets up and leaves the room. Grant is astonished. And the reader is led to expect some sort of tie-up between the cairn story and the Martins. Only later does Grant learn that Martin is the father of the living woman's child and when he does everything seems clear to him. But I find I haven't written down what he thought was clear and a new paragraph could express it – and at the same time recapitulate and tie up. Thus it would make these points: the sister's jealous care of her brother, her neurotic desire to save him from an "impossible" alliance, drenched suddenly with the fear of the effect on her brother should Anna and her child do away with themselves as had the mother and child in the stone cist. No wonder she had abruptly left the room (Grant would conclude).

That's the main human tie-up. There is the more ubiquitous one of Martin and the Neolithic. But actually the book is full of symbols or bits of myths. Accordingly there is nothing that the reader cannot go on thinking or wondering about. The Silver Bough comes in through the child and ultimately links Donald to Anna, and so reconstitutes the family – the father, mother and child. The inner pattern – or plot – is beautifully intricate, like Celtic interweaving – but you can't blame me for that! – so long as I the writer am telling a straightforward story about people and their doings. In fact the writer is so practised or realistic that it is not sadism that finally hides the crock of gold but dull history, for no archaeologist has ever actually discovered a gold hoard in Scotland. But if he did, the chances are that it would be like the one in the cairn. Could I be fairer than that? (And if I also give the lovely legend of the crock a further life, would you blame me!)

The criticism of yours that *really* worries me concerns the flaying. I, too, hate it. I hate the violence that is on the verge of destroying our world. *The Shadow* was written with that hate as its invisible text. Yet psychologically it is the only specific bit of known and practised violence that could affect Martin in his relations to Anna and indeed to life generally, as it did. It would take me too long to give my reasons. I *don't* want Martin to be merely a mystery man. He is the highly sensitised type, intuitive and subtle, who has been driven by our age to nihilism. I suspect it is a much commoner disease among really fine minds than may appear. But I cannot deal with this at any length in the book without affecting its balance, so all I can do is let Grant surmise the actual trouble according to his capacity to apprehend it, for he carries the book on his back. All the same, when I hear from you again I'll go carefully over what Martin has to say in the book and recast some of it.

I must get the book – perhaps the proof copy? – looked over by an archaeologist, for I have no practical knowledge of the subject. It's not so much that I'm afraid of my facts as of some minor slip or implication. About the dog – I believe they ate him in Paleolithic times, and it's a fair guess that he was domesticated in the transition period between the Paleolithic and Neolothic. But then – didn't you ever try to domesticate rabbits or pigeons in Atomic times? Or at least the transition between TNT and the Atomic! Haven't I said somewhere in the book that the archaeologist hands over to the poet? I could hardly say the novelist!

But I have said more than enough. Perhaps you could also get one of your readers' reactions to the points you raise, before I get down to final re-reading?

Wishing you a quick recovery to full strength – even overproof.

Yours,

Neil M. Gunn

DAVID MacEWEN, born in 1910, was the second son of Sir Alexander MacEwen, one of the founders of the Scottish Party. Trained in the law, David spent some time as a journalist, and then joined a legal practice in Edinburgh.

TO DAVID MACEWEN
BRAEFARM HOUSE, DINGWALL   13/2/48

My dear David,

I'm prepared to take you on at golf any day and amaze you in a different fashion even if I haven't had a club in my hand for 10 years. Of course if you opted for clock golf on your green, with liquids off, I'd think none the less of you. I can remember your hitting a ball on the odd occasions when you hit it, though less clear about its direction. But against my remorseless slicing you never had a chance. Daisy says you have developed a lovely easy style. I found she was referring to your writing. No wonder, I said, when the young devil had a sitter. But then I had a shoot this last season. What between poachers and other vermin, game has all but vanished. Here's a problem for you in the ethics of pukka sport. (Incidentally I could never understand the mentality of poachers.) Imagine yourself (= put yourself in my place) walking along when a rare cock pheasant astonishes you by coming out of the bracken at a distance of 20 yds. The pheasant is so astonished that he stands and looks at you where you stand looking at him. Over the rise and out of sight is the keeper with his dog. Beyond the keeper and further from sight is the pukka major, your co-tenant, who never shot a standing bird (a sitter) in his life, and hopes to God he never will. Far behind you at home is Nesta, bless her soul, who has told you you must get a pheasant because she is expecting someone, and who has more than once indulged in hollow laughter at an empty bag. At any instant the wild old cock may pop back into the bracken acres. Query: What tactic do you now adopt with regard to that pheasant? You will at once appreciate that the difficulties of Plastic Scots[34] has nothing on that.

Your poetry in the early days wasn't so bad as all that! Congested a bit, perhaps, but it had the stuff in it. And now you control it as it comes through. You are writing very well. David, I am sorry to have to say that I was relieved when I saw from the opening remarks on a certain Highland novelist that it's yourself that was after doing it.[35] If it had to be done, all right, but let it be by someone who can handle a club. And if some of your best shots were done by the imagination, you can always plead that you had to use wood when the going was difficult. Your last putt won the match and left me laughing. Able stuff so you can be certain I'll make you pay for it. I may be in Edinburgh on March 12th for a meeting, so Nesta and you will have to come and eat with me somewhere, but I'm not sure of times at the moment.

I hope you appreciated my quotations from Jung. They were fair into your barrow, anyhow. (. . .)

Salute, David! And keep that pen of yours in action.

Neil.

TO GEOFFREY FABER

BRAE, DINGWALL, ROSS-SHIRE   10TH NOVEMBER 1948

Dear Geoffrey,

I am glad you liked *Behind The Wave*.[36] As you say, it was not an easy job to weave such diverse themes into a credible whole. I appreciate your three points of criticism and if Alan Pringle sends the typescript back, with any remarks he may have to make, I'll go through it again in a final revision.

Actually my real trouble lies in having cut the stuff to the bone (though it may not read like that); and this explains why there is not more, e.g. about the two characters you mention, Ellen and the Assessor. The utmost I can do about such characters is to add a few lines here and there; otherwise it would mean dealing with them at length, as I have done with Dermot and Christina. This could be done, but it would need a much larger book, and I don't want that for all our sakes. Perhaps I am over-modest in such matters! for in a letter from Naomi Mitchison about *The Silver Bough* she says she so fell for the book that she wants to know a whole lot more about everything and everybody in it. I warn you that if ever I write a really long book the blood will be on your own head.

Joking apart, I doubt if I can do anything about reducing the club talk to which you refer. Let me confess that in addition to the different themes which more obviously weave themselves in and out, there is also a theme of my own with a sort of invisible existence. I seem to have been pursuing it now through three books. In *The Green Isle*, I start off with it in paradise. In *The Shadow*, I bring it to earth, to be seen through the feminine eye (the cerebral male with his power theories in the head appears bent on sending us to an arid hell). And in *Behind The Wave*, the matter is brought to the normal city levels, with secret service excursions and alarms and what not. Here the club talk is also (for my own purpose) cut to the bone, consistent with saying what has to be said – at odd moments and in different ways. So I am sorry you find the talk too much, for the fault then lies with the juggler, who again feels that an ampler book might have carried it less conspicuously. All I can say is that a book like *The Shadow* has had an extraordinary effect on some young intellectuals who have been through the arid ways. And I wonder if the sales of a book like *The Green Isle* haven't astonished you? In short, I wonder if you may not take a chance on the talk?

The title, too, is a difficulty, because I mean it to be an answer not to the Gaelic part only. Let me be naive enough to confess when I'm at it that *Behind The Wave* was not thought of in the original conception as a thriller but rather as a serious (cannot think of the right adjective) book with the excitement of a thriller.

But I've said enough. Send it back and I'll have a severe look over it.

Yours,

Neil M. Gunn

TO JOHN GRAHAM (EDITOR OF EDINBURGH UNIVERSITY'S STUDENT PUBLICATION *JABBERWOCK*).
BRAEFARM HOUSE, DINGWALL, ROSS-SHIRE   15 DEC. 1948

Dear Graham,

What about calling it *Calvinism and Critics*.[37] I admit you made me think of calling it *Calvinism Outside In* but that had better wait for longer treatment! I am glad it has proved of some use to you in meditating on the Devil. So far as I know (which is never very far) the approach to the business is new and, if I may say so, badly needed, for we do tend to get tied up with an internal argumentation which doesn't carry us over any border. If you don't mind my referring to your excellent letter it might even apply to it. You talk very truly of the recurring sneer of the English reviewer at the Celtic twilight as an interesting if rather irritating aberration that may be part of the realistic revolt against romanticism. But one step further on, and what the Englishman calls Celtic Twilight is to us something as natural as a plate of porridge. The romanticism is his. We can talk of giving the Devil his porridge with at least as much realism as the physicist uses when he gives some nucleus a whack in the eye with a neutron, for both Devil and neutron are inferences, or inferential substances, which can produce on their respective planes, equally good or hellish results. I need not elaborate the argument – I hopefully leave it to you! But whatever we do here, don't in this matter let us give in to any Sasunnach text-book concept of romanticism. We need a new standpoint in our criticism, one that will carry it with some assurance – even manners across all borders! Make it your new concept of the old *Edinburgh Review*. You talk of back scratching among our Makars as a sort of reaction to the neglect of English reviewing. But how much is there here for the psychoanalyst? With a clearer vision of our own authenticity, would we not be turning the psychoanalyst on the English reviewer? When I was writing the article for you, it chanced that I had beside me the review of my last novel by the *Times Literary Supplement* and *The Scotsman*. They at once yielded examples of what we're getting at. For I am not referring, need I say, to any question of quality but to one of fundamental attitude. Quality is always where we find it, but fundamental attitude is fairly constant. Nor should we really discuss, as you do, the harassed journeyman reviewer who deals in cliches, for he is precisely the kind of bloke who exposes the symptom. Had they put a really clever critic on to my book he would have concealed the symptom better. I am not having one at the TLS, which, in its time, has been very kind to me and even "chosen" a novel of mine – when it has conformed to the accepted "chronicle novel" pattern. Now I am writing this to you – in somewhat congested fashion, I admit – because I feel you are getting at something in criticism and because I feel that a new realm of it for Scotland may be opening out. Your historic treatment of the Deil is necessary and will be excellent – but I'll see you hunting out the modern application. By the way, it mightn't be a bad idea if you sent a copy of *Jabberwock* containing my article to James Bridie and asked him for a

guest's contribution on THE DEVIL. You might even say
that Neil Gunn suggested it! But I must finish now though
perhaps we might have a talk about all this sometime – perhaps
when I come to Edinburgh for a British Council meeting.
Probably in the Spring, when you might find time to have
dinner with me.

Good luck to the good work.

Yours,

Neil M. Gunn

TO J. B. PICK

BRAE. THURS.   (1949)

My dear John,

You've done it! And I am full of relief. Before, I may have
been conscious of encouraging you, but now I throw you over,
and if you sink it's your own dam fault. This is a novel.[38] It
crawls with life – like a warm heap of fermenting microbes. An
inexact metaphor – to one whose metaphors are just first class.
I was nearly half way through Hutchinson's *Elephant and
Castle* when Daisy finished yours. She wouldn't say anything,
but I know the signs. I started and finished it yesterday, and we
had a very late dram in compliment and she was quite excited
over your accomplishment. Hutchinson is also a terrific fellow
for using metaphors, and very brilliant they are. Yours are not
brilliant; they just spout warm life into warm life like a
fecundating jet. You had four in a row that made me laugh
outright. I'm afraid you are better at it than Hutchinson. So I
wash my hands of you – until I find you going wrong, when
you may expect to get your daylights scattered ruthlessly. I am
particularly pleased that I didn't interfere when at one point
you said the book had stuck. Your plot is excellent and you
work up to a worthy climax. I took a breath and wondered
what-the-hell when you had that fight as Dave and Phyl were
going to Dave's house. It's too abrupt; you don't make it clear
enough, its simple mechanics and personalities. However,
blessedly it had nothing much to do with anything and you
weren't forcing a climax, so I'm saying nothing. Also – when
I'm at it – I could have wished you had shown Dave in an
integrated happy mood – say when he was with the girl in

Leicester – for every time we meet him he's in a mix-up and turmoil. However, so much is implied that I'm not suggesting lily-painting. It goes. It has interest and grip. And you have brought off the two themes – pit and film – like hand and glove (your metaphor-spewing affects me). In this connection you have used Lewis with a negligent excellence. And all from the Pit to the Coal Board are not delineated, told about, they're just there like one's porridge. I had a moment near last page – so you do keep it going – when I wondered if from some high concept of tragedy after the classic fashion you were going to leave the lad in the lurch. But not you, plucky fellow. The happy ending, as ever was, thank God. For it's dead right *for our age*. And the lassie not having gone on the escapist train to nowhere – what kept her back is about the only *positive* thing left us. For life will go on. You were (critics will be) left with the feeling that in *The Lost Chart* I hadn't solved our problem. What have *you* solved? What has the Creator *solved*? We'll leave it for the boulevard. What you *have* done is shown a human warmth; and that humanity would have come through even if you had had a few vultures in the pit's cage, not to mention on a tin shanty's roof.[39] Which reminds me. Probably the perfect title for the book would be *The Cage*. For Dave is certainly caught in the cage of his own emotions, not to mention the Pit's cage. However, I merely throw that out in the hurried by-going. I merely think it should be a short sharp title, thus partaking of the nature of the writing itself. Of course the only bit of writing I stumbled over would have to be on the first page. What I have to endure! But you talk of a wildly *groping* hand – for an infernal clock – and then knock the clock over with a "straying" wrist. And not quite content with that you say the dream eluded him "as the clock had done." I rather fancy that a dream eludes in a silence unknown to the higher fever of an alarum clock (...) When I can think up a few destructive things to add, I'll add them! At the moment I can't be bothered. (. . .)

Tell me what happens to it. Should it ever come to the point of being sent to Faber's, I'd write Geoffrey Faber himself. This would mean nothing beyond ensuring a very careful reading by Geoffrey. I have heard it said that Faber's are not good *novel* people. So think it over – and hold your horses, an all, until you do.

From amid the thunder of hammers and hoovers Daisy sends very genuine cheers, an all, any road.

Love to Gene.

Neil

(. . .) And for heaven's sake get Gene to make *all* ink corrections on your typescript. We did not even try to decipher yours, which look like the drunken footprints of a pterodactyl. (You and your metaphors). (. . .)

TO GEORGE BLAKE

BRAE, DINGWALL, ROSS-SHIRE   6/5/49

My dear George

We have to leave this house on May 28 and have bought a very small cottage on Cromarty Firth a couple of miles north of Dingwall. It has the attraction of the sea (and some fishing) on one side and the noise of the public highway on the other. But for a season it will serve. So we're clearing up and last night I was making a complete holocaust of all MSS, letters, and what not. The letters were business ones strung on a wire hook and I began casting an eye over some of them in your fist as publisher. They covered the *Morning Tide* episode and the difficult *Lost Glen* follow-on, mixed with Nationalism, and I was struck afresh by your understanding and kindness, and thought that, well, I must really tell George how nice a fellow he was once upon a time. And here's me doing it. I'm afraid, George, your general humanity and particular concern for an author come through unmistakably. You just couldn't dodge it if you tried.

But old Pat's hand-screeds had me shaking with laughter. He seems to have been haunted by one whom he calls G. M. T. (sunshine) Thomson who had an umbrella. He assumes (wrongly) that I had heard "the lastest one" about a haggis in a latrine. But if only I could tell him what *Sun Circle* was about so that he could pass on the news to witless book-sellers . . . I was sorry to commit such beautiful stuff to the flames.

We were delighted to hear a fellow J. K. Cross talk so

enthusiastically about your new novel on the air and hope it's doing well.

Daisy joins me in blessings on you both.

Yours,

Neil

TO MARGARET MACEWEN

KINCRAIG, DINGWALL   11 APR. '50

My dear Margaret,

That was a very charming letter, thank you. If you had been on the spot, I should have thanked you with more elaboration. A very bad correspondent, I am. Perhaps having to write so much about nothing much is enough. Though I seem to be writing less and less – like yourself with politics. I think the piano is a beautiful solution of all the time-wasting impertinences of politics. Not that I expect you quite to agree with me; and anyway there would have to be such long and involved definitions of terms – and then of the definitions. I'm afraid the last General Election didn't draw me over a doorstep. I have been disappointed with Labour and Scotland, oddly enough. And you needn't smile, for you're worse. People will so insist on being totalitarians that I am finding less reason than ever for abandoning an early and enlightened anarchism. And what was the book that had a quotation from *The Serpent*? Couldn't have been one on anarchism, though I get an old country philosopher in that book to apply it to a Highland community. And don't tell me it had anything to do with psychoanalytic probings into the body politic! Actually there is a very distinguished psychiatric gentleman who thinks vastly of *The Green Isle of the Great Deep*.[40] That my provincial simplicities should wander into such strange countries! "It just shows you", as they say hereabouts – though exactly what I can never grasp. But enough about books. Daisy has it all fixed up with your mother for lunch here today, but it's cold and she has decided – wisely, we agree – to postpone her visit. I'm afraid we move about very little, and sometimes feel guilty that we are not so good at the entertaining as we ought to be.

We are both going to Edinburgh for PEN Congress in August, but let's hope that won't interfere with having at least a glimpse of you. But that's a long way off.

I'm glad you're finding life pleasant – even if work is heavy. And that you should have had such a pleasant thought for me fair warmed my heart. It did an all. May even a small warmth abide with yourself.

Neil

TO GEOFFREY FABER
KINCRAIG, DINGWALL   22ND OCT. 1950

My dear Geoffrey,
And now you have set me a bit of a poser. I realise my novel[41] is of an unusual kind but I had not thought it would be difficult for you to follow. As I have no thought at the moment of another novel, not of the traditional or more popular kind, as you call it, you will have to bear with me, if you can feel that way.

Now it would be a help to me if you could explain why you find it difficult, why you think it would be a "puzzle to most of the English public." I don't want it to be a puzzle. If I puzzle you then I have failed as a craftsman. If I could find out my weakness here, I might be able to do something about it. A writer can't help having new slants on things, even on the novel; but he does want to be understood – as far as his unfortunate nature can! There may be obscure or difficult passages, some points that I may not have made clear. If my attention were drawn to them, lucidity might emerge!

May I, to begin with, give you a simple notion of what I have been trying to get at in the book? Where most novels of the more ambitious kind today deal with violence and materialism leading to negation and despair, I thought it might be a change if I got a character who would wander among his fellows looking for the positive aspects of life. Is it possible to pierce the negative husk, the dark cloud, even for a few moments and come on the light, the bubbling well at the end of the fairy tale? Do folk still do it, ordinary people? Can this feeling be conveyed, the moment of wonder, of integration? Not in any high falutin or mystical way (I don't think I use the word "mystical" once) but close down to the earth among human happenings of a credible kind, a shepherd among the sheep, a fellow telling his story in a smuggling bothy, a sportsman looking through trees, trees themselves, or a dog rose. And not as a thesis, but as something felt by the way, so that when it is quite forgotten it is still implicit. For this, the principal character must appear to have a wide knowledge of life, actual and historical, so that the whole may not seem merely naive. And it must be carried through in the spirit of comedy because of a gaiety at the heart of the notion. Does this convey something of the book's "unifying idea"? For the rest I have tried to make each incident or adventure in this quest as humanly interesting as possible. (I actually took one incident – the fishing boat in the storm – turned it slightly and sent it to my American agent who has sold it to the *Saturday Evening Post* for $1000).

Now I can quite see that a quest of this kind is very different from the ordinary "plot" of a novel. But I'm afraid I can't see how that structure can be radically altered in this instance. And in any case the story of a man on a quest is an old one – and even successful one. So if this was your only difficulty, I realise it wouldn't have puzzled you. There must be something else. Either that or you were being polite! And I can take all the knocks going!

After plot or construction the other ingredient of the recognised novel – love interest, and here I admit I have been very – if not shockingly – unorthodox, for the love of a married man for his wife (and them nearly fifty, God help them) permeates the whole book and comes to a life-saving climax at the end. I should blush – particularly after having read some recent novels praised by the higher critics where a girl seems to be going to bed with a different man, and vice versa, on every other page. A full man might be pardoned for wondering what would happen to them if they had to wash their own bedsheets. Anyway, in comparison, my idea might positively be called revolutionary – blessed word.

Levity apart, do you think you could, then, be a little more explicit about the puzzlement? Could I here or there make things clearer or more pointed? Once or twice I admit there is a symbolic note as in the introduction of the goat – the spirit of totalitarianism that's pursuing us today – but even here I could be more explicit without tearing the texture, if it's really needed.

Finally, and assuming the whole well done, do you think a touch of puzzlement is against sales? If so, tell me why *The Green Isle* has done so well, when everyone who has read it told me it puzzled them (with the exception of a well-known Harley Street psychiatrist!)[42] while *Young Art*, immediately appreciated and even loved (I get letters about it from abroad) never got beyond its first printing? Again, in *The White Hour* I hesitated over including a story called *Blaeberries* because it's little more than a mass of colour, full of symbolism and yet Odhams Press have just asked me if the second British Serial rights are available. Can you appreciate, then, my puzzlement even in the matter of sales? So please do give this matter your thought and me the benefit of it.

Yours ever,

Neil M. Gunn

TO GEOFFREY FABER

KINCRAIG, DINGWALL, ROSS-SHIRE   13 Nov. 1950

Dear Geoffrey,

Many thanks for your letter about *The Well at the World's End*. I appreciate your remarks, and just because you are prepared to publish it as it stands, I am anxious to do what I can to meet your criticisms in every possible way. It was good of you to enclose Alan Pringle's report (. . .). I decided to check his first criticism: "Now the story begins," he writes, "with A Man and Woman . . . they are enigmatic people; and it seems to me a weakness to begin a mysterious novel with enigmatic people. It is true that attentive reading will reveal (later) that the man . . . and that his wife (but is she his wife?) . . ." Now the simple fact is that the first time the woman appears, which is at the very beginning – to be precise, the fourth line of the first page – she is called "his wife." On page 2, a paragraph begins: "It was his wife who had gone to the door . . . Marching on in front went her husband." Mr Pringle has read the book with such obvious care that I am sure he will be astonished at these accurate quotes. The trouble is: so am I. So I cannot help asking myself if the reader, expecting or hoping for a different kind of novel, may go on missing the earthy facts, however clearly I state them . . . You see my difficulty? I am not trying to be enigmatic: the very opposite. But I cannot write this book in any other way . . .

Yours sincerely,

Neil M. Gunn

TO GEOFFREY FABER
KINCRAIG, DINGWALL, ROSS-SHIRE   11TH DEC. 1950

(. . .) In his Report Alan Pringle, referring to the wild flower which Fand had stuck in her husband's buttonhole, calls it "her symbolic flower" and, later, when the flower has been lost, asks "what then does it symbolise?" The answer is: nothing. I never call it a symbolic flower. His wife puts a rare wild flower in her husband's buttonhole at parting and at the end of the day he finds he has lost it. That's all (. . .)

TO NAOMI MITCHISON
KERROW HOUSE   14/11 (1950)

Dear Naomi,
My thanks for your letter, even if you did take the wind from me for a start. For of course I do mean the living Fand[43] at the end. In fact, I called her "living". Yet I do see what you mean. And it's flattering of you to suggest that I would have made him taste the milk – following on what you say about my treatment of the senses and inanimate things, but let me tell you that even if I had you would still have had the same doubt, you would have seen him imagining even the taste. Nothing short of interference by the unfortunate author would make siccar. It is the penalty of "atmosphere", I suppose. Yet somehow it shows a rare sensibility and subtlety in yourself. Which is you hoisted by your own "sight". So don't you try to throw things at me.

And Zarauz[44] makes it worse, much. My God, it shakes me. For the near-drowning incident there has nothing to do with what you didn't tell me about yourself. Yet it's true in detail – the only time I have ever copied life exactly in a book – and the Scot who came charging naked down the beach is the fellow to whom I dedicate the book,[45] and the fellow who was nearly away with it was myself. I have only had one narrower squeak in drowning, where there was nobody to help and I lay among the tangle for a while in a bad way. But Henry's sherries were a marvel – in the cafe on the west side. I could do with one of his bottles now.

One more point – you wonder what would have happened if Willie did not recover in the "ghost" incident. That, too, is *based* on fact. In fact, Willie did recover, but the shepherd who helped to frighten the wits out of the three carpenters was in a bad way until he did. He told me about it and how he felt. The house on the West, where it happened, the haunted house, was vacant for years. But when I was round there recently, I saw it was occupied – probably by servants from the South! (. . .)

Yours

Neil

TO GEOFFREY FABER

KERROW HOUSE, CANNICH   12 MARCH '52

My dear Geoffrey,

Your suggestions for a new royalty scale have hit me in the wind. Our former housing conditions were very unsuitable and I had to buy this new place and put out some cash on it. So the knock is most unhappily timed! However, that is personal and by the way, though it does put an edge on the unfairness that cuts an author's income while wages and salaries all around him are doubled or trebled. And it doesn't help much when you say that though the royalty has been reduced the selling price of the book has gone up and therefore the author may still be getting as much as he did in the good old seven-and-sixpenny days. My wife, who has to run our home without any staff, knows only too well that it costs about three times more to do it all round than in pre-war days. So the reduction in means is very real. And I'm not talking of increased income tax over and above. So there is a gnawing sense of grievance that the burden isn't spread evenly. The author's wages and your profits are hit, but everyone else concerned with the making and selling of a book gets an increase. And when you say that roughly out of a sale of 6,000 copies of a novel at 12/6 you make a profit of only £7, then someone's increase must be rather terrific. If the poor fellow at the bottom, the author, is always going to give in to reduction while the others go ahead, how can he help asking where it – or he – is going to end? (. . .)

Yours sincerely,

Neil M. Gunn

TO GENE PICK
KERROW   24 JUNE, 1952

My dear Gene,
   Many thanks for returning the proof – and for your note, which at once disturbed me, for I, too, wondered who could be hunting old Sandy in Italy![46] It was one of the things I meant to go into more fully but didn't. I took the hunters to be Germans up in the north of Italy round about 1917 when they and the Austrians did in fact overrun a considerable swatch of Italian soil. I confess that my memory made that swatch much bigger than it actually was. Still it could be enough. There was a lot of enemy submarine work going on around and in the Adriatic. In short, I'm letting the thing stand. My vision of the incident was oddly enough peculiarly vivid; and I think there may have been some obscure prompting from the old subconscious about the north wanting the sun, but that would need a few drams to evoke.
   I was very interested, too, in your query about a possible Christian infiltration into Sandy's make-up. John in his fine letter about the characters in the story did not mention or assess Sandy and I had a feeling that I knew why. But it's all very difficult. Sandy for me was *the* character and if he fails the whole book is a bit futile. I suppose I must have been trying, however unconsciously – or half – to get a glimpse of that peculiar quality that we have – literary gents in general, I mean – called "goodness". Sandy was very bothered by it, particularly when the blessed thing would act in spite of him. It seemed to me finally that it is not a specially Christian quality, not of any particular creed, but, rather literally primordial. It probably had a very long innings in paleolithic times, the ages of the hunters. It is at the root of the myth or archaic heritage (forgotten memory, so to speak!) that makes even respectable anthropologists babble o' the Golden Age. However, that's all beautiful argument and argument is easy. Evoking the thing itself is the bother. And the biggest and best novelists have always been wise enough to avoid the attempt. Anyway, I do mean that this "infiltration" of goodness belongs to us all and is not of north or south, so there you are. But now the next thing: assuming it could be evoked (for I am placing no value on my effort) would we like it or would we react against it,

finding it too soft, too kindly; finding it too much of a good thing? I am beginning to wonder. I am beginning to wonder if our talk of wanting this goodness isn't a bit of a fake, a literary gent's nostalgic moment. I was greatly interested in the Thomas Mann broadcast talk that John sent, wherein that world-eminent bloke came to the final conclusion "about it and about" that "good" and "kindly" are the profound and meaningful words. Is he just being simple and nice or can you tell me where in his works I can find this wonder-essence naturally evoked?

If this "goodness" could be shown in a character like old Sandy, would Thomas's smile before it be one of pure wonder or of kindly condescension? But Mann is a great and big man, bless him; most of the normal critics will have no difficulty in dealing with this soft bit of provincial sentiment. So I'm not expecting much!

If there may be a sort of nihilistic sound about all these words, at least the sound was in my head when reading Sartre's *Iron in the Soul*. Jean Robertson sent it to us and I've just finished it. But I had better not start on it or I mightn't stop for a long time! Some time John will have to do a real criticism of this kind of stuff. He's sure a remarkable fellow – Sartre, I mean – and the way his intellectual imagination (if you see what I mean) works up conditions inside his head is wonderful and even stunning. I was so stunned that I missed some "good" character that John spoke of. His use of language and image is quite simply stunning. It's the modern use of the old purple passage; but whereas the old purple passage was laid on with a "poetic" brush, Sartre's purple is shot at us through a tommy gun. Even in colour itself or the use of it, all is violently intense. A stickit painter is coming out of a restaurant when "it was as though someone had operated on him for cataract . . . colours drummed in every object with a mad pulsation . . . world thrilled and vibrated until it must burst . . . everything on point of exploding, of falling down in an apoplectic fit . . . shrill cacophany of brilliance, whirled and dazzled like a merry-go-round . . ." (At this point the painter "indulged in a shrug"). "Colours had thrust at him from every side, bursting like tiny flasks of blood and gall . . . the spread of *Nature's* green, crude, unrendered, an organic secretion like honey or curdled milk . . .". And so on. Wonderful. But all that did not happen to the painter coming out of the cafe; it was worked up inside

Sartre's noddle. And every now and then he has the trick of underlining a word to make sure you get it. Then the quality of the thought following on these smashing intensities doesn't really amount to an awful lot, however clear or modish it may look. For example, the aforesaid painter next goes to an art museum. But he doesn't want to see the old masters. "*They* had the good fortune to be *achieved*. Somebody had taken them, inflated them, breathed life into them, pushed them to the very limits of their nature, and now, their destiny accomplished, there was nothing more for them to hope, save to be preserved in museums." Revelation! Quite. But is this really what happens? It was put more succinctly by a bloke who said that a work of art is dead immediately it's completed. One sees the thin little element of surprise they want to convey. But really! Yet it sounds banal, so unsurprising, so provincial, to say that a work of art does not exist until it exists, and only after that does it do whatever its job may be. And it will do its job best if put in a place where we can all see it. That place is a museum. Just as in literature, that place is a book. To say that, for example, Lao-tzu had nothing more to hope, save to be preserved in a book, makes about adequate fun of the silly little thought. And Lao-tzu lived about half a millenium before Christ, who also *achieved* some memorable remarks.

But this is boring, and you'll forgive me. Only I confess I was thinking of John, too, for that lad has a lot of necessary work to do in this milieu. I am only mentioning a certain aspect of Sartre, but something has to be done about all this violence; it has got to be seen in all its disguises. (. . .)

Jean Robertson[47] enjoyed her time here very much, not to mention the distinguished guests, starting with yourself. I caught a salmon. Last night we were dining at the big house farther up the glen. Very nice folk, and helpful.

Cheers for you all.

Neil

TO J. B. PICK
KERROW. MON. (1954)

My dear John,
    The bow and arrows have arrived, with Zen in the eternal background.[48] This is very good of you, and I dance my

THE FULL-TIME WRITER

solemn gratitude before the target, like the Master who didn't
believe in words. Though I'm afraid it wasn't a tapdance he did.
But perhaps I'll compose his dance – for Gene's adjudication.
So many games are just pastimes, as you so exhaustively know.
I had a session with your new book[49] the night Daisy spent in
Dingwall and I was alone with a silence more potent than the
Master's. It's a most engaging work with a humour that
enriches itself with a bland restraint. Perfect manners. On the
way to Zen, I mean. I found myself lost once in a peculiar
phantasy arising from your game of Teams. No Bach, who
should have been playing outside right, with Handel inside.
What weaving of incomparable dribbles would have been
there! When Bach got the ball Handel could sit down for a rest,
and vice versa. No going off like members of the Dynamo
team. The trouble with Bach, I found, was that when he had
woven his wonderful way to the goalmouth, he didn't shoot,
he wasn't finished, he began to turn back, making beautiful
rings not only round his opponents but his own side, until
Beethoven yelled, "Herr Gott, don't you know where the goal
is?" but Bach merely thought that the goal was where he
finished. One member of the opposing team, by the way,
yelled at Beethoven, though for what reason I do not know;
"Ya! You great Beetroot!" It was an extraordinary game.
At a critical moment for his side, Tchaikovsky let off some
fireworks from his "1812" and blew the ball the length of the
field and scored. The goal was not disputed. I think everything
– ultimately – depended on the referee, whose name was Zen.
He never spoke, just placed the ball and whistled, and I got the
very odd impression that the game would be played to a finish.
You'll play more wonderful games yet. When you're commis-
sioned to do a book on gambling . . .

We enjoyed our weekend with you very much indeed and
hope Gene has recovered – she expended so much on kindness.
All I can see of David is his smile. Daisy has sent for Yeats and
that other book. She has more scope when I'm tethered.

Neil

115

My dear Gene and John,
  Many thanks for your cheerful letters. We need all the cheer
we can get! I stuck the Northern Infirmary[50] for a full week
and then – yesterday – beat it. The intensive treatment wasn't
doing any good so I said to the specialist I'd like a spell off
before he started a new treatment. Simple fact is, as he frankly
admits, that they don't know any cure. But they have theories!
I was feeling so woolly that I misjudged a bloke's bumper by
half an inch and tore the back mudguard of my beautiful car. I
didn't take any particulars, and, as I am due to pay first £5 in
any Insurance claim anyhow, I'm not bothering to report the
affair. Bad luck has been dogging me so assiduously so long
that I'll soon think twice before I'll blow me nose! A big repair
is suddenly needed to the house, an expensive business. And so
on. Have just got a letter from Maurice Walsh, thanking me for
my new book[51] and regretting that it will make no money.
He struggled valiantly to find out what a lot of it was about.
I suppose he's dead right. I shouldn't like to have to tackle
reading it myself. You should have got your copy, too, but you
haven't to read it, glory be.
  Which is enough in the way of grumbles.
  My head at the moment is not clear enough to read any
book. Had some fun in the hospital trying to follow a tome on
History by Karl Jaspers, the existentialist. The ends of the grey
matter wouldn't knot so to speak, not readily anyhow, but I
liked something in the stuff. I was going to have been there for
another ten days and was on the point of asking you about
two new magazines (*London* and ?).[52] But here we are again,
getting ready to fetch the milk on a frosty morning. Haven't
written anything for a long time, and I'm afraid it will be a long
time before I do.
  However, we have a wonderful self-compensating mechan-
ism in this household whereby when one goes down the other
goes up! – And here's a phone call come from my brother who
is coming for night.
  So cheers to you, and enjoy the bright hours,

  Neil

THE FULL-TIME WRITER

TO MAURICE WALSH
KERROW HOUSE, CANNICH, BEAULY   OCT. 1954

My dear Maurice,
    When I get a book of yours I put all else aside and don't stop
until I finish it. Which I have just done. I confess I smile to
myself, for now you'll get a little of what the critics, not to
mention ordinary readers, pass on to me – for dealing in extra
dimensions. We looked in on Neldie in Forres a few days ago
and she, in her old form, said she was getting a book from you
which you said she probably wouldn't like. How I know the
feeling that made you say that! I can imagine how Chambers
felt, too, and as a piece of book production I don't think much
of it. Disturb the old anthill by probing here and there and
you're for it. That kind of thing I have taken for granted, and
shoved into an empty pocket, for a long time. However, I
wouldn't prophesy about nothing. So good luck to your new
effort.[53]
    I am so taken with your effort that I would like to talk about
it in all kinds of ways, and criticise it, and wonder about this
and that. Which only happens when a fellow craftsman is really
interested. I once wrote a play and then, like you, turned it into
a novel (*Second Sight*). You have kept to the form of the play –
three acts, with entrances and exits an all – far more rigidly than
I did. Your conversation has something of the stage speech.
For full flavour it would have to be spoken. So spoken, your
added explanations of feature, tone of voice, etc. would have
been unnecessary. That, I can see, would be the fascination of
the stage. The vivid would come through sheer. But, of course
– and, oh Lord, I have had plays produced – yours would
require actors of genius. It's all dam difficult, and all we can do
is have a shot and take whatever may come. You have packed
your characters with vitality and that's wonderful. Because of
the subject matter you have dealt in essences – the poet's way.
Yet you have kept your characters distinct, like a novelist. To
an age grown casual, cynical, uncaring of the destruction of
life, your intensity may be disturbing, and the reaction to
disturbance of that kind is often an easy mockery. But that has
always been. Where it is not, perhaps one should question
one's work. But it would need talk! And my God how you talk
anyhow, you quiet dark man. When you forecast much more

talk in Hannah's house I could not help laughing. Indeed I could see myself there, listening, and not a word out of my mouth – beyond a few casual remarks on simple subjects like Buddhism and esoteric Christianity. However, on one thing I would have nothing to say at all and that is your marvellous descriptions (my pen has dried up) of inanimate objects – if they are inanimate – like the inside of a room when there's no one there, the twilight in the window, or the afternoon light on a lawn. Sure, your characters blather away about Nothingness. But what if the Nothingness is an experience of that kind of light or half light? When we talk of nothingness what are we doing but showing the inadequacy of language for traffic in such dimensions? But some of you will go on talking. So I had better stop. Thank you for your book and its communion. Daisy will be into it soon. She often talks of you, and we wondered about going over to see you at this time, but somehow the time has slipped past, and you'll have plenty of visitors. I haven't written a word for a long time, and have no thought of any kind of book. Somehow the urge has gone and for nearly three months I fished and caught salmon and paid my rates with them. By the time I caught 50 they were really coming up! I confess I got tired of it in the end. We are now settling in for the winter. There's a lot of redding up to be done about this place, and after that I may read a bit and take the day as it comes. The trouble about them extra dimensions is that once you've gone a bit into them, most other things seem a bit shallow: Or is it just that one has to go on growing – as your book suggests? I remember an old saying of yours about the fellow who had to wander because round about him were just the fat cattle and the lean cattle and the women kissed before! It seemed a simple enough saying then, but maybe it's complex. (. . .)

Daisy sends you happy messages and hopes to hear from you.

Yours ever,

Neil

And congratulations once more on your courageous adventure.

TO J. B. PICK

KERROW HOUSE, CANNICH, BEAULY   (AUTUMN 1954)
SUNDAY

My dear John,

(...) The part to which I took very great exception in your
letter was that which suggested 1) I should begin to do some
work on 2) of all things, wise insights and wisdoms.[54] Apart
from destroying my somnolent ease, what on earth do you
mean? All I know in that way could be shoved down on two
pages. And yet into me you put that gnawing bug. I all but
killed it by doing an article on "Deer-stalking" for an
American magazine, with payment now en route of $1,000.[55]
I wouldn't get that from Sayings, not if I had the wisdom of
Aquinas, not to mention Solomon and Bertrand Russell,
Hume, Kant, Hegel, Spinoza, Plato, Confucious, and Uncle
Tom Eliot an all. So clarify yourself.

Love to Gene,

Neil

TO C. M. GRIEVE

KERROW HOUSE, CANNICH, BEAULY, INVERNESS   27 NOVEMBER 1954

Dear Christopher,

Put it down to curiosity, but I should like to know just what
you meant in the recent broadcast discussion when you placed
my work in "the nineties". It was obvious to any listener that
your criticism was meant to be damaging, if only from the way
Edwin Muir and Douglas Young at once countered you. But
apart from that – and I mention it because they sounded as
surprised as I was – what exactly did you mean? The nineties
surely stand for an ultra-sophistication, for men like Beardsley
and Oscar Wilde, for an aspect of urban civilisation that must
be about the very antithesis of the country which I have tried to
evoke in a score of novels – economics, background, traditions,
history, people, in detail from the first-hand experience over a
lifetime. You may not like what I have done, but what on earth
has it to do with the nineties?

That you may not have read my books I quite understand.
Why should you – or anyone? But when you proceed in that
discussion to voice the need for a rigorous criticism with
integrity, you will realise, I hope, that at least I am driven to

wonder what it all means. I say this quite simply and without
"personal" feeling. "Personalities" in matters of criticism are
as unnecessary as they are tiresome. But I confess I am curious.
So for the meantime.

Yours

(Typed copy, unsigned. Ed.)

TO C. M. GRIEVE

KERROW HOUSE, CANNICH, BEAULY, INVERNESS-SHIRE 15 DEC., 1954

Dear Chris,

I am just back from Edinburgh and find it good to get your
letter. On Saturday I tried to contact Norman MacCaig but
learned he had gone to see you. I had to stop in Edinburgh
because I was attending rehearsals of my broadcast on the
Clearances. Than writing, how much better to have tossed a
few theories and ideological differences into their appropriate
limbos (though you are beginning to sound suspiciously like a
fellow who has found heaven – though you always were
idealistically inclined) as we used to do in talk long ago. I have
such a pleasant memory of those adventuring times that I did
not want it to be confused with or damaged by ambiguous
snatches of criticism heard on the air or elsewhere. Somehow,
when I wrote, I had not thought of an unscripted talk which
would then be cut to a time measure, but now it explains a lot.
My ear caught your expression "the nineties" and I wondered
what on earth you were getting at. I still rather wonder, of
course, but your emphasis now on Celtic Renaissance or
Twilight – does at least give me your drift and rouses some of
the old mirth. It would need a night! Indeed I can vaguely
remember a night when after dealing fairly faithfully with the
said Twilight you came to its support with a poem by Fiona
Macleod on, I think, Women. Our agreement was complete. I
even wrote a short story about it, from the subjective angle,
which appeared around that time in the *Cornhill*.[56] . . .

But please don't think I am taking your "opposite points of
view" and all that too lightly. An argument never came amiss
yet. I am merely just a little astonished at the rigid way in which
you stick to your own thesis. You positively sound solemn and
intolerant! Surely even in your Marxist dialectic you should
make some effort at getting your thesis and its anti into a

synthesis. When you talk of irreconcilable opposites I begin to wonder about your dialectic. But then I admit I have the kind of mathematical mind that gets bothered over a lack of rigour in reasoning. Even in that broadcast you said that art came from the unconscious, but, a little later, that materialism was all. Which is like having rationalism and irrationalism at the same time. Not a bad idea when it is taken far enough! I could trot out analogies from the sub-atomic world of physics. Your rigid standpoint and the opposing one you condemn may be but two aspects of a whole. The word synthesis has for me sometimes a "synthetic" flavour, but the physicist's complementarism is as acceptable as his experimental results. He does the things and shows you the results. When thought or criticism takes that kind of slant I am there. In fact I find scientific penetration here – as at the other end with its four-dimensional time-space continuum – more fascinating than most modern poetry I have read, to put it mildly. You talk of the "scientific attitude to nature". Of course. But what I'd like you to tell me then is where poetry comes in. What can the poet *add* to the physicist's equation? To what is already perfect in form and communication? The content can't be tampered with. What is it then that the poet adds and how do you include that within your concept of materialism? So with nature in the obvious way. A colour photograph beats any artist or any poet set on describing what he sees. If the poet *should* add nothing, then what is his function? For do you think that I, or any tolerably educated person, am going to have the poet's words on quanta and waves rather than the physicist's? And when I come to Renaissance of any kind or time I am bothered in the same way. You are against Edwin Muir, you say. And presumably also against T. S. Eliot and Joyce and Proust and Dostoievsky and all those who have been concerned with the spiritual and the humanistic. Do you include them in the nineties also? In whole or in part – and where do you draw the line? And can you be so certain of any given situation seeing that science moves? The rationalism of the last century is not now to me what it was as a lad. Things have happened to the constitution of the atom since then! But I have said enough, probably – or not nearly enough. But it springs from a very genuine interest in what you may have been thinking.

I know quite well what you mean about my name not

appearing in Renaissance articles abroad. In the current *Listener* I see a new Oscar Wilde society has been formed in New Delhi. Oscar will beat you to it yet! Even if I am never asked to speak at an Oscar society. Which sounds like the time for another round.

But – more important – it was nice to hear from you and know that you are alive and kicking. Daisy and I are pretty fit at the moment. We had a badish spell some months ago but are now getting around in good style. I think I got my trouble from chasing deer over frozen mountains. The years of the Lord have a way of getting on your back.

(Typed copy, unsigned Ed.)

TO J. B. PICK

KERROW.   8/3 (1955)

Dear John,

You're sure working! It's some consolation for me to know there's another slave like myself, and doubly so when it's the other slave has done it on me. Yes, you've set me going, so I hope you're in as many difficulties, incredulities, absurdities, nonsensicalities, and impossibilities. But no, I couldn't have the heart; not even in the case of an enemy, hardly even John Redmond or was it Raymond?[57] (. . .).

However let it be said at once that when you come around 20th we'll be right glad to see you – at least Daisy is quite sure to hoot with welcome towards you; by that time I may have a dubious eye for you as a taskmaster, but the sight of Gene will more than make up. So may you complete your double task like Hercules. Which reminds me of Hercules' club in J. C. Powys' *Atlantis* which I must have been skipping at same time as yourself. I did my best, but I wasn't at my brightest when reading it, and somehow I had hoped for something special, for I have long had a feeling that I should have liked to pay tribute to one whom I might have called the greatest original in the English novel since Thomas Hardy. But I may come at it some other time. He is so diffuse that you would need to be like a wonderful windy day yourself, or just as anyone will need to be when they, if ever, approach this hotch-potch into which you have so guilefully and criminally thrust me nose first and heaven knows what's coming after. For of course I can't write down wisdom, as you know only too well. But assuming the thing will have a shape it will be an autobiography, a detective story, a Freudian analysis (of Freud), a spoon for physics, a critical commentary on Yeats, Proust, Wordsworth, Rilke and uncle Tom Eliot, a high dive and a long swim into anthropology, poaching, church attendance and sucking eggs, and a way of using these and much more in a sustained, convoluting, forward-and-backward search, with a ruthless precision in the complexities of expression, into the nature of Delight. Now you've got it – without the short story which I'm planting in the middle of the plot like a flower pot (for something must be plain). And the title, the one and only certainty so far, *The Atom of Delight*. I can hear your resigned comment, "He was bound to land among the atoms sometime". Well, I sure have. Ay, it's sad. I shan't be surprised if its half-concealed logic works up into a simple, naive philosophic system, and you know how a system chokes the wisdom you are always prepared to salute. Though I'll do my best with camouflage. If only – if only – I hadn't the vanity which has hitherto made me finish once I start! For I *have* started. But I may achieve the sophistry which could well find an end anywhere. I don't feel myself in honour bound by nothing.

And now, my God, here's your apparently innocent letter with its talk of Ouspensky and G.[58] There's something deep here and damned. Omens around and totems. Here is a cunning design to make me include Ouspensky also. You can't hoodwink me. Very well. I'll send out a tentacle and haul him in, once I've dealt with Rilke seeing himself as Christ. Anything else? Rags and bones!

Oh and by the way, have you got Herbert Read's book on Wordsworth? *Not* that I want to see *it* but I think it was in that he quoted *a poem* which I want. The poem (Wordsworth's) was about a young man who rowed out into a lake in a small boat, and as he rowed a mountain peak began to look at him, until at last he turned and rowed back hard to safety. It's the best example of animism I know, and I can't find it in my *collected* volume of Wordsworth.

But really don't bother about it.

Actually I have done a couple of articles for home consumption, for cash, but the cash offered is so small, after America, that – ah well, it will provide a sherry for Gene. And these BBC folk begin to worry me. I really am very worried. They are bringing a van to this house with a recording box in it and they want me to talk for several minutes into the bloody box. About Scotland. It's frightful. How can you expect me to drip wisdom under that threat? – I mean, of course, how can I write about atoms? I am really having a shocking time. Me, who was free for over a whole year! But I admit I have a chortle at the thought of how Geoffrey Faber may be shocked. It will stagger him. But I'm afraid I have been building a phantasy.

I enjoyed your Ousp. and G. comments. But I've written enough for the moment.

I hope our drive will be free of snow by the time you roll up in your Rolls. I have been trying to do something to it today. Thank goodness we are having unfrozen weather and no more snow.

Daisy sends merry messages. My love to Gene.

Yours,

Neil

John Macnair Reid died recently, so an old literary friend is gone.

WILLIAM MONTGOMERIE, born in 1904, poet and collector of folk-songs and rhymes, had made a discovery about *Hamlet*. It concerned the odd fact that there is both a dumb show and a play-within-a-play dealing with the same material. Why? Montgomerie thinks that they were making different points. In the dumb show "Claudius" poisons "Hamlet's father". But if in the play-within-a-play the "nephew" who poisons the King were dressed as Hamlet, this would deliver a clear warning: the victim here is Claudius himself. The letter is included to show Gunn's openness of mind and willingness to interest himself in other people's ideas.

TO WILLIAM MONTGOMERIE

KERROW HOUSE, CANNICH, BEAULY, INVERNESS-SHIRE   25 AUG.'55

Dear Montgomerie,

I find your analysis and interpretation fascinating and convincing. Perhaps, not being even a rudimentary Shakespearean scholar, it is easy for me to have an open mind – but it's not

necessarily an easy mind on things of this sort! Before tackling
your work, I read *Hamlet* again, and again I sort of took it for
granted that the customary interpretation of Dumb Show and
play-within-a-play was near enough to Shakespeare's apparent
single intention of letting Claudius know that he, Hamlet,
knew what had happened; and though a double-barrelled gun
is not unknown in sport, still I must confess, taking it all in all,
that there did seem to be a lot of confusion about – not at all the
kind of performance from the most deadly marksman of all
time. You have cleaned all that up, for me anyhow; and, so to
put it, the great marksman has come into his own. And, even as
your by-product, the subtlety and penetration are delicious.
Even your psychiatric quotation comes in pat as a knock on the
head, and, if I may say so, as a novelist I am not unacquainted
with the gulf between a mental construct and a living
experience. *Your* double barrel has scored with both shots: on
Shakespeare's craftsmanship and psychology in depth. This is
exhilarating, and I have always found that where exhilaration is
unity of achievement is not far off. Anyway, my thanks for
letting me see this. Have you shown it to Shakespearean
scholars, like Dover Wilson? (. . .)

Yours,

Neil M. Gunn

TO J. B. PICK
KERROW. TUESDAY   (1955)

Dear John,

(. . .). But let me be as simple as this to begin with: When I
read your article I know there is something missing – as it is
missing in all such articles – and it is the fundamental emotion,
desire, urge, which compelled it to be written. If that element
were present the thing would be whole. Now I cannot begin to
enlarge on that or there would be no end to this letter. I know
that such an article is not meant to be more than an intellectual
assessment, a finding, out of a background of experience
life-long. But it is no more than that – which means it can be
extraordinarily difficult reading for those not skilled in its
kind. And for those so skilled it can tend to become another
intellectual exercise. The more experience is left out of this
kind of exercise – the emotional factor – the thinner it becomes.

Theories – and so on. You were critical at once when in my last novel[59] my conversation about such difficult topics as bollards and second landscapes was too abrupt. Your instinct was dead right because you were wanting me to get the thing *whole*, the reality of the emotion that produced the bollard. Now that's exactly what I want you to get, with the ideas contained in your article. Now I am not concerned with the article as a particular kind of form, with a particular kind of content. We know all about that. What I am concerned about is that you should get your fundamental concepts *plus* the dynamism that produced them into one *whole*. If you can do that then you are doing something bigger than can be found in a philosophical article, for such an article at the end of the day can be no more than an assessment of what has been done or at any rate of what has been experienced (though *done* is definite always and *experienced* can be fanciful). In short, by achieving the *whole* you would be fulfilling your vocation completely Q.E.D.

But how? Hold your horses, now, these impetuous head-strong horses of yours. For the time has come to illustrate my remarks. Though first, I suppose, we should really have to have a canter through the realm of Art. For Art is where the emotional factor is, the dynamism that shoots the spark across the plug points and makes the whole contraption go. Man has come to think he has *made* that spark. In fact it is the fundamental stuff of the universe and here he has been clever enough to direct it. The artist deals with this kind of fundamental stuff. You're an artist and you have got to deal with it, and you have got to deal with it more than you have ever done before. It has got a value for the whole greater than any other because it keeps the whole going. Philosophy seems to have fallen by the roadside along which science is pushing, perhaps to cut its own throat. But enough.

Now where are we about your article? Just here: its contents are truth, but you have got to make that truth dynamic. The only way you can do this is through a creative bit of work, artist's work. Can you do it? I think you can. Why do I think so? Because I listened to your ideas about mechanics who found their vocation in making a motor car by stealth and because I read your short story. For the moment it does not matter to me that your short story ended badly and that your letter about it said this and that (which, if I may say so, I had already apprehended). We can discuss that. I am not questioning the validity of what you were after (though I could discuss that, too, of course!) The story has a tremendous emotional drive. The dynamic stuff is there. That's what matters. And why at the moment am I thinking of that particular bit of writing and relevant notions for a novel rather than other work? Simply, I suppose, because the ideas of vocation in your article are here given a living ground.

How to do it? Just work. The satisfaction of vocation. Have a go. But I can take it on myself to issue a few of those maddening little bits of caution and advice.

Possibly I wouldn't have blethered so much about emotion or dynamic impulses did I not feel that you handicap yourself somewhat in this region by a reticence which is all the stronger for being innate. You have got to give your characters their emotional head. It is almost unthinkable that you will err too much in this way. I know there are many ways. Hemingway dams the stuff up – in order to produce a hefty head of steam. All right. But the stuff must be *felt*. It's got to be there – if not the whole time at the pitch of your short story! You are never ever superior to your characters. You may wonder why you should bother with this often footling character or that, Phyllis or Dan or whoever. I don't know the answer to that wonder myself. All I can do is borrow from you and say it is part of the mystery. Van Gogh or Degas or blokes of that ilk make their simple even "primitive" characters part of the mystery. They would never do it if they felt superior to them or even impatient with them. But some kind of illumination results that goes beyond the characters and the painters. There is something very profound in your acceptance of this as part of the mystery. But acceptance *in action* is not easy!

Take your time. When one rushes against time, or has unduly the feeling of rushing against time, time has its revenge. What is here is largely an attitude of mind. Time sets up of itself a rush in the creative mind once it has got going. To blazes with it! The only way to knock time sideways is to take your own time. That of course is a counsel of perfection. But it can find unexpected riches in the interstices of time. Every artist has this bother.

Now a particular thing. In this article you have the "unifying idea" for your novel. So you can afford to forget about it. It will come through in spite of you. This is specially said to you. I would probably have a character who voiced it a bit. So may you. But this is only a bit of the whole. However, I need hardly have mentioned that. Though I suppose what I am trying to say is that more will come through than you are aware of. I want it to come through, too. Because I know quite simply that it is important, that it has a value which cannot be questioned because it is in a profound way part of the mystery. Your article does one good. Somehow it makes the ground solid under the feet and, with that ground underneath, they can go forward, the burden of the clamant ego lightened and fresh air thinning the old congestions. If only I could think of something to write about, I believe I could write myself!

The fishing is about over, and now I must spend a few solid days in the garden which is in an incredible mess. Daisy has to take it easy by doctor's orders. She has been overdoing it. She's awfully difficult to tie down. But I am trying, Gene, to be very firm. We must certainly cut out having visitors for a long time – I mean visitors who stay for weeks. Daisy thinks Gene just about the sweetest girl she has ever had in her house. Men apparently don't seem to matter so much!

I was very interested to hear about your one day a week at school. I would be all for it. Actually I have the greatest difficulty, though you mightn't think so, in offering advice. And there is a way in which it is into your barrow. Anyhow, you'll learn something – as well as the kids.

A long letter – and not the kind you expected, perhaps.

With all our best wishes,

Neil

I doubt if Daisy will ever be able to read your fist – unless typed!

TO J. B. PICK
KERROW, SAT.   (1956?)

Dear John,

(. . .) Even my pen has forgotten how to squeeze out ink, for not a word have I written for many months. Perhaps I am going through some transition period and have not yet found the new job. I have regretfully eliminated two physical-labour jobs. Reading can't be called a job, I feel; anyway, I have never really taken to it. So what it's going to be I don't know. Anything but writing anyhow. I fancy gambling might have been fascinating, against a background of peculiar detachment, but I should have thought of that earlier and become a successful author with the stocks and shares to move about on the Exchange board, with litanies on dialectical materialism being murmured, off. That might have been wonderful. Instead of which I'm just reading old Ouspensky again and not-aiming an arrow in Zen archery. At which point Daisy came in and on discovering that I was writing to you, said: "Tell him that when they come they can *all* go to bed and *I'll* look after them." And out she went with a laugh. Just like that. She is in fair fettle, I confess. And a woman comes in to help. We haven't been anywhere except to Perth mod. I saw a Bridie, in distressful circumstances. *Baikie Charivari*. David Stewart, of Perth rep., came to lunch (after we'd been up for most of 2 nights) and invited us to a matinee. We were to be greatly entertained; so went with the company in their bus to Dunfermline to see their evening show (of *Baikie Ch.*) While they were making-up I took dinner. Fatal. For when I got into the warmth of theatre, sleep hit me with cruel rods. Poor old Bridie! And then I was asked afterwards to explain its enigmas!

Neil

THREE

———————

AFTER LITERATURE
1957 to 1963

KERROW HOUSE, CANNICH, BEAULY   (EARLY 1957)

Dear Naomi,
   Thank you for your little letter about the book.[1] I hope you
stick it to the end. I know what you mean about too much
psychology and too little physiology. I have tried to give a sort
of balance for the whole man, even if at the end thought ran off
into odd dimensions. The trouble is one of length. You see, the
blessed book is over 100,000 words! It was tempting to amplify
at every point. But I wanted my main stress to be positive
(hence title). We have been getting so much of the negative
stuff, negative emotions, and diggings into the futility of the
Outsider, that I have grown bored by the whole unending
performance. It has become so unfashionable to be positive, so
positively indecent to be optimistic, that I just said so long to
all that. I know I am in for it from the critics. I don't care any
more. I am even getting the notion that the one thing Scottish
writers can be, over against the existentialist French and their
English copyists, is positive. (. . .) Then again, the London
critics have their notions of the provincial. What one of them
(Tynan, I think – drama critic on the *Observer*) said about
Bridie and *Mr. Bolfry* the other Sunday just made me feel mad.
Not merely its superior complacency, its nitwitted arrogance,
but that air of the new Bloomsbury looking down on the
narrow ignorant "provincial" – but I'd better not start. I know
it doesn't matter. But it matters enough to make one wonder
what does really matter. And that's our job. (. . .)
   Neil

TO NAN SHEPHERD
KERROW   27 JANUARY 1957

My Dear Nan,
   (. . .) my experience with *The Atom* has put a full-stop to
book-making. Not that much was needed. And – apparently
like yourself – I am now retired. By "experience" I mean the
book has been ignored by critics and the lave. Which is not a
complaint, but a fact that makes sic writing unfruitful to all, for

133

wasn't it the learned Doctor who knew a man a fool who didn't write for cash. And I have the by no means unpleasant thought that even while I was writing these turgid (if I may borrow your word) swatches I was fair killing the cash. But don't think I did it deliberately – which might sound masochistic – but only because I was enjoying myself. To hell with the Pope – or was it Freud? That was a delightful mood.

All the same, I think you may be forgetting somewhat how much "ideas" meant to your early years. And autobiography – if I may use the word – isn't a novel exactly. Again, from the beginning systems of philosophy or psychology were troublesome to me for two reasons: because my mind could not accept premises and so got bored, and because (for now we come to it) they did not (necessarily, by structure) stem from their author's *experiences*. So I thought I would write something that did, and even use the earliest experiences to show they persisted and interpreted the later ones. Which took me into some weird fields, I admit – knowing all the time that the mixture of categories (autobiography, Freud, etc.) would revolt the literary pure of heart, but feeling – and still feeling – it was worth it, poor as the accomplishment was, alas! So, as I say, I have no complaints. Most of us did our stoic best. . . . And as for poaching forays – I seek for one regret in vain! (. . .)
Yours,

Neil

TO J. B. PICK
KERROW HOUSE, CANNICH, BEAULY   (1957)
MON. MORN.

Dear John,
    That film fellow,[2] amid a hubbub of folk and whisky bottles on Saturday, never gave me a chance to say anything, for instead of coming to catch trout, as expected, he suddenly caught a sleeper for London, and left me chewing my cigar with the fairly distinct impression that I had said I would go to London on Monday next (July 1) rather than have a posse of scenario writers to see me in Cannich. I did say that I couldn't go to London without Daisy. He merely said "Fine! Excellent! Would you like to go to Savoy – or – " I thought a change. . . . Anyway, I gather that it will be a quiet little place called The

Mayfair, or something like that. In short, seeing that Gene and you couldn't come to see us we thought we might go and see you – need I add at their expense![3] However, I did make it clear that all this commits me to nothing. The wary Highlander did contrive to make that clear! He took some notes and said I would be hearing from them after he got back. So at the moment it does look as if you might be seeing us both next week sometime. Don't ask me how all this has apparently happened. So far at least. I mean, I'm never astonished at what may happen next. Roughly, the position is that they are interested in my script and before taking any steps about it, they would like me to discuss it with their principal scenario writer and others (including a choice of possible producers). If after all that I am prepared to play, then things like an agreement and so on should follow. I feel like one of my own fish on the end of my own line, and full of possible evasive action. But it's sort of complicated because I got Maurice Walsh – and he got me – sort of involved. But I'll be after telling you all about it, no doubt, in due course. After Daisy has absolutely prohibited my appearance in plus fours, she then asks me what she should wear. So I am in a very complicated position at the moment, Gene. So I am postponing at the moment any consideration of Ouspensky's *The Fourth Way*. Did I tell you that I saw Maurice Walsh for a few hours the other week? At 78, he is looking well and fit.

Anyhow, John, I'll find out something about films – and in due course I should see how they may react to your idea about car-building and racing.

Looking forward,

Yours,

Neil.

We may be staying about a week.

ALEXANDER REID wrote an unsigned review of Gunn's *Wild Geese Overhead* in *SMT Magazine* for November, 1939. Neil went to the office and sought him out. Reid was a poet who later became a dramatist (*The Lass Wi' The Muckle Mou*, *The World's Wonder*), and wrote the radio version of *The Well at the World's End*. He died in 1982.

TO ALEXANDER REID

KERROW HOUSE, CANNICH, BEAULY   9 APL, 1957

Dear Alex,

I do apologise for having kept these two books so long, but I put them aside after a first wrestling match, in order to have another go later when the dust subsided. Not that I can claim to have held my own, for their handgrips are more elusive than young eels. But I thoroughly enjoyed some moments. The real difficulty with a book like Huang Po's[4] for us of course is that it is composed of essences of thought delivered to different and always specialised audiences. But at least I did satisfy myself about such an affair as that heron experience[5] and just how it comes in. In fact, unless one has had some such actual experience as I tried to describe at length, I just cannot see how anyone can get an inkling of what Zen adepts are after. And by the way, think of my getting from far Zenland a copy of the English magazine *Encounter* for January last, because of an article in it called Zen and the Mood of the Universe![6] Also in that magazine an advertisement of the highbrow quarterly *Chicago Review*, devoted entirely to articles on Zen. What next! (. . .)

And all good wishes,

Neil

TO MAURICE WALSH

KERROW HOUSE, CANNICH, BEAULY, SCOTLAND   SAT. SEPT.1957

My dear Maurice,

Here's a copy of the screen play, which I've sent to the film people. I'll let you know their reaction when it comes. From previous comments of theirs, I should say they'll go ahead on it, probably about May of next year. So we have plenty of time for the book.

I should like you to have a go at it. We have been in many ploys together, and this collaboration on the writing side would be a copestone. We would invent a name for this poaching sally – author's name. The opening is certainly right into your barrow, for your description of the Highland scene has never been bettered. Supposing you make a start on it – right up to the end of the bothy scene? If you could include the bits of conversation, that would keep the film straight. But you'll know all about that.

To say you haven't a kick left – nonsense. We'll both have a kick left to the end, with God's help. Then about it being Scotch whisky – damn it, aren't we the same Gaelic stock? Beneath all, isn't that the truth, let politics bedevil it as they may? We know what we know, and one can help the other. In fact I wouldn't have started on it in the beginning, but for the thought that I was going to enjoy myself helping you. And had it been an Irish subject you were on, I'd have backed you to the hilt. Anyway, think it over, and if you are in the mood for talk, Daisy and I could be coming over to see you in the first days of October, as before. But now, listen, Maurice – if you don't feel like being set upon, just say the word like a good fellow, and we'll bide our time until your resources are able to cope with two persons who wouldn't have more than one Irish punch of a night, unless maybe for the small one, of which Daisy has such fond memories. And it's she made me say that. For it's the great concern for you we have. So if you feel like it, let me know soon, so that I may book a sleeping berth on the Dublin steamer. We could talk then – and if you didn't feel like having a shot at the novel – or part of it – to hell with it!

I was very interested in your remarks about the cash takings of *The Quiet Man*. And I'm glad to be able to tell you that there may be a small royalty in it – after *all* expenses, etc., have been cleared. But I'll explain all that when I see you. (. . .)

Yours as always,

Neil

TO J. B. PICK
KERROW HOUSE, CANNICH, BEAULY   (1957)

Dear John,

(. . .) Another comment on *The Atom*, and your responsibility thereanent: in a letter just received from a lad who goes peddling books on a pushbyke (sic) through the wilds of Scotland. Incredible that such trades should exist today – and wonderful. "I had among my customers yesterday an ex-radio operator, living far from sea in Perthshire, who was much impressed by your *Atom of Delight* and who as a fiddler (he plays at the local dances) felt he'd made progress only after studying a book by a professor of a Continental conservatoire, whose methods (or advice, rather) he thought to be about on a par with that of the Master of Zen Archery." The peddler himself is now reading Herrigel on the Art. The opening sentence of his letter: "This is to express my gratitude for all you have given me in your books." Remarkably intelligent letter, notwithstanding. But you see where you have sent Zen!

My part-time job? Don't know yet, but when I was writing to you I got a letter from a noble lord in your city[7] asking me if I would be prepared to do some advising on whisky-making! It wouldn't take up much time and wouldn't make use of my name – so he may even know some of my peculiarities! I have acknowledged and shall let you know if anything comes of it. But meanwhile, confidential. There might be some cigarettes in it, if not a steady bottle. It would be amusing if I had to go to a conference in London! It would be such a delight standing Gene and yourself one.

Spring is coming, as you say, Gene, and I'm afraid Daisy and I had one of these wild assaults on the earth that hasn't done us any good. But we'll recover.

Which is more than enough for the moment.

Fond regards to all,

Neil

TO NAOMI MITCHISON

KERROW, CANNICH, BEAULY   7 DEC '57

Dear Naomi,

Many thanks for your interesting packet. First about your book of Scottish short stories,[8] which I am glad to hear is coming out. About reviewing – I simply have no editorial connections of any kind. Otherwise I would have been happy indeed to have selected yours for treatment. If *you* don't know how the reviewing racket is worked, what of me, lost in a glen? Of my last book, *The Atom*, there were about 5 reviews (yours excelled) and 3 newspaper notices in *all* the publications of these islands. If I were to do another book it would be even noticed less and might embarrass my publishers, so why do it? So I'm doing nought. And I don't say this in any critical or bitter spirit. That's the way things are. If one's work is running counter to the prevailing current, one mustn't expect much. If this sounds pessimistic, let me assure you it is far from it! But time is needed and a searching out of what matters. Then something may be written. And if this sounds to you like Highland sloth, hold your horses: Anyhow, I'll find my way of saying something about your work. For there's something intilt that I find more than distinctive. I'm looking forward to the short stories, for I *know* that they'll contain the essence. You'll be hearing from me. It's only at such a moment that I wish I had editorial or reviewing contacts. Otherwise, I have no interest in the racket at all. Some Sundays ago, I saw two of the big shots riddling Colin Wilson's second book, though a year before they had acclaimed his first as a masterpiece. By chance I read both books, and thought the second much better than the first. After all and as a youngster he is trying to get at something, which is more than can be said for either P. Toynbee or C. Connolly. The reviewing racket at its most elevated or worst. I agree – I know only too well – that if a book of value is critically ignored the author suffers in his pocket. Well, all right. He has got to get his bread and butter somehow. Some months ago, Daisy and I had a delightful holiday in London at the expense of a film company who were wanting my advice. So it goes. (. . .)

Neil

TO ALEXANDER REID
KERROW HOUSE, CANNICH, BEAULY, INVERNESS-SHIRE 17 APRIL, 1958

Dear Alexander Reid,
    I have found your letter and enclosures very interesting (not to mention my surprise at finding one person in Scotland who has read *The Atom of Delight!*) I like the quality of your stuff, its attack in breadth, sure apprehension, understanding. When I opened the pamphlet and found the quotation from Aldous H. I chuckled and sat up. It couldn't be that here was another Scottish writer interested in such material! And I wondered at once if you thought Huxley ever really "got" the Divine Ground. However, I'd better answer your letter or we're lost.
    First, then, personal detail for that article of yours in S. M.[9] for I can see you want it soon. I have been asked before and shied off, for the personal embarrasses me a bit. But the way you have treated Orwell is as provocative as interesting. For

example, your reference to his anarchism rang a bell in my strath somewhere, then I remembered my novel *The Serpent* (not having read my books since writing them, I forget what's in them), turned it up and found from p. 175 some talk on anarchism in relation to old social conditions in a Highland community. (It was reproduced in an anarchist newspaper).[10] Here, then, is the Equality you talk of in your Orwell article. But in this particular instance of mine you will see that it stems from experience. Here was an actual society living in a specific way. The character who discusses it went through his "socialistic" phase in Glasgow. Empirical (a word I use so often, I'm afraid, in *The Atom*). Accordingly Equality becomes the fundamental norm, and Inequality – class distinction – the something that's got to be searched out and understood. This *reversal* of the usual attitude to class-distinction and its politics is not fanciful, it's quite real. And I have wondered why no critic has ever at an odd moment spotted it in much of my stuff. Particularly when it comes to talk of communism, etc., for here is something to go on – not just theoretical talk, but an actual ground – even, dammit, a Ground! Your talk on the "individualist" comes out of it, as you know. And the way you have caught it in Orwell – Eric Blair – naturally interests me. Now to make of all this, reasoned subject-matter for a novel, would by your definition be pseudo-art. What matters, of course, is the human relations that result. For example, I wrote a novel, *Young Art and Old Hector*. Now the relationship here between an old man and a young boy is almost unnatural from the point of view of a class-distinction public school society. At the best, a bit too good to be true, therefore sentimental – as one friendly critic assured me. This annoyed me a bit, so I conceived the idea of letting these two characters drop through the bottom of a pool into their Gaelic Paradise (The Green Isle of the Great Deep), run on totalitarian lines, with the latest politico-metaphysical theories buzzing around, just to see what would happen to them. Naturally I first read every thing I could find at the time on the conditioning of the human mind – Russian purges of '37, Nazi-ism, etc. There wasn't a great deal, nothing like what we now know in the realm of fact, but in the realm of the spirit nothing much that I could now alter. Here again it is the *reversal* of attitude, or approach, compared with Huxley's *Brave New World* and Orwell's *1984*. Not – need I add – that any comparison is intended! What I'm trying to say is that from an initial or intuitive conception of Equality one starts with a *positive* over against a *negative*, and not with a negative or destructive description of human relations over against an *implied* positive. In the case of our background the positive was a reality. If I'm over-simplifying, overlook it. But there is a distinction here. Not, for the writer, that it pays cash! For, of course, the negative, the destructive, is always more dramatic – or, on the ordinary level, more sensational. But when it comes to the dear old mystical level, then inevitably the further the negative, the destructive is pursued the worse it gets, until the reader of our day becomes uncomfortable in the presence of the positive, until words like beautiful, good, decent, have sort of to be spat on – as some of our Sunday critics make clear. So cheers for your use of Beauty and Keats! Then again, the terms "provincial", "primitive society" – don't we know them! You would think that Lao-tsu, the Indian esoterics, Christ, had lived in highly industrial civilisations. But blame yourself for making my typewriter run on like this. I have never belonged to any anarchist or communist party, I should add, though anarchism in some form has always seemed the final hope for humans who wanted to retain maximum individuality or freedom, consistent with duty to community. (. . .)

(. . .) Congratulations on editorship of the *Saltire*! May you make it prosper. About suggested article by me – I just don't know enough about the mystical in Scots literature and haven't got books for reference. Besides, the kind of reading I've been doing on the subject for the last year or two ranges outside Scotland – from far Japan! Also, all practical on my part, empirical, and that's a long story. Haven't done any more writing on subject, as reception of *The Atom* has put any follow-up out of my mind. When do you want it? I should like to help. We might discuss it – and that's why I'm writing this at speed, for I should be in Edinburgh for whiles on Saturday and Sunday, 26th and 27th. (. . .) So over to you at the moment, for I have got to keep an appointment on loch and I'm late. All the best,
    Yours,

Neil M. Gunn

TO J. B. PICK
KERROW, CANNICH   18/1/59

Dear John,
   There were a few sentences in your last letter which I did not
mention in mine because I wanted to think them over. I have
now done the thinking, so you may as well pull yourself
together and look out! But first you must let me repeat what
you said: "Perhaps one day I will be able to think of a book that
I can do and will *work* – slowly to write something . . . would
please me . . . but doesn't seem to come." Now if you were
really prepared to work in that mood, taking time, no haste, at
something you deeply cared to do, something big and difficult,
difficult because it would stretch your faculties to the utmost in
intellectual and emotional range, and something therefore,
because of its *meaning*, that would give balance to your
workaday world, then, assuming the robe of the Zen Master
(not unconscious of his stick), I am prepared to tell you what
you should do. But let me repeat, I am taking it that it was the
real "I" in you that expressed that simple, wise aspiration, and
that you are prepared to let urgency of time vanish in the
creative effort.
   Let me, for illustration, show you just two preliminary
shaping notions that guided my thought: when you went to
Cambridge you *chose* to read history; you have *actually*
written a historical novel of merit. After that I began to think of
you and of what old Gurdjieff would have called your
"magnetic centre". And on top of all that I remembered your
natural and native interest in Cromwell and Fox and that most
remarkable period in English history, which included surely
every conceivable aspect of the human spirit in action from
fanaticism and frustration, governmental and private, to Fox's
Inner Light. I have been looking up the period and am amazed
not only at the all-inclusive range of human thought and action
but at its sheer equivalence for our day – and, for that matter,
for every turbulent period in man's history, everywhere. And
here you have it, on your own soil. So, writing it, you would
not need to think of today or any far yesterday; indeed the
more you forgot them the more they would be *now*.
   Why I think of a novel is because pure history would restrict
the range of your faculties. You have got an intellectual centre

("It's a fine day, Gurdjieff" – one must at least acknowledge the fellow, en passant) of such fine precision that by a sort of sheer honest artistry in its expression you would tend towards final *intellectual* statements. Now your innate ultimate operation is not such, as such, but for Truth. And Truth, in its absolute *experience*, is as emotional as intellectual. And instinctive – with a cheer for that third centre! And if we stick in "intuitive" somewhere, we're coming at the whole man. Now I'm not really talking Zen or Gurdjieff here – I'm telling of something I believe I understand, from boys cracking nuts to heron's legs. If you understand it in the same way, well, there you are. If your first reaction is to fly off the handle at the "impossible", then sit down, empty your mind, then let it slowly fill with the calm conscious, and regard my notions with becoming detachment. Is there any other thing you would rather do – assuming you might conceivably do it? Turn it over. Make sure. And so exercise the "slowly" of your expressed thought, in the first instance! Then and first you could do a bit of reading. And I would here particularly suggest not historian's histories, but any intimate personal diaries or such of the period, where individuals (*characters*) come alive. Now as I must make it clear to you that I am not just talking out of my head – a practice, alas! in which we are both so adept – let me refer you to a short story of mine in my last book of stories. Read it (for I can't) – it's called *Montrose Rides By*. Well, from some MS source material of the time, I was handed the complete picture of the old woman and her hotel. Note *some* of the actual detail. And the Inverness Bailies of the time too – *real* names of townsmen. Now supposing you find some such source material and you have a character who goes to an inn – there it is! Thickening of texture – the coming alive of subsidiary characters – and so, with luck, of history. And who knows what principal character may come alive at you, too? Anyway, there's a direction for preliminary reading.

I am chary of throwing out any sort of guiding line, for I would rather let your imagination come on it. But as I know you can discount the inept, let me suggest a young woman on the royalist side who *feels* for her side with every aristocratic (and I don't mean *merely* class here) element in her. This aspect of the conservative best, mixed, muddled, but alive with some aspect of the spirit that has meaning; confused, intolerant,

THE SELECTED LETTERS OF NEIL GUNN

perhaps, but holding to something. The irrational that somehow achieves the rational of the feminine.

Her opposite number, as the movies so beautifully say,
would be a young man who was moved by what Cromwell
stood for. That is, he knew it better than he could tell, or even
Cromwell could tell. He could well be one of Cromwell's
aides. I could even imagine him, in a moment of doubt about
his attitude to his lady, doubt of himself, of everything (except
the love of which alas! there could never be doubt) being
present by chance when Cromwell and Fox met and talked.

But perhaps I have said enough for one morning. It will be so
much easier in due course to talk.

Thank Gene for her charming letter. You may tell her that
there's a small tuft below my nostrils, but nothing that anyone
could really call a moustache. However, there's no good my
hoping for a real moustache, because Daisy has said she is
going to make me quite better. Already I resign myself to the
loss of my moustachios, and as for Sir Cumpton's beard – it
fades like the smile of the Cheshire cat.

One last thought: I realise how big and difficult the project,
particularly as you must give your days to your work. Perhaps
impossible. But look at it. And then have another look. No
harm in *looking*. And anyway real good in doing some
preliminary reading of the time, instead of so many books
today. Who is General T. S. Auden-Montgomery anyhow?

Neil

TO J. B. PICK
KERROW HOUSE, CANNICH, BEAULY   1 MAY/59

Dear John,
(. . .) Now about Little, Brown in U.S.A. – the firm and fine
terms of the Agreement cheered me vastly. An excellent firm of
publishers – and you are following in my footsteps, for they
published my first, *The Grey Coast*! What you have done
about this, including your quoted reply to your "American
agent", is just right. Fine. The only thing that has disturbed me
is Gene's remark about Little, Brown wanting to see more of
your work. Now you must listen to me. *Don't* send them
any of your unpublished MSS. *Don't* send them anything. Tell
your American agent, if pressed, that you are engaged on

another, and what you hope to be a greater work than *The Fat Valley*. That's all – and enough to keep them expectant. This is no reflection on earlier work. You are simply now in *another* field of work, and I know that it will go down in America and Germany. I did once tell you that in my view *The Fat Valley*[11] should be taken in America. My intention here – which I didn't tell you – was, after you had done the round of British publishers, to send the MS. to my agents Brandt and Brandt, with a special recommendation. However, all that doesn't matter now. Only, it's sometimes difficult for me to shove my oar in if I don't know exactly where the boat is! Giving advice can be a tiresome business – especially to the recipient. But I am now going to give you some – should it be my last – and I hope it feels as tough as the Zen stick.

You are now at the second most important turning point in your life (the first was when you met Gene). You must take it from me that in your working life the opportunity has now come. This is *it*. I never told you this before. So it's very important, because the real opportunity, when missed, rarely comes again. Why it is the real opportunity I may tell you some time. Meanwhile, true realisation lies in your next book, so I must talk to you, not about the book itself at the moment, but your approach to it. You know how in Ouspensky, Gurdjieff (may his astral body rejoice), after a proper interval, decided to tell each of his group his "principal feature" or "chief fault". Well, let G. now tell you yours. It's impatience. This usually leads to irritations, superficial aggressiveness, and such like negative emotions in most folk. And usually they make for variety or spice or what have you. But in writing they worm their way down through upper frustrations to chill the vital warmth in which creation takes place. And *you* cannot afford to waste this warmth, because you are going to be a writer of significance, and perhaps high significance. So you have – and it's a terrifying cliché – to possess your soul in patience. I know that Gene and you thought I was being lightly banal when I wrote of emptying the mind, being nothing, or writing as a hobby. Of the three, I was the only serious one, positively solemn. But in your quiet places, where the witness is, you know this.

But I shan't be serious again – for a while! *The Fat Valley* will do better in America than here. And it might do very well in

Germany, not merely because of its locus, but because you handle the grim theme with a lighter hand than the German writer could, with a movement of style that is not only in the writing, but in the physical bodies. The gamble in America is that they tend to go all out for a book, or they don't. (. . .) Our greetings to Gene and the young warriors.

Neil

TO ENA MACLEOD
KERROW HOUSE, CANNICH, BEAULY   4 JUNE '59

Hullo, Ena! And how's yourself? These BBC blokes were here last night, holding a thing in front of my mouth and making me answer questions on the spot – about scenery! Let me forget it. Well, look! On Sat. June 20th, I have to do a theatre in Pitlochry with the Arts Review boys. Now if you'll be at home, we could motor direct to you on Sat. arriving after lunch some time, and Daisy would stay with you while the Edinburgh wallahs picked me up and whisked me to Pitlochry for the night. I believe it's a new play by somebody I've never heard of and historical, so I don't know that it would interest you very much. Anyway, that might be at 8 p.m. (when I'm in the theatre) the Saturday Night's Theatre play from London will be my *Drinking Well*, and I would like Daisy to hear it. If it wouldn't bore you to listen – that would be fine for me, because then I would have a report by two brutal experts, if you see what a poor long-suffering chap means. On the Sawbath I'll be carried by car to Edinburgh in a conscious condition. I hope to see a film, after which we go to the BBC studios and say what we have to say for the air. My particular contribution will be criticism of a book. Then I should get back to Perth on Mond. – or Tues. – pick Daisy up, and hit out for home. How is all that by you? Let me know soon like a good girl, because I'll have to fix up with Edin.

We were up in Caithness for a few days; it's a tough country. But we'll give you all the news anon, I hope.

Love from Daisy,

Neil

AFTER LITERATURE

TO ENA MACLEOD

KERROW HOUSE, CANNICH   14 JUNE (1959)

My dear Ena,

Why there should be complications about a simple little affair, it's the God of all Highlanders alone knows. But now we have got to go so far on Fri. the 19th that it would be as easy for us to reach Perth that night as to get back home, and as it's only two cylinders out of the four I'm sure of I'm planning to get the overhaul done in Perth, as it would take more than a day to do the job properly. So if around 6 p.m. on Friday would find you at home . . . But if inconvenient, drop a p.c. I'm really very sorry to trouble you like this, Ena, unused to it as you are. . . . Even the broadcast of *The Drinking Well* on the 20th has had to be postponed till July 18th because of some political complications high up, which require the 20th so everything is, so far, going strictly according to schedule.

Our blessings go direct anyhow.

Neil

TO ENA MACLEOD

KERROW HOUSE, CANNICH   16TH (JUNE 1959)

My dear Ena,

She had a sweet voice as she told me over the telephone that she had tried to book me a bedroom at Pitlochry, Dunkeld etc. for the night of the 20th (Sat.), and failed. But this charming BBC Secretary in Edin. (her big noise was in London) assured me that she had been successful at last in fixing a room in the Salutation Arms, Perth, for that night! So I put it to her very seriously how odd, if not peculiar, it might appear to many, who know no better, that I should so to speak be in the Arms of the Salutation while my wife, round the corner of the street, was – well, alone if she saw what I meant and in very serious tones she admitted she saw it. And indeed we discussed the implications of this intricate problem of human behaviour ignoring the pips that went pipping, until at last I left the final decision to her and she decided that she had better cancel the Salutation Arms. So please do understand that when I turn up at midnight, Sat, on your doorstep, I am not to blame. And please do not wait up for me. If you put the outside mat under the key . . . But of course I'll be seeing you before then (I touch wood). As for my car, the garage hand assured me that the faster I went the less time the engine would have in which to leak. So it's all plain sailing so far.

Love from Daisy.

Neil

TO J. B. PICK

KERROW HOUSE, CANNICH   25 JUNE '59

Dear John,

(. . .) Daisy wasn't too fit some little time back and we got the doctor in, and at the moment we're expecting the result of the medical investigations. But they'll be out of date, for she's fine again. She stopped over in Perth, while I went on to do a theatre, films and a book for Arts Review, and having a clear day all to herself she went to shops and bought two pairs of shoes, etc. etc., and these material things must have had vitamins in them in a fashion that would have baffled Ouspensky in his sixth dimension. Then we stayed with Neil Paterson in Crieff and at a dinner party she told stories about her having lunch somewhere and overhearing two old ladies talking about me on Iona on the Third, and said one of the ladies: "I saw Neil Gunn on the street and he had his wife with him: what a pity she dyes her hair!" Daisy went back to same place next day and again same two ladies who had been to see (as Daisy had) the film about a room on the top,[12] the night before. Said one: "I think it was far too sexy, and though I may not know much about sex, I know a little."

By way, I had been writing Neil Paterson when your previous letter came in and I quoted your remark on same film to the effect that he had improved on the book. He's a nice fellow, and I spent hours and a lot of drams telling him he should also be doing his proper work – his *own* writing. Same with Alexander Reid in Edinburgh (dramatist) who is trying to find an hour now and then to write a novel, but he has to keep his family alive. He's giving up editorship of *Saltire Review* – too much work and time for too little. And Ronald Mavor (Bridie's son) who is dramatic critic on Scotsman – and had sent me a play and a bit of another. What a relief to me to find he has the stuff in him! So, my dear John, here I was (in the

luxurious position of not doing a blessed thing) urging upon
them the sacred word – work! But perhaps you have heard me
at it? Anyway, I'm trying to tell you you're not alone. And
when all your ships come in – as they will – I can but hope that
you'll remember a poor old fellow and him living on the Old
Age Pension – though I confess I was cheered lately by the
great political news that Public Assistance may be increased by
9/- a week.

So you see I can't even begin to tell you about Enlightenment, for the lawns round about here have whiskers on them,
with buttercups and daisies in them. And it's me now for the
real hard work, you lazy devils. But I think of Gene's smile and
that's an inspiration, thank God.

Neil

RONALD MAVOR, James Bridie's son, himself a playwright,
was for a time drama critic of *The Scotsman*. In the Autumn 1958
Saltire Review he published a satirical article "Angry Young
Mac", about which Gunn wrote to him. One result was Mavor's
attempt to introduce Neil to the "Beats".

TO RONALD MAVOR

KERROW HO, CANNICH, BEAULY, INVS-SH.   2 OCT 59

Dear Bingo,

(...) It was good of you to send the books. A provincial who
hazards opinions on Lit. must be brought up to date. You are a
thoughtful fellow. I got half way through Kerouac's *On the
Road* and stuck. But I'm not of the beat generation, so give me
time. I'll make it. Dashing from bed to bed at 80 m.p.h., with
pauses for swigs from bottles, is very exciting. As the advert.
puts it: "There's Yes to drink, drugs, sexual adventure and
poetry . . ." and they are never satisfied. Fine. And well done,
too. I think the repetition got too mechanical for me – the very
opposite of the spontaneous in which they think they are
indulging. I fancy Kerouac has a notion that he is showing Zen
in action. I find that very amusing. But I saw it coming long
ago. We are in for an awful spate of it. Though the Frenchies
have been working through it.

I then tackled *The Catcher in the Rye* expecting the same,
but read right through. Laughing and being moved, to the last

word. How pleasant to enjoy a thing naturally. Are we getting out of the way o't? He's a skilly lad. But I hope we'll have time for a talk, and I hope you will look upon it as your duty to continue to further my education. Not but that a certain charming young woman could do it better . . . however . . .

My hand o' write is uncertain from navvying, heaving a salmon rod, and just about doing everything that is poles from Literachure.

Good luck,

Neil

TO J. B. PICK
KERROW   10 NOV '59

Dear John,

(. . .) Our own news is hot, if non-literary. We've sold Kerrow at a good price. Alone I did it, with a charming lady from a Manor in Kent (though I suspect she's Highland). Having seen over the house, she wanted there and then to sign on the dotted line. So I sent her to my agents in Inverness. So within a day we were homeless – though my native cunning reserved the take-over until 15 May next. Which suited her. Then I got going. And within two days, heard of, and inspected briefly, a house on the Black Isle and got my agents to sign on the dotted line for it, with entry on 15 Jan. All within the week. Was Daisy at top doh! For the new house is her dream come true at last. So we cross our fingers against snags which cannot be foreseen!

The new house is a neat compact cottage of 3 public rooms, 5 bedrooms, flowers, shrubs and over 5 acres of woodland, sitting in the sun, facing south over the Beauly Firth, about 2 miles by the shore road (quiet) from Kessock Ferry and Inverness. Daisy suggests that "cottage" is perhaps not quite the word. But I insist on calling it a small cottage. After all, it's only got one bathroom and one cloak room. You don't need a bicycle to reach the telephone. In fact, the telephone in the new place is both downstairs and up. You see what I mean? Compact.

Well, anyway, Gene will understand that there has been some excitement here over a few busy days. I suspect Daisy of having long furnishing schemes in her head, for sometimes she says something about something apropos of nothing relevant, if you follow.

So there it is. And the moral: the totally unexpected can happen in an astonishing way. Never forget that.

Nothing otherwise startling, though I'm doing my best to gather wealth in a non-literary way. Queer things happen if you keep at it, I find.

Daisy sends greetings to you all from top of the world.

Yours,

Neil

TO RONALD MAVOR

KERROW HOUSE, CANNICH, BEAULY   11 NOV. (1959)

Dear Bingo,

I hasten to thank you for a very nice lunch and for introducing me to so charming a girl that my eyes have been the better for it ever since. I do not exactly reserve my opinion as to whether you deserve your luck, but you may take it that the aforesaid eyes will continue to observe your career critically, if not more so, or more than ever, or doubly. Doubly, I think.

I hasten also – haste being a true Highland attribute – to return you your books. I always thought the word beat (beat generation) meant beaten, but, from a garbled something I heard, can it conceivably mean beatific? I stagger. When I get my wind you can hit me somewhere else.

I have just read your *Scotsman* review of a late Ibsen effort. Some time I must read Ibsen's late or last plays. They might draw me back to an interest in Literature. Anyway, they might. Or maybe it's just that you did your piece so well. But not altogether, I fancy. Maybe there's a way that would be on the way for a fellow who knows summat about Zen gardens, though he's not stopping in them.

Are you working? (. . .)

Daisy sends you the happiest greetings.

Yours,

Neil

TOKUSABURO NAKAMURA, Professor of English at Tokyo University, wrote to Gunn in May, 1955: "It is with an ineffable sense of awe that I am writing this letter. The sense of awe

comparable with that of Kenn when he first beheld the salmon
trout in the cool Highland river." Over the next seventeen years
Nakamura wrote regularly, often enclosing expensive volumes of
art reproductions. In 1962 he published a treatise in Japanese on
Gunn's work, and in 1965 sent him an English translation for
comment.

TO PROFESSOR TOKUSABURO NAKAMURA
KERROW HOUSE, CANNICH, BEAULY, INVERNESS-SHIRE

30 NOVEMBER, 1959

Dear Professor Nakamura,
(. . .) Why you should wish to write an essay on my books
remains obscure to me, though I am moved by your remark
that you "like my works because you like them." The only
kind of reason that matters! Would you mind if I told you the
kind of essay I should enjoy reading? In an early letter you said
that a book of mine reminded you of your boyhood in Japan. If
you cared to treat this poor subject from that point of view,
finding parallels with your own Japanese background and
traditions, attitude to nature, animism, Japanese writers and
painters, social life, delight in life, and so on, how interested I
should be! As I have already said you know enough now about
Scotland, about Gaelic as a complete language, about the
Gaelic background in place and time (*Carmina Gadelica* is rich
with old lore). You have all the essential facts and can make the
necessary comparisons. I am aware that I am not a scholar, and
that you must forgive me for preferring liking to analysis! But I
should like you to think over this suggestion. Even if I am
thinking only of my own pleasure! (. . .)
About Scottish books I dislike: only those that falsify our
true tradition, whether by becoming too sentimental or
nostalgic about it on the one hand or, on the other, trying to
disparage it. As such they do not exist as literature, and even if I
could remember some titles I should not ask you to waste time
reading them! (. . .)
With our best wishes,
Yours,

Neil M. Gunn

AFTER LITERATURE

TO GEORGE BLAKE
KERROW HOUSE, CANNICH   2ND JAN 1960

My dear George,
   You certainly had some news for us, but how relieved we
both were, too, to get the news after the op was over and your
self on your pins and manifestly prepared to do battle, even
unto London. Good for you! And game to be handled by a
Ghana princess *and* to enjoy it. I have heard of fellows in their
middle age taking odd fancies. I can see I'll have to have a small
talk with Ellie on the side. Not that I know much about middle
age yet, but I hear things. For example, two or three years back
there were two fellows who lived alone in a small cottage by
one of my salmon pools (which is another story), and one of
them was 76 and the other 80. On one evening when the younger
chap had not turned up for his supper the elder put on his fore-
and-aft and set off for the hotel pub. Sure enough there was his
young brother making a night of it with the boys. The elder
was a grave man with a really long white beard and he boomed
to the errant one: "Isn't it time you were thinking of saving a
little for your old age instead of squandering it in this way?"
   And so, having warned you, I'll pass on, for I don't want to
have to boom at you.
   Now about this Mrs. Marie Muir. You see, George, it's like
this (and as a Highlander there isn't a twist in me, as you
know.) I have so persistently refused to appear in any public
discussion group (and particularly on local occasions which
would always have prior claim) that, with much sorrow, I was
compelled to decline the distinguished honour of her PEN
invitation. Boom away at me if you like. For it's me that knows
my own shortcomings and limitations. You talk of an ivory
tower, with an assurance that sounds a little ominous to me. I
have never seen one myself, and I hope you are not thinking of
breaking out in some new direction or dimension. Though I
confess there's a small ivory figure of a Chinaman that sits on
my mantelpiece under a Japanese picture of a heron, and the
sage silence of his 2½ inches is something I whiles ponder on.
Not that I can ever hope to emulate him – except in writing.
There, I have been on his level over the last two or three years,
and very pleasant it's been. And there – God between us and all
harm – I may stick.

I admit the thought of you in the chair was a lure and a temptation and had it been a blether in the ben end of a pub or even in a quiet, small BBC studio, I might have fallen: but in public – no, George. And no more can I say. (. . .)

Yours ever,

Neil

IAN GRIMBLE was born in Hong Kong of Scottish parents in 1921. He gained his degree in history at Balliol College, Oxford, and his Doctorate from Aberdeen University. He joined the BBC in 1957 and set up the first local VHF station in Britain, covering the area from the Moray Firth to Orkney. Grimble visited the Gunns in January, 1959, to record a talk. Later he became a successful presenter of history programmes on Television, and has written many notable books, including *The Trial of Patrick Sellar*, *The World of Rob Donn*, and *Scottish Clans and Tartans*.

TO IAN GRIMBLE

KERROW HOUSE, CANNICH   FEB. (1960?)

Dear Ian,

Daisy won't allow me to do nothing about something for a long time. Och, says I, the lad will be looking in. But seeing you haven't, I'm doing something about a lot, for I've enjoyed reading the two books very much. As for their comparative merits, they will be both the same, especially the first one – in the words of the judgement of the West Coast expert who was called upon to adjudicate upon (if "upon" it is) two boats, each built by a rival boat builder. Finally, after he had put them through their paces, he said (for terrible was his position) "They will be both the same, especially MacTavish's." Why the name MacTavish has, in the context, an extra humour, I don't know. It's terrible, the people we come out of. Maybe, then, it's the young girl and the land of the first one, for in some of my writings the girl was a boy, so I've enjoyed long and comparative thoughts and insights, and at least here it can be said that boy and girl are equally here, especially when they come together. Which is more than a couple of boats could do whatever.

Thank you greatly for letting us read them.

I wrote to the Japanese professor about the tape-recording ("Iona"), politely requesting to know if he would do me the honour of accepting it. Back came his answer saying that though the native politeness should compel him to refuse three times, he dare not risk it, so – so just "Yes". And I can feel the bald naked monosyllable of Western uncouthness doing him violence. However, I had told him (perhaps to shield myself, as in the case of the boat critic) that both the tape and the suggestion anent presenting it to him had emanated from you, so I must in honour quote from his letter: "How can I express my grateful feeling to your BBC man who suggested to give me the invaluable tape? If you would condescend to give me a suggestion I would be overjoyed." Over to you. (. . .)

Yours,

Neil Firbolg (remnant of ancient race among mere upstart Gaels) (– and parvenu Norsemen)

TO JOHN MACKIE OF SEAGER, EVANS & CO

DALCRAIG, KESSOCK, INVERNESS   8 APRIL, 1960

Dear Mr. Mackie,

I have got the sample of Tormore[13] which you asked Mr. Henderson to send me, and, after due deliberation, have been telling him that I am very pleased with it. It is a clean drop, without a trace of that "guff" which haunts some Speyside stills – it may be for years, if not for ever! For what my opinion is worth, I think it will mature fairly early – and by that I do not imply that it is lacking in body but that it is well bred in the sense of not having objectionable characteristics to be bred out. This, I suppose, means that it will mix in perfectly with your notions of a Long John blend of a light and distinctive character. But I am not thinking of your mere blends at the moment; I am thinking of what a delectable dram this will be, as a single whisky in eight or ten years' time out of, say, a second-fill sherry cask! Here's to hoping that in less than that time I may be able to say to you: "I told you so." Moreover, I shouldn't be in the least surprised if in years to come when consumer cash is still more plentiful, a single whisky of fine character will be sought after at any price. So however we look

at it – troubles and expenses and all – I think your fundamental purpose has been well and truly achieved. (. . .)
Yours sincerely,

Neil M. Gunn

TO IAN GRIMBLE
KERROW HOUSE, CANNICH   (1960?)

Dear Ian,
   (. . .) Myself, I admit I'm not really good at the books nowadays. When a new one comes I sort of give it a distant glance now and then over a few days until I get used to its being in the house. Then, like a dog at a hedgehog, I may get near enough for a sniff. Daisy sends her special thanks. Hope to see you soon,

Neil

GEORGE BRUCE, born in 1909, first met Neil Gunn in 1940 when he was a teacher of English at Dundee High School. In the 1950s he became a Programme Producer for the BBC and joint editor with Maurice Lindsay of the radio magazine "Scottish Life and Letters", to which Gunn contributed. Gunn later took part in Bruce's programme "Arts Review". The film *Light in the North – Neil M. Gunn* was written by Bruce and shown to Gunn a few months before his death. George Bruce's *Collected Poems* were published in 1970.

TO GEORGE BRUCE
DALCRAIG, KESSOCK   10 JUNE 1960

Dear George,
   I just didn't know how you were to give a head and tail to the piece, much less a body. In simple honesty to the public, the *Radio Times* should announce: once again out of Nothing, Wizard George Bruce makes Something. With sub-heading: Ten Minutes of Scottish Life and Letters. Instance: last night I was particularly anxious to hear Norman[14] on Edwin Muir and the other bloke on Forsyth's[15] Clyde film, so went out to take a stroll among the roses and the rain ten minutes beforehand to

freshen me up – and got back in time to hear you talking from the chair in the closing minutes. What did five roses do with half an hour? Ask them if they know and they just nod in the wind. Even writing this: the starling on the right side of the window (I thought he was an old bachelor) has just taken her new brood into the wide world and the thrush on the left side has appeared with a grub for a half-fledged family in the bush of winter jasmine. Half a look – a look with one eye – and she popped into the bush. It didn't take her long to sum me up. Besides – but if I go on *you'll* lose half an hour. For that's the way it's lost. There's nothing mystical about it. Cheers. (. . .)

Neil

TO IAN GRIMBLE
DALCRAIG, KESSOCK, INVERNESS   14 NOV. '60

Dear Ian,

(. . .) The tortuous courtesies of the Gael! But you have written to Prof. Nakamura, who is even more tortuous than the Gael. Quote from his last letter: "To my dismay I made a great mistake in my last letter. I used a wrong expression. I told you a young wife of a . . . University Professor hearing your tape-recording said 'Your voice is vigorous but warm.' Now in Japanese 'warm' means 'conveying kindly feeling or human emotion or friendliness.' To my horror I found the word 'warm' in English usage signifies 'excited, animated, enthusiastic.' Please excuse me." (. . .)

But enough of tortuosities, except perhaps for one small further one. As a clairvoyant Gael, would you say that the young wife, already referred to, is a good-looker? I merely ask out of detached interest in the distinction, as a matter of English usage, between "warm" and "excited, animated". . . . Myself, I always thought that "warm" meant no more than warm. But then when a simple fellow gets mixed up with Gaels and Japs his usage, so to speak, becomes uncertain.

However the end of his letter restored my Zen serenity, with its delightful usage of "Yours thankful." At which point I should give you your first small exercise in Zen. When – it may be in the morn or again at eventide – you look upon nature, and, looking, empty your mind to a stillness, the inner silence, *then*, while you are held by the silence, inner and to utmost space, breathe upon the air "Yours thankful." When the magic has worked you'll realise you could never have said "Yours thankfully". Try it. Anyway, when you have done this one dozen times you *may* earn the right to learn the next step.

Daisy is looking forward to hearing *your* voice. So you can go into the whole business of a BBC voice again. She is busy arranging for folk to come here, because they asked us there, and so I'd better put my tie on this minute.

Our kind thoughts,

Neil

FRANCIS RUSSELL HART was born in 1927. He gained his degree at Harvard and became a teacher of English. When he wrote to Neil Gunn on 11 July, 1961, about *The Green Isle of the Great Deep*, he had just moved from Ohio State University to the University of Virginia, Charlottesville. In 1972 he became Professor of English at the University of Massachussetts, Boston. He and his wife Lorena first visited Gunn in the summer of 1965, and several times thereafter. Gunn addressed him in early letters as "Francis", but later changed to the preferred form "Rus". Hart is the author of *Lockhart as a Romantic Biographer, Scott's Novels, The Scottish Novel*, and co-author of *Neil M. Gunn: A Highland Life*.

TO FRANCIS RUSSELL HART

DALCRAIG, KESSOCK, INVERNESS   25 JULY '61

Dear Mr. Hart,

Your letter hit me like one of those astonished moments that now and then hit Art, and if I had had to write another story about him would have gone on and written itself. Oddly enough, too, I seem to have delivered myself in a recent issue of *The Scottish Field* (interviewed by a Scots poet) of a few remarks on (inter alia) critics and criticism to the effect that I know the critic by the quotes he chooses and that American criticism is on a high level. Almost looks as if I had been asking for it – and now have got it! When I read your initial excerpt from *The Green Isle* I knew you "had it", as we say in the Highlands, and could do no wrong, "whatever else". And this had the element of astonishment, because it's so long since I'd written the words that they were new to myself – or almost, like a memory not altogether mine. I even began to go over the passage, wondering how I could improve it – and couldn't alter a word. And I doubt if that's as bad as it sounds, for I suppose a writer is reluctant to read what he has published lest he trip over imperfections and inadequacies too often for his comfort, and is accordingly relieved to find something that gets by. And I doubt further if that is altogether vanity – for does it not link up with your final words on the perfection man seeks? Whether a prose passage or a Utopia – well, in essence is there such a difference? Which is the sort of imprecise observation that brings on a dialectical storm, I know; still, I am rather with the mathematicians here who use the fundamental given, and when a man cannot do much with the given, the innate urge, I agree with your conclusion that the flaw is in himself. But I'd need to take that a bit further – and may some time. For the moment I am satisfying the urge to write at once and salute someone who has stirred up the old atom.

However, I must confess, unfortunately, that my knowledge of Utopian literature is very slight and that most of the works you mention I haven't read. But at least there may be, for you, this critical virtue in ignorance; you contrive to make me feel that I know the essence of them all. I particularly delighted in the quotation from Margaret Mead, its sheer aptness and the masterly way you handled it. The more so as I know some of her best work. As for your anticipation of angry marginalia: I am too conscious of the way the balls and clubs are kept circling by the juggler to breathe a word!

All the same, had you been sitting here with nothing better to do I think we might have begun to evolve the notion of Huxley's "alternative" in other directions – even an extra-dimensional one, which would be less theoretic and more empirical. The awful difficulty with fellows who *know* things in the head only is that they cannot believe that they cannot understand something you have experienced totally because to them you cannot communicate it in their rational terms. I was amused to read in the current issue of *The Listener* a letter by his brother Julian telling off the chemistry boys for suggesting "that biology is but 'applied' chemistry." Julian: "The impossibility of 'applying' the results of the study of a lower organisational level to the understanding of phenomena at a higher level . . .". But I'm afraid my dabbling with such notions in *The Atom of Delight* killed that book, so I'd better stop.

Besides, it's always the human living level we come back to, thank the Lord, and I may amuse you some time by telling you how *The Green Isle* came to be written. However my concern for the moment – I have been away for a few days – is to assure you that I am honoured by what you have said and written and if I can help in any further project I shall be very pleased.

I hope you are settling down in your new place – may it be nearly perfect – and with every good wish.

Yours sincerely,

Neil M. Gunn

TO J. B. PICK

DALCRAIG, KESSOCK   SAT 2 SEPT. (1961)

Dear John and Gene,

(. . .) Lately in fact Daisy has been getting tireder and tireder so I fetched the doctor. He took a blood test and as a result she has now started on a six weeks' course of injections. After that, he'll take another blood count and continue as necessary. The doctor said that the condition of her leg resulted from anaemic condition, and that she must have a long rest and no visitors, as any extra labours set her back. (. . .) Yesterday afternoon, e.g., we were going to do something in the garden, but she had to give in, suffering from pain in head. So I got doctor to come along. The concealed swelling turned out to be fibrositis. She was so relieved of a deeper fear that she said "The pain is nothing."

Thank you for the Zen book. I haven't read a book in a long time, so this one should do until next Easter, unless you want it back quick. I was sorry we missed Zen on BBC TV last night, but doctor was here. Did you see it? I'm afraid, John, I have got quite out of even the notion of writing, so couldn't think of anything for anyone to write about. However, when I've got the temper of your mind over a day or two, you never know what might stir up! Easter seems an appropriate time for being born again. By way, another literary gent has got interested in *The Green Isle*. An American – asst. prof. in English Dept. of University. He really bowled me over and asked to read a paper "at next December's national convention of the Modern Language Assn of America in the Literature and Society Colloquium on modern Utopian literature" he adds that "I immediately expressed a desire to concentrate on one of the most profoundly exciting books I have ever read (three readings haven't shaken this) – *The Green Isle*." He enclosed a 20 page typed thesis on subject which he hopes to get published in one of the "scholarly or critical quarterlies" – and asked permission to go ahead. But his real aim is "a critical appraisal" of my whole box of tricks. Dear me and well well!

Our garden has been – and still is – full of colour. Daisy sometimes, as she looks at it, has visibly nothing to say. I think she gets the "other" radiance. We can now pull the plums off and eat them warm. I can see there is no hope of an early flitting from this place.

Our love to Gene – and may the boys wax.

Neil

TO IAN GRIMBLE
DALCRAIG, KESSOCK   27 NOV. '61

Dear Ian,

We are back after our tour, in which I had a few minor misfortunes, including the loss or theft of a new coat and hat and blackened finger nails from a slammed car door. In fact I had so many mishaps that a Skye man in the Kyles of Bute sprinkled me with water from a bowl which had silver in it, and muttered Gaelic incantations over me. From that moment the mishaps ceased, and we drove home like a bird.

I have a few incantations of my own, and I hope you may feel the better for them. (. . .)

Yours,

Neil

TO ALEXANDER REID
DALCRAIG, KESSOCK, INVERNESS   30 NOV. 61

Dear Alex,

It's a pleasure to watch your flawless playwright's hand.[16] It has the ease, the inevitability, that gives speed – or pace, do you call it? – plenty of time to take the humour along. Not to mention implications – positively part of the athletic muscles. The centuries click into place quite naturally – human nature being much of a muchness yesterday, today and forever, apparently. When I read in the ordinary way my mind will sometimes want to alter this or that, but not page after page with you. The theme, too, as you know, is at the core of things and meaning for me. So I enjoyed myself through all the varied and dramatic action – right to the end, and then in that last long speech by Gordon I began to wonder – afterwards – if he could pull it off, fully. Possibly, in this, I am being affected by my own experience in novels. *The Atom of Delight* was a flop – in the sense anyhow that the reading public weren't interested. Even the critics – only half a dozen of them noticed it, the regular southern critics ignoring it completely. Even novels like *The Well at the World's End* and *The Other Landscape* didn't fare much better. And here I find you at the same kind of well! So forgive my uncertainty. You'll know, because you know about theatres and audiences. But the only suggestion I can make to you is to work over that last speech. You have certainly prepared for it dramatically, because Gordon is not only wounded but excited by the "water" discovery, and the crust of his normal reserve thus being broken, what's deepest in him will pour out. Still, work over it, cut an odd abstract word or phrase. This is the kind of play I should love to succeed. And a play it is for an intelligent audience – not a film. The trouble with you and me is that we have got used to this kind of thought or vision, and we are astonished when others don't *see*. So keep this in mind, as you work over the speech with all your dramatic guile and invention. I enjoyed the second reading even better than the first. All power with you.

Neil

An extra word or two, as you may well ask what I mean by "abstract" word or phrase. When I read the sentence: "It was an idea cooked up in my own head *out of the stuff of my own preoccupations*" I *felt* that the words I have underlined might not be necessary. Depends on the mood of the speaker, I know. I suppose what's really worrying me is the thought that of all the writers in Scotland – and most other places – I know, only you and I are concerned with this break-through of vision, this instant apprehension of reality. It is really the Zen *satori*.

Though I was attempting it long before I heard of Zen. And in a novel one can come at it and come again, with all the rhythms and skills one may have. How often, for example, I used the experience of the nut-cracking boy (quoted by you in your birthday tribute) – yet quite obviously its significance was never grasped by readers of *The Atom*. That's what makes me feel an incompetent critic now. At the same time what I do know is that what we are trying to express, or evoke, is of fundamental importance. "Without vision the people perish". Everyman repeats that in complete belief that he understands it, so for him there is no nut to crack. There's our rub.

We must have a talk about it some time, and even attempt to assess fellow writers in terms of it, and ourselves. At least we have achieved the detachment for that.

But enough. I'll be glad to hear from you sometime.

TO J. B. PICK
DALCRAIG, KESSOCK   2 APL.'62

Dear John and Gene,
    When I read out Gene's Daisy said, "What a sweet letter!" Then she saw John's, said "Spiders!" and fled to the kitchen, leaving me to decipher. Which wasn't really difficult, and I duly read it out, too. You see, I'm just back in the role of secretary. Though I got a frightful row a few days ago. When I saw the way clear, I sneaked out to the tool shed, and with woodman's axe, saw and clawhammer, made my way round the outside hedge to a spot where the wooden uprights had got knocked down during our absence and taken the anti-rabbit fancing with it; my object to knock the wood away from the fencing for time being, and so still keep rabbits out. After a short while I realised I had better try to get back to house before passing out, but didn't she see me coming like a tottering scarecrow. But, while trying to tell me the kind of idiot I am, she also fed me a dram, and back I came. She refused to listen to my theory that a person with low blood pressure merely passes out for the time being. In fact, I have noticed when it is a case of practical realities, she pays no attention to theories whatsoever. This often restricts life's action. But one can always fall back on philosophy, with a touch of regret for human limitations. So to speak. Anyhow, such is the comedy

of our days, and it would be much more amusing if the days were decent. Across the firth, as I write, a thin cover of snow comes half way down the slopes. Never has there been such a long winter in this part of the world. The garden is weeks behind. We're both itching to be out and doing things, and I can hear the rows I'll get, before hand. Somehow I have gotten a real interest in things that sprout and grow; but I'd better stop such small talk and ask you, before I forget, and on her orders – when is Whitsun? Give's your dates. Our only fixture ahead is for last week in May, when Neil Paterson and his wife are expected for 2 or 3 days – though that's not quite fixed yet. Anyhow, when you give us your date that *will* be fixed. So don't forget. Soon.

You know, John, you made me take down *The Lost Chart* and have a look inside, for my memory couldn't tell me anything about it. I think I had a feeling that it was merely some kind of thriller, as well forgotten. And then there were the old sun and moon, the salute and the curtsey. I got now and then even a queer half-translated feeling. However, I'm mentioning it now, because you speak of your lack of interest in the darkness and of difficulty in expressing the light. The point is (and even Daisy wouldn't call this a theory), a person who has the light in him doesn't have to try to express it, because he will express it in spite of himself. That's final! Let him be deliberately concerned with darkness only and the light will find the most subtle ways of entry – between the lines, round the edges of the dark blind or as a glow through it. This is a fascinating subject – carried just a step farther. But first – lest I forget – send the two starts you've made a week or 10 days *before* you come. That will save time – and give me a chance to think – intuitively, perhaps. Anyway you've stated your problem, and by carrying it a step forward I mean that we might try to conceive a new form for its solution; or perhaps just a new angle of vision on the old tao. Possibly we both feel that something new is needed. Meanwhile you might read the new Aldous Huxley novel which I see is called *The Island*. I've read a review of it by Cyril Connolly in *Sunday Times*, and am a little amused at his treatment of same. But it's *his* (Aldous's) solution, his way of getting the light through. Are there new ways – or, as in his case, less old? Creatively considered, it's a fascinating problem. And never finally without the *possibility*

of solution (for those to whom it means the highest) because
for each one there is the distinction of his own way, the
individual way, and the more individual ways that can be
expressed, the richer and better. I know that you have now
won a fine lucidity and simplicity (= refining until only
essence left, and expressed with ease). (And I won't modify
that word "ease" either. If Daisy saw this handwriting, her
comment "I'd prefer John's spiders".) Such a lot of stuff to talk
about. Get stirring, and prepare your diverse cases.

Have written enough for one go, but prepared to come back
weightily if threatened.

Love to Gene. And next time I write I'll detail all our duties
when you're here – of course remembering that I'm always not
so strong as I was!

Neil

TO RONA MAVOR, ENCLOSING LETTERS FROM
JAMES BRIDIE, WHO DIED IN 1951.
DALCRAIG, KESSOCK, INVERNESS   25 APR.62

Dear Rona,

I am sorry to be so unfruitful in the matter of letters, but all
too obviously the bonfires o' the flittings, as beforesaid, did
their fell work. Such as there are belong to an early period and
got mixed into some Nationalist stuff with which I was much
concerned for many years (and for which O. H. scolded me) so
that I now wonder, taking my Civil Servant's job into account
also, how I managed to write anything at all. But I saw him
fairly often. We were both, for example, members of the
British Council and before a meeting I never failed to tell him
he must be there. And he *was* there; which I rather fancy never
failed to astonish him. After he departed, I hadn't the heart to
attend a meeting for years, so perhaps there wasn't an extensive
correspondence, though I do remember things in his letters,
fresh critical assessments, etc. so wittily pointed that they still
make me laugh. There are bits in the letters I enclose which will
bear me out. And these bits, referring to persons still alive, are
not for printing. Sometimes he miscalled *me* and then I said
things about *him*, as the letter about "Smut" makes only too
clear. I hesitated over sending it, but it is so deliciously healthy,
so needing to be said, that when I came upon it it had me

laughing all over again. He was a lovely man, as the Irish say. I really had a great admiration and affection for him. He was the only man who ever made me feel that literature – writing – was a ploy, an adventure in common, like poaching; not a serious business but a foray in delight. Anyway, by saying some such thing I could goad him to his spontaneous best. Which makes me appreciate how letters sometimes can hardly be understood, without knowing a lot more.

However, I'm hurrying this for there may be a paragraph here and there for your purpose. But you'll let me know how the project develops.

Daisy joins in all the best,

Neil.

TO J. B. PICK

DALCRAIG, KESSOCK   23 JULY '62

Dear John,
Overlook delay because I have not been in good fettle these last few weeks. Had the doctor in couple of days ago and he has taken 3 different samples for analysis, and I should know result in a few days. Sort of seasickness affair, with lassitude and no power of concentration. (. . .)

Now about your own distinguished piece of writing.[17] For it is really good stuff. You have refined to an apparently easy simplicity, and what you put over really matters. I do not know anyone who can write better than this, who is so at home with what is literature's (and life's) concern. I simply do not know where this quality and length of story would be accepted, and would doubt if anywhere. It's the kind of thing that with 2 or 3 more of same length could make a book *when* you have published a notable novel or two more. (. . .)

I do wish you could get a full novel on the go. It would somehow help *me* if you brought it off and became famous, at least a name that mattered. When Gurdjieff talked somewhere of the need for a Master having one behind him on the upward steps if he himself hoped to reach the higher levels, there was more than summat in it. Not that we need have personal traffic with word "Master"! Gurdjieff's main notions stem, I should say, from Zen.

Thanks, Gene, for photos. You wonder how I so magically vanished from your side, in one. I merely decided I was not worthy.

Neil

TO ANDREW HOOK, ORGANISER OF THE WRITERS'
CONFERENCE AT THE EDINBURGH FESTIVAL 1962
DALCRAIG, KESSOCK, INVERNESS   17TH AUGUST 1962

Dear Mr. Hook,

Many thanks for *The Novel Today*. I have been reading it with great interest and, if I may say so, appreciate your own contribution to the old commitment debate. The whole affair has a wonderful variety, and gives real information on what countries other than one's own are doing in the novel. Even the West Indies article which starts off with mention of "more than a dozen" novelists. Accordingly I do feel it's rather a pity that you weren't better served by your Scottish contributors. After all, the Conference is about the *novel* today, not about poetry and poets, and surely there should have been one article devoted to Scottish novels, as there is one so devoted in the case of each of the other countries. Just as I am pleased to learn what is being done in, say, the French novel, apart from the few "innovators" whom we have already and so often heard about, equally the novelists of other countries might like to hear what Scottish novelists have been doing, but all they get about our living novelists are three dismissive paragraphs by David M. Craig of a truly incredible "superiority" and ignorance. As the last word may seem excessive let me illustrate by quoting half of one sentence about my work "the farm woman in *Morning Tide* (1932)* is never 'Mother' or 'Mrs. Mackay' but 'the mother' – archetypal and featureless." First, the "farm woman" is not a farm woman but a fisherman's wife and the early part of the book describes a terrific storm at sea in which her husband and son are in danger of losing their lives; secondly, her name is not Mrs. Mackay but Mrs. MacBeth; thirdly, she is invariably referred to by her family as "Mother", and when they address her directly I write "Mother". Any reference to "the mother" of this family is normal usage and has nothing at all to do with "archetypal and featureless". Do

*should be 1931 (NMG's own note Ed.).

you think it would be really possible for anyone who had actually read the book to make such mistakes? Again, if I were to take the other half of the sentence, like ". . . nationalist problems or escapes into mysticism" the thing becomes rather shocking. *The Drinking Well*, with which he is apparently dealing, is concerned with commitment to the social complex, with a close analysis of a specific economic basis, and also the commitment of the individual to his fate (your twin theme). And as for "escapes into mysticism" . . . as if mysticism were like taking a bus to Portobello. Alas for the East and its milennia of mental discipline and evolution. Lord, it staggers me. He also, I observe, refers to drama in an extraordinary footnote without mentioning James Bridie, Alexander Reid, and Robert Maclellan. And his references to poets curiously omit such names as W. S. Graham, Norman MacCaig and George Bruce.

However, to return to our theme, the novelists. I am aware that the two or three academic critics in Scotland have no time for the Scottish novel, only for genuflection before the Poet. But you could have got a foreigner to do it, like Kurt Wittig, whom both MacDiarmid and Edwin Muir have praised. He had no difficulty. Or a living Scottish novelist like Naomi Mitchison, Eric Linklater, or Neil Paterson – to name three who have world connections and have written novels with backgrounds in U.S.A., China, ancient Rome and Greece, Spain, etc. Surely they are at least on a level with many of the novelists mentioned in each of the other countries. Incidentally, I should be amused if a French delegate referred to Gide's recent resurrection of Hogg's *Confessions* . . . Indeed I am prepared to lay a bet that there is no theme or contention or "innovation" mentioned in this programme of yours that I could not illustrate from a Scottish novel written in recent years.

Usually I take no notice of personal criticism but here I do feel that for this conference we should have given a reasonable and critical display of the Scottish novelist in print for the convenience, if nothing else, of our guests. There is still the public debate.

Wishing your conference a lively success.

Yours sincerely,

Neil M. Gunn

AFTER LITERATURE

TO FRANCIS RUSSELL HART

DALCRAIG, KESSOCK, INVERNESS, SCOTLAND   27TH AUGUST 1962

Dear Mr. Hart,

I was beginning to wonder if you were still in it, as we say in the Highlands, when your surprise packet arrived.[18] It came at a time when even a small dram of the true spirit would have been welcome – and you drop in with a full bottle. I had the odd illusion when reading your pages of being spoken to by my second self (if I may invoke *The Atom*.) And the companionship somehow was natural and rare. Put this down, if you must, to a general condition of bodily weakness – or to a convalescence on the way (I hope) – for earlier this year I was in an Edinburgh hospital for seven weeks and underwent a couple of operations;[19] and when I got home, and after a time was feeling pretty good, I one day started with a harvester's scythe swinging into nettles and docks in a corner of a field of mine and was so enjoying it that in a minute the sky was swinging, too, and the field. After the world had settled, over a while, I got the notion of going north to see a boyhood river (*Highland River*) and smell the air off the moors. Once again I was beginning to feel good – but enough. At the moment when yours came I was able to bite my thumb if I sat down to it. I have confessed to being every kind of ass and so on, but I am not really deceived, for in this condition there is a lot of rare light about. *The Atom* still does its stuff. When I read your understanding, I agreed with "implausible epistolarism of the first part" of *The Shadow*. When I was writing the book, I did not think so, simply because the book began writing itself that way, and I did not "think" at all. But, afterwards, I got your "implausible" note not so much as it were on the psychological side as on the sheer physical. Nan[20] could not have commanded the bodily pith to do the writing, and accordingly – and with dim psychological factors added – would have sheered off from any attempt. Now, do you know, I am not so sure. For here I am in my present condition, going on like this to you (and ready to start off into pretty elusive stuff) – while I just could not even begin to write a long-promised article on whisky for a highbrow quarterly. My hand just couldn't move to its task. Then I rather think that a woman needs, more than a man, to communicate – particularly in such circumstances as

169

Nan's. But I should have made it clear (perhaps I do, for it's a long time since I read the book) that Nan wrote in bits at a time – and found *no difficulty* in doing so. However, that's of no importance, for what I did find useful in the epistolary method was the extreme clarity that often comes in convalescence, for by means of it objects are seen with an astonishing particularity: a sort of purification of vision. Always I have had to curb this tendency to describe objects in this light (you are, by the way, and if you can forgive my saying so, extraordinarily perceptive in your description of *seeing* or visioning) . . . and now I'm beginning to wonder if it's something of this kind that distinguishes the *new* and revolutionary, as critics call it (the avant-garde fellows) in the work of writers like Robbe-Grillet (I don't happen to have seen any of his stuff?). All I know is that what is often called new and revolutionary in our day (like the incantatory in Joyce) is just about as old as human time. As for "gimmicks" and things – but let me stop, or I'll be going serious next.

Though I hope it's clear now how much I appreciated your generous assessment. And I was particularly pleased that you started on that "regional" note. For just now the Edinburgh Festival is on, with its Writers' Conference – a gathering of novelists from the nations – and at least the London tribe have shown their contempt for regionalism. (I had better not start on the said tribe!) But you have many surprises, starting with the title and its "fiction of violence". Indeed this almost shocked me, for clearly I had the fond delusion that I did not deal in violence! Which sounds like a giveaway of something. My wife (who is typing this, bless her!) was struck with admiration by the way in which you kept the theme going and used quotations like chimes. (. . .)

But more than enough. (. . .)

I must get Huxley's *Island*.

Another book? No. Had I had two or three as interested as you a few years ago, there might have been.

Thank you again for your tonic company at the right time. I shall always be glad to hear from you.

Yours sincerely,

Neil M. Gunn

AFTER LITERATURE

The letter which follows was written to Professor P. H. BUTTER, of the University of Glasgow, biographer of Edwin Muir (*Edwin Muir: Man and Poet*, Oliver & Boyd, 1966), enclosing a letter from Muir to Gunn about *The Silver Bough*.

TO P. H. BUTTER

DALCRAIG, KESSOCK, INVERNESS, SCOTLAND   (6 OCT '62)

Dear Mr. Butter,

I knew Edwin Muir over many years, one of our last meetings being at Newbattle Abbey when he was Warden there. He invited me for a weekend so that I could meet and talk to his students, and I got great pleasure out of this visit, for I saw Edwin going about his business and Willa as the gracious chatelaine. I always had a deep admiration for Edwin Muir, and I remember once saying to James Bridie, who was a vastly intelligent critic of Scottish writers, that Edwin could come into my mind suddenly like one of the old Druids, a small wise man who had winnowed his wisdom out of an immense experience not only of life and others but also of himself. He knew himself in the ancient and profound sense. Perhaps this casual way of talk was hardly for the middle of Princes Street, Edinburgh, so we drifted into a more suitable place, but it was the kind of thing that could happen on meeting Bridie and remembering Edwin Muir. Bridie was immediately sceptical about my Druids, of course, but I knew him well and how to shock him at a start off in order to get the best the quickest. We wandered for a while in strange country, for Edwin's country has a touch or look of eternity about it, remote somewhat from the theatrical stage of our angry days. So there is really no limit to the unexpected turns in talk, the sudden visions, momentary illuminations indeed, when Edwin sets the wind going. There is a feeling of tremendous scope about him, far vistas, and sometimes one is hardly sure whether a vista backwards is in space or time, or forwards for that matter, nor does it matter much anyhow, for the experience one undergoes, if really beyond words, is yet strangely precise.

But this is difficult country, though the most fascinating in the poetic realm, if one has gone far enough to glimpse an odd landscape in it. Anyway I feel quite sure that no one ever gets there until he has gone beyond his own ego. Thinking of

Edwin Muir, I can believe the Eastern sage who said contrari-
wise that egotism is the only sin. Yet at the very moment when
one sees how egoless Edwin is one is most deeply aware of his
unique individuality or being.

This radiant country towards which he was travelling, no
matter the accidents, became so much part of his essence that it
could present pictures in his dreams. Perhaps I could try to
instance this by mentioning one of his poems. It happened
many years ago when I was serving on a Government
committee and had to be in Edinburgh frequently for meetings. Edwin then had a job on the British Council (just after a
difficult and even distressing time in Dundee) and it gave me
great delight when he and Willa joined me in a meal or a drink. I
looked forward to these meetings and talks. I remember, then,
on one such occasion wanting to compliment him on a new
book of poems, called *The Narrow Way*,[21] and getting round
to it by first mentioning a short poem which had particularly
struck me. While reading it, I saw the sea water, blue-green,
sunlit, in motion, before my eyes. But may I quote it:

The Swimmer's Death
He lay outstretched upon the sunny wave,
That turned and broke into Eternity.
The light showed nothing but a glassy grave
Among the trackless tumuli of the sea,
Then over his buried brow and eyes and lips
From every side flocked in the homing ships.

Edwin told me that the poem exactly described a dream
which he had had. I know we talked of the wonderful clarity
and radiance of the light – of the sea – which remained in our
minds from early boyhood days in that northern world. But I
cannot remember if I mentioned a word in the poem which had
affected me, that word "homing". I may have been diffident
about mentioning it because I felt that such a word gave a
warmth to radiance, appeared to add human experience to
austere vision, and that some of his poems might gain by
having it here or there, if only in the sense of gaining more
readers. I know this kind of criticism is difficult if not dubious,
but possibly it contains the one point I could look at here for a
moment in a personal way. I don't want to repeat words like

eternity, austerity, symbol, heraldic, which keep recurring in appreciations of his poetry, as if what he emotionally experienced or saw was always given a timeless shape, was translated from the fluid movements of life in the living moment into a permanance that abides where time and eternity cross. We know he had that kind of vision and could himself abide for moments in that place. But when we cannot enter into that place, into that condition of being, where what is fixed is not fixed but held in dynamic suspension, in the radiance of revelation, then we may find his poetry strangely static, lifeless, carrying life like a memory to the place beyond, where it remains forever "frozen". Hence the apparent lack of human warmth, so that a word like "homing" stands out and is received somehow with gratitude.

But that the lack is only apparent can be seen from a letter which I got from him after he had read a novel of mine, *The Silver Bough*. I'm afraid I am not a keeper of letters,[22] except by accident, and this one fell out of the book, where I had left it after checking some point in his letter, I suppose. Its extravagant generosity embarrasses me over again, but I cannot think of any more authentic way of showing his human warmth in action, its depth, even its height all the way to the sun! Here he is being naturally himself and as naturally generous to another. Clearly, too, concepts like time and acceptance are not in the nature of philosophic abstractions but realities experienced in his inner being. A poet's essence must also be the essence of his poetry. And in fact the essence is always there, any "lack" being due to the reader's blindness. I am tempted to say more about this, because an intelligent reader may well be blind, until, reading on, he forgets himself, then *sees*, and enters in. I know of no poet of my time, not even Yeats, who so intuitively pierced through human obscurities to the ultimate light.

Sincerely,

Neil M. Gunn

TO J. B. PICK

DALCRAIG, KESSOCK, INVERNESS   17 OCT. (1962)

Dear John,

I've got wandered a bit about correspondence, and don't remember just where we stopped. Anyway, Daisy is home and making steady progress; still frail, of course, but beginning to be full of orders, as though enjoying hearing the sound of her voice again. Don't think I told you of the long anxious time after the operation, when first she got a painful internal infection, then thrombosis in one leg, and then pleurisy. I was beginning to be afraid someone would cough half a mile away and give her double pneumonia. The medicals were very good, even if the surgeon went off to get married after the operation. I went every day by car and back – beside my own telephone. I was well looked after by our daily dame, who came all alive under the responsibility, and was about as much concerned as myself: this helped Daisy apparently, who was inclined like a silly ass to worry about me. The older some couples get the worse they get, I do declare. I never felt so utterly helpless in my life. However, as I say she is beginning to boss again, and has just told me of some poor old fellow who got breathless and dizzy, like me, then "did something extra and popped off dead." That's her reading the lesson. However, we have made a pact for the moment to behave sensibly and get well and strong together, growing in beauty side by side. In other words I'll have to do as she says, and she'll do as she says anyhow. Her sister Molly is with us and a treasure. So now you're about up to date. (. . .)

Overlook brevity of this hurried note, but Daisy's being suspiciously quiet somewhere.

Neil

TO TOKUSABURO NAKAMURA
DALCRAIG, KESSOCK, INVERNESS   23 OCT. 1962

Dear Professor Nakamura,
   (. . .) However, I have had one consolation in these recent worrying months, for I have been seeking the spirit that inhabits your painting and poetry and, perhaps more particularly, that extraordinary manifestation which in our western books is called Zen. Somehow I have got out of it all a curious sense of companionship. I am not concerned with any specific religious or metaphysical considerations, only with an intuitive apprehension of what lies behind. This is very elusive and very difficult, but not altogether foreign to me, because from an early age I seem to have had some glimmer of it – as a short

chapter in *The Atom* about the Nut and the Stone may make clear. (. . .)

(Typed copy, unsigned. Ed.)

TO J. B. AND G. PICK
DALCRAIG, KESSOCK,   THURS. (NOVEMBER 1962)

Dear John and Gene,
    We appreciated my birthday greetings from you very much. A year ago the year started very well in Edinburgh, indeed memorably;[23] but after that it began interfering with our physical well beings; but our spirits kept up, and here we are, looking out at the sun on the snow and the rich autumn leaves and feeling grateful. Daisy is definitely and visibly improving, though of course she tires very easily; but the surgeon warned her about it, saying she *must* remember she has had a major operation and won't get her working strength back for at least 12 months. She must go slow, have no visitors etc. etc. . .
    (. . .) She uttered a verse of poetry this morning in the real Zen manner, crying from her room to mine:

"Oh, I see a lovely spot in the sky
Yellow yellow yellow
on top of the wood."

She doesn't even know that she did it yet, for I just growled back at her not to get up until I got the house warm. As for myself – though I confess we're getting a bit tired of mentioning illness – the doctor has started a series of ten injections, one a week, to bring up the blood count. After that there will be no holding me back or down. (. . .)
    Got interrupted there yesterday by Daisy who said it was half-day for the Kessock shoppie, so off we sallied – I rather think really, Gene, because Daisy has bought a new hat (the first for 50 or 15 years) and wanted to wear it. She fair loves it, and all she needs is a horse to be a Cossack. She bought it in Inverness on my birthday, so it's in some mysterious way a sort of birthday present and she insisted on paying for it. Of course she's quite wealthy now because she cashes our National Pensions at local P.O. and keeps the lot: £6:1:6 a week. But she buys me food out of it, so I can't complain, I suppose. (. . .)

Daisy asked me how your Irish novel is getting on.²⁴ She likes it. I do feel that you should concentrate on one thing at a time, because you have so little time. I remember long ago your saying you were waiting for a new book of mine because you were wanting something to read. Only now can I appreciate that you may have meant it, because I know how I should appreciate the *companionship* of a book from you. I don't think it would greatly matter what form the book took, if your true mind was in it. I've got a new Zen book (small), but it's translated from German and full of Teutonic abstractions. How wonderfully free of such was Herrigel. I must try to read a bit now that snow has come. (. . .)

Love to Gene.

Neil

TO IAN GRIMBLE
DALCRAIG, KESSOCK   28 NOV. (1962)

Dear Ian,
Here's your five bob as ever was. It's been staring at me for a few days, but I've been busy trying to tell a chap about his play and odd things of that kind. I have a vague memory of borrowing in order to tip the night porters (perhaps a revealing trait – in that I have often returned late (or early, is it?) and been so soberly lit up that I felt a warm common humanity with the toilers of the night!) Anyway, it meant that on this occasion we had such a beautiful night that – didn't the Greeks throw something valuable away when Fate was kind beyond their deserts? I'm sure there's a Celtic parallel to that. And, begod, it strikes me: didn't I do it without thinking of the Greeks? And without throwing it away? such as it was. A whole new mythology (or old) brings itself to light before I can write it down. (. . .)

Neil

TO TOKUSABURO NAKAMURA
DALCRAIG, KESSOCK, INVERNESS   23 JAN. 1963

Dear Professor Nakamura,
(. . .) As you may be wondering what sort of political notions I had myself I should be hard pushed to find a word for it

though probably that word is anarchism! Have you got a copy of a book of mine called *The Serpent* (in American edition *Man Goes Alone*)? In it I describe how a Highland youth found socialism in Glasgow towards the end of the last century – really a fairly historic description of the beginning of socialism in our country. Later in the book, when the youth has become an old man, he looks back on the past of his own glen, and uses the word anarchism to describe its economic way of life (. . .) Anyway, you can generally rely on my applying a Highland touchstone to most problems. And I hope that thought amuses you (. . .)

With all good wishes to you – and to your country, in which may freedom continue to grow.

Yours sincerely,

Neil M. Gunn

TO J. B. PICK

DALCRAIG, KESSOCK, INVERNESS   19/2/63

Dear John,

Would you mind sending back at once that little book on Edwin Muir by Butter? George Bruce has been on phone saying one of his staff is coming up *in a few days* to interview me about Edwin for some programme or other – which means he'll fire questions at me etc. I don't like that kind of thing, particularly as I seem to possess only slim volumes of Edwin's poetry, and no prose. I might be asked, too, about Butter's book, and Butter is a well-meaning fellow, who is still on my mind, and asked me about Edwin's letters, and I haven't looked properly yet for them.[25] He's doing a book on 'em. And so on. Dear me.

Your letter, with Gene's addition, is still on my desk. It has no date. When I went down for *Sunday Times* (in milk box at gate) on Sunday last, I got the odd illusion that I'd gone down yesterday for last week's. If you follow me. We have been hibernating – suspension of time. Curious state of non-being in being. Our talk consists of same sentences – about the weather – day in and day out, so it's all the same day. The first time the weather man used the phrase "freezing drizzle" we awoke and laughed, but he's gone on using it, day out and in. In a search for a light touch, a gaiety, I hope I don't call Edwin's timeless poems a freezing drizzle. The met man also cheered us with "freezing fog", and I should not like to talk hopefully of low depressions off Orkney, or even of high depressions, for that matter. What a wonderful ass of myself I could make, in endless sentences of involved imagery without thought. Furthermore, we had expected to hear from you that you had gone into your new home. And I was going to celebrate with a poem. Now it would be a freezing drizzle, so I'll forbear . . .

Anyway, that's us that was. Daisy feels often pretty good, but she tires very easily, and her heart can be a flurrying nuisance. If I'm not making any progress in physical prowess I'm inclined to blame the weather which doesn't let me exercise or walk much. I don't like gradients. Haven't the breath for them. We'd have gone south to sun before this, but didn't want to be too far from Daisy's doctors so soon after her op. But next winter, if we're not frozen drizzles, we'll depart like the birds.

Don't write, and don't read – apart from Stock Exchange and Zen paragraphs. I tried several new novels, but stuck. I find "brutal frankness" on covers doesn't attract any more. But I read nearly whole of a French novel on sex theme – described on front cover as "fast moving and improper". Such a delightful change from brutal frankness, and with so decorous a frankness and no neg. emotions. Let me add two Eastern sayings of profundity: "Every day is a good day" and "The flowering branches grow naturally, some long, some short."

Love to Gene.

Neil

TO IAN GRIMBLE

DALCRAIG, KESSOCK,   2/3/63

Dear Ian,

I could do with one or two more sarcasms from Rob Donn, for times I am hard pressed by a one, Janet, myself.[26] Only thing is that when she read the sample you sent she laughed shamelessly. Little time ago I was pouring a dram for her into a measuring glass (invalids mustn't get too much) and, for her, stopped at the mark, but unfortunately when pouring for myself my hand momentarily shook and thus drowned the mark well and truly – and I heard what may be called an inadvertent cough. Thereupon I began arguing my case so well, that, bedam, didn't I pour the lot into the nearly full water jug instead of my glass. You should have heard her mirth. Rob Donn sounds a good poet to me. (. . .)

Neil
Greetings from Janet

TO J. B. PICK
DALCRAIG, KESSOCK   4 APL '63

Dear John,
    After a 3-course breakfast in bed, there was a 6-course lunch, cream confections I love with afternoon tea, and an 8-course dinner. The surgeon was very pleased with the result of his handiwork and refused to take a consulting fee in his own home, so we invited him and spouse for dinner, which lasted over two hours, and afterwards I had mellow old malt sent to him in a box. We never had less than two guests for lunch – Daisy's boy-friends and their wives. I got steadily weaker but held out to end of a full week. It may be that I was more full than the week – of food, I mean. Now home, and slendering, and none the worse, even the better. Which shows you something or other. Anyway, here we are again, and me getting told off in the same old way for doing what I shouldn't. I haven't written any poems, but I may some time. They'll be Zennish, I fear. Like this one this morning:

> The world of dew
> Is a world of dew:
> That's all it is.
> And if I'm right
> That's all I am.

Which isn't quite nothing yet, but at least aiming that way. I have had a glimpse or two of the perfect nothing – maybe.
    But I should have started by thanking you for your beautiful letter. What you should do is get a cottage somewhere in North for your summer holiday, so we could visit by car. Long outings. Daisy has got a touch of phlebitis in one leg again (she had it in hospital) and is resting it all she can. A car is a grand resting place. Being slowed up, I thought a newish Jaguar going

at 100 m.p.h. would sort of average out my pace, but Daisy is terrified at the thought. The trouble with the small cars is that they all squash my hat. Daisy wants to stick to our old trusty friend for this year anyway until we get our breaths back. Maybe she's right. However, a holiday within bens and glens is what you all need, so you should be thinking about it.

I'll be hearing about the Irish book when you're ready. "All action and no texture" sounds good to me, and frightfully modern. I can't read anything, except maybe about a frog that jumped in a pond or thereby. But perhaps in a long talk we might evolve a new way of the ways for – take off your bonnet – Western civilisation. You can tell Gene that not having seen her for so long belongs to the Jaguar class of my disappointments. George Bruce refused to destroy my blethers on Edwin Muir. His face so fell at my suggestion that Daisy rushed to his assistance. And T. S. Eliot is giving an interview on Edwin so all should be well. It may not appear until autumn. Write soon.

Neil

TO J. B. PICK
DALCRAIG, KESSOCK   11/5/63

Dear John,
I found your reflections on Gurd.[27] and his critics very interesting and thought I should interest you by two cuttings from *Scotsman* on three chums of yours: Yeats, Sir Cumpton, and M. Maclaren Esq. The young man who did Yeats, also did the Gurd volume you mention, in *Scotsman*, and when we saw it Daisy phoned bookseller to get it for us, but it hasn't arrived yet. To quote from young man's review: ". . . here is second volume of *All and Everything*; the first, the cosmological epic entitled *An Objectively Impartial Criticism of the Life of Man, or Beelzebub's Tales to his Grandson* (1950); the third and final volume, *Life is Real Only When I Am*, is being prepared for publication by G.'s pupils." I don't suppose you've seen the first? Apparently though G. is a "most exuberant and unconscionable comic liar" he also has some good points. So let me pass on.

I haven't opened *In Search of the Miraculous* since the cat climbed the Rhu rowan tree to have a look at the Merry Dancers (and I shouldn't mind if we were turning from that

rowan and going inside at the moment to have a look at Gurd!)
But you've brought it back and I feel like a few words. Indeed I
feel like a whole lot, for I've been wandering in some odd
"marginal lands", as the farmers say, for a longish while, and I
fancy I had got a fairly consistent picture of G. I don't think he
was thrown out of a monastery or school. He wandered from
monastery to monastery – or master to master – learning all he
could, just as Zen boys wander to this day, even Zen masters.
The quest of the truth – without end. Why he doesn't name the
places, I think I understand, and some day, if you care, I'd try
to clarify this and other difficulties. As for his charlatanry,
it's not quite the word. In his time he acted many parts.
Play-acting. Something akin to Yeats's masks. Again, why so
wise a fellow should do this is not difficult to follow – though
by "follow", of course, I don't mean progression of rational
steps so much as getting the *feel* of the doing. His second self
could direct the posturings of his first self or ego, and even get
some pleasure therefrom in certain company! I'm not unduly
flummoxed by this! What's a little more difficult to weigh was
his final treatment of Ousp. I remember feeling some cruelty in
it. Not so much deliberate or malicious cruelty as a total
withdrawal of himself from O., and a lack of interest in O's
hurt feelings. But here we have to understand the kind of
impact O. was having all the time on G. There was a sort of
humourless mathematical integrity in O. that whiles must have
become a bit wearing to the versatile G. However, it goes
deeper than that. What a novel it would make! for the really
profound issues I haven't even touched. As for the critics, they
just can't help. As I laboured to make clear in *The Atom*, you
(or G.) cannot convey to anyone what that one hasn't in some
measure experienced. The awful thing about established critics
is that the original *given* capacity, however slight, to respond
to a G. experience, has gotten atrophied. But my hand begins
to wobble, so enough. Yet it is for some mysterious reason
comforting to learn of the not-atrophied. Even my professor in
Tokyo says his students are looking forward to a lecture he's
preparing to give 'em on *The Atom*. And I thought the book
dead as mutton.

I haven't read a book for many moons, but am looking
forward to G.'s *Meetings With Remarkable Men*, which
should arrive before Daisy and I go into Inverness Infirmary

on Tuesday. I tried for a private ward with two beds, so that I could read G to her; but when she heard me she chortled, saying my arm would be all bound up or fixed to receive blood transfusions, so I couldn't read. However, we've just heard from Infirmary that two private wards are reserved, with consultants laid on. I was pleased at being able to motor Daisy to Inverness on Wed. last for consultn. She's been suffering continuous pain. Surgeon diagnosed kidney infection, but X ray pictures needed, etc. So complete check-up for me and possible blood transfusions to keep me going. With luck, we'll be in for only 3 or 4 days, so you may be hearing from me in a week or 10 days. Meanwhile if you've anything to say about your literary gents, say it, for I find it good company.

My dear Gene, the notion of a Jaguar was the last rebellious fling by self No. 1, and I've given it up, for it mightn't be good for any one if driver sat staring at nothing while going 100 m.p.h.

Good luck to you all,

Neil

TO IAN GRIMBLE

DALCRAIG, KESSOCK, INVERNESS   MON. MORN. (27 MAY 1963)

Dear Ian,

We've been in the berluddy wars of no-health (to borrow a Zenism) and finished up jointly over a few days in the Inverness Infirmary. When we got out Daisy caught a flue just to keep the ball going, and now is up for the first time and crawling around. I crawl around also. So it's a great world, beautiful with greenery and birdsong. And although we couldn't crawl much slower without stopping, we still decide it's a beautiful world, and even if we got no better we'd go on living in it. (. . .)

Write soon.

Neil

TO J. B. PICK

DALCRAIG   2/6/63

Dear John,

It's good of you to wonder how you could help, and we appreciate it, I assure you. But we manage along nicely. The daily help came every day and back in evening, when Daisy was laid up, and the land girl slaughters the weeds and sows the seeds. Also Daisy has a sister in Inverness and a free-lance niece in Dingwall,[28] and both always anxious to help. But we manage wonderfully, and only have occasional regret, as when a friend in a garage in Inverness phoned me that they had a Jaguar, only done 6,000 m., for sale. There was a deep stirring; but, as Daisy said, the old thing we have drives itself. Mark you, I don't like giving in, but whiles lately I didn't feel like driving a wheelbarrow. But after giving my solemn oath to Daisy that I wouldn't do a thing for four days, I must confess that after 3 days I feel able to think again as far as Inverness! But it'll be a while before I get there. Daisy is up and about again; and with a bottle of pain deadeners goes about her flowers, which she thinks the finest in Britain. (In the middle of that last sentence, the door was flung open and a head appeared saying, "Ha, I just wanted to see what you were up to.") Which is more than enough for us. The sun is wonderful these days and we go out and in. Sometimes in a deck chair I listen to all the birds and the wind in the trees, and am with them and out beyond them. You say "a bee in a dandelion". Sitting on doorstep yesterday forenoon, I saw a huge bumble bee anchor himself to surface of plastered wall, hot with sun. Wonderful to see how his proboscis slowly folded inward into sleep. Clearly he hadn't been home all night and was still heavy and fuddled. Then he stirred and got on to a clump of small flowers (cotoniaster) and lay cushioned on his belly divinely. But no – no real rest for a poor old fellow. And then I observed two tiny pink ants crawling into and out of his armpits. Wasn't it terrible? I felt for that country bee so intimately that I cursed the bloody little web-spinners . . . And then I thought of what he would say when he got home to the foreman of the hive, the shop steward or the rep. of the T.U.C. Think of the honey-sodden poor old chap blabbing about having been tormented by pink ants . . . So don't shake a bee off a dandelion. You never know.

All of which reminded me of your remarks about the next book you'd like to discover in yourself. You're like the young fellow given a koan by the master – like the one when the master held up one hand and asked him to describe sound it made. Herrigel in one of his two small books[29] discusses it at length, and how pupil almost driven crackers by his efforts at solution, at last gets light, breaking through sweat, and so on; but he doesn't give an inkling of what solution, Herrigel doesn't. Anyway, I had a go myself, without any result of any kind for a long while. Now what I'm going to say next you'll understand (in true Gurd. sense) because I remember your once quoting from a book of mine about someone in it who listened beyond the silence (was the scene a moor at night?) to the far silence. (You're a master quoter). In a word, I began to listen even to the no-sound beyond the unheard sound that one hand makes. And of course the word "unheard" immediately evoked Keats: "Heard sounds are sweet but those unheard are sweeter, wherefore ye pipes play on . . ." (Don't tell your Eng. lit. friends that I remain capable of repeating the "Ode to the Grecian urn" to myself for sheer delight. They might think I suffered from pink ants. (Further parenthesis: *not* pink ants, but pink spiders. Our ants are black and immensely swift. Freud would probably explain my lapse by saying I didn't want, unconsciously, to say spiders to *you*.)

Now where the heck was I? – as I asked the recording machine when telling it about Edwin Muir. Oh yes. But first I need not explain the immense difference between "working out" that no-sound and actually experiencing it: therein the whole rub. To proceed to your koan: You have now to go on applying Judo to all your thematic alternatives . . . until the theme breaks and throws *you*. By August that should happen. Then we can go into mechanics of plot. (. . .)

But I'm going out in sun again for few minutes with my shirt off. So no other topics till next time.

Neil

TO GENE PICK

DALCRAIG, KESSOCK, INVERNESS   TUES. MORN. (SUMMER 1963)

Dear Gene,

Daisy read your two letters and thought you a sweet kind girl, or words accordin'. Write her another little one sometime: Ward 9 (Room 17), Royal Northern Infirmary, Inverness. You and John were the last visitors she saw, and now I go for a *short* spell in afternoon and her sister Molly in evening. She gets very exhausted. Yesterday she had to confess to houseman that she was utterly exhausted and he took some blood for test. Nothing but fruit juice, but some of it *does* stay down. The dietitian tries many liquid foods, and Daisy knows by first sip if it will make her sick. Sickness – retching – leaves her clean done. Have just had phone answer from Infirmary that Daisy had good night without sickness. They give her injections now for sleep, etc. But I have a sort of feeling that she's holding her own now, and I'll tell you more in a day or two.

I eat like a navvy; or pretty nearly; but doesn't make any difference to blood count. However, I'm fine and Daisy tells me to tell you that she's very bright – and that's the truth. Tell John to write about Scottish Studies etc, and I'll reply at length.

Neil

TO GENE AND JOHN PICK

DALCRAIG, KESSOCK, INVERNESS   11 SEPT '63

Dear Gene and John,

Many thanks for your Heinz and letter which postman left on backdoor knob yesterday and which I got this morn, so I was able to tell Daisy this afternoon and to read John's letter to her, which she thought full of wisdom and understanding – for one so young! It's the kind of letter, with its dark and light, which is instantly hers, like well water. Alas, I hate to tell you that she has now got jaundice, and any affection of the liver is something I won't think about – until I meet the surgeon in 2 or 3 days. I can only live from day to day. She was very tired and couldn't find any resting place for her legs and body. The jaundice does help to explain her nausea and dislike of food. I'll be phoning my brother John later and he may be able to come up for a long weekend, though his own wife is far from well. There has never been a promising symptom, but it got the knock, so I'm just holding on now.

Somehow I liked your letter, John, not because it flattered my efforts so much as indicated regions of the mind that matter. Same with Francis Hart's article, though here it did please me that he dealt with some of my later books, and on a level which took a certain achievement for granted. I have never had such understanding from Scots critics; in fact, either misrepresentation and false statements or no notice. (*The Scotsman* had a column on the "Studies in Scot. Lit." but did not mention the article on me.) But abroad – Japan, U.S.A., Germany – and yourself – it's different, and it gives a certain warmth to have such friendship. By the way, I noticed when reading your novel that it had not only a certain distinction in the writing but was pervaded by a sort of quiet authority which it was good to be in. Perhaps all literature does is give you a few friends. Or words like that. I don't even need to find them for you. I'm going to read it again, if only the next crisis would pass. And Daisy says she wants to read it. You may remember she liked the opening part.

A poached egg on top of the spinach it will be, and my blessings on you all.

Neil

Perhaps I'm not fair to Scots critics because I remember unsigned reviews in *Glas. Herald* and *Scotsman* that were understanding. I was thinking more of later and academics, like Craig.[30] Not that it matters, of course.

TO J. B. PICK

DALCRAIG, KESSOCK, INVERNESS   SUNDAY/MONDAY (SEPT. 1963)

My dear John,

Your serial on *The Key of the Chest* grows more fascinating with each instalment. That I must have written the book makes no difference apart from thoughts when writing it. There's a sort of no-mind place where things are or appear. And what stands out here are your reflections, as for example, about a new romanticism (and we don't need any analysis of that word) *and* your boredom with lust, doom, violence and the absurd. I confess I got rather a shock when I saw the title of the American's article on *The Key* etc. (Francis Hart) with its word "violence". But in a last letter of his he says that once he's done his book on Scott's novels, he'll "go groping for the significance of the fact that only in Scotland nowadays can one find the serious search for the meaning and continued vitality of Innocence, now that America has cut itself off from Huckleberry Finn and declared 'an end to innocence'". Which rather astonished me too! but, after all, which does show that there are those here and there in the world (he and you and I, and Nakamura, as samples) who are concerned with the same fundamental values. And that there always have been from Laotse (and no doubt long before him) onwards, including Goord and Oosp in our day – to whose "negative emotions" I have been giving some attention, with result that I cannot find an instance where said n.e. do not lead to sterility and destruction. If literature exists *only* to tell about them, then, as you say, there ain't no point in writing at all. I have gone a step or two beyond that; but let me have my serial, too!

When I saw Daisy yesterday, she got sick and after a little asked me to leave. But she doesn't get sick quite so often, though the paroxysm drains her energy so much that – I don't know. I try not to think about it, if only for a little while, but I'm soft. Your note with cutting about neo-cytamen has just come in, Gene. I'll keep it by me, and if only I'll get her back we'll do things. John my brother may be here for a spell. Neil Paterson, on flying back from Los Angeles, phoned me he was coming up to see us, so he and Rose were here for three hours on Saturday – at least in Inverness – and were allowed, not being locals, to see her for a few minutes. Unfortunately, the Station Hotel was over-heated for me and I had to get out for air, but I kept on my feet!

Neil

TO GENE AND JOHN PICK
DALCRAIG, KESSOCK, INVERNESS   (OCTOBER 1963)

Dear John and Gene,
   Last Sunday surgeon told me that there was no hope.
   Yesterday her words came through to me still.
   John my brother is with me.
   Love

Neil

I have just heard from sister in hospital that she is very weak this morning. I cannot write.

FOUR

ALONE
1963 to 1973

My dear Gene and John,
   We have got back from the south, John and I, and I now
must begin on the pile of letters on my desk, for they say such
lovely and true things about Daisy, that I must acknowledge
them with my own hand. No one has written what you have
written in ultimate understanding, and yet it's what has moved
them to write. T.S.E.: ". . . I remember her as very charming,
very beautiful, and with a most delightful way of speech. . . ."
You can see Daisy smile! But Eliot adds how much he regrets
that his wife and Daisy never met. As you say, John, it's that
deep still place where she always was. I have just had a cable
from Nakamura (whom I haven't had the heart to write for a
long time) addressed to "Neil M. Gunn Esq." and saying more
than everything in three words: "I am sad."
   Thank you for your homeopathic efforts. The specialist, Dr
Douglas Ross, gave me stuff to take. But I'll tell you more
when I can write. And I'm keeping in mind how you dashed to
a place called Crewe. Perhaps sometime you could dash again!
   My love to you both for you inhabit my mind so naturally.

   Neil

Dear Christopher,
   Many thanks for your letter of sympathy and understanding. Daisy was always with me, over what now seems a whole
lifetime, in all our wanderings about the Highlands, and is so
identified with all I see and hear, that it's going to be difficult to
be alone. But at least there are memories, as you say, and they
are gleams that whiles light up the darkness of no-meaning.
   I haven't been very fit physically over the last year or two,
but I may improve, and the old mind is as adventurous as ever,
if in country that may not interest for writing's sake! I am glad

to hear that you are keeping wonderfully fit and interested in many things.

May this condition continue.

Again with my thanks for words that come back from over a long time.

Neil

TO J. B. PICK
DALCRAIG, KESSOCK, INVERNESS   (JANUARY 1964)

Dear John,

S.S.L.[1] has just arrived and I have "tipped" in the Erratum note on your Lindsay. (. . .) I think I always found something slightly repellent in the harsh names of the characters, with their curious "L"s, and elsewhere, too, occasionally, as if the vision was too nightmarish at times, his nightmares too personal to himself. But it's so long since I read the book. Perhaps, too, I was often puzzled a bit. In some of your quotations I still am. The world that is "*rotten* with illusion from top to bottom. . . . Behind this sham world lies the real, tremendous and awful Muspel-world, which knows neither will, nor Unity, nor Individuals: that is to say, an inconceivable world". (P. 179, from his *notebook*, so presumably not fictional). The world of "appearance" is an Eastern concept, of course with Reality behind it, and very ancient, and Lindsay does nothing to help us to a Western angle of vision. "Neither will, nor Unity, nor Individuals. . . ." The words bog me. And if in fact these non-attributes of the *other* world mean anything visionary or paradoxical to Lindsay, why then does he go on to call that world "inconceivable"? One can go on, however vaguely, from a world of appearance, of individual beings and things, to a total Whole or Unity. The paradox that One is also not-One can "mean" something, however elusive. Even Marx could go from his thesis and anti-thesis to a unity or synthesis. Then again this other world of Lindsay's, his "real" world, is "tremendous and awful". Well, that's not the experience of your Goords and Oosps, not to mention old Zen masters, who gave wallops right and left. But apart from such light-hearted thoughts, I think we could say that the actual experiencing of states of being that inhabit the other world momentarily are characterised by a profound sense of harmony, integration, unity, well-being – not "awful" etc. In fact, lower down your page, Lindsay writes "Quickly and unexpectedly Lore stepped . . . into a free, pure atmosphere. . . ." Though that is in a character's dream. Still he (Lindsay) had the notion, or conception, if you like. Anyway, clearly there is something to be thought out here, and possibly his notebooks would help. (. . .)

Pen dying, too

Neil

(. . .) It occurred to me that perhaps Doctor is giving me B12, because that's for groggy blokes. . . . He's that kind of doctor. He's been away at small-bore rifle competition and came 3rd out of 500 competitors, including British International Team. In special match Scotland v. England he was the highest scorer over all. I had given him *Zen in Archery* some time ago, and he was vastly interested. He reckoned, he told me, that 3 times out of 100 he knew exactly where his scoring bullet had gone, before looking down telescope. He actually spoke of the target and himself being one in a way he couldn't describe. How's that?

TO MAURICE WALSH
DALCRAIG, KESSOCK, INVERNESS   3 FEB.'64

My dear Maurice,
    I hear you are back in dear old Ard-na-glaise, where we spent many a good day, and I am delighted to think of you among your own folk. Indeed I have been thinking a lot about you – and about the past – these last days and I must say that whole area from Lochindorb via Forres to the whole Laigh o' Moray has a golden glow over it. And no wonder, for through golden autumn weather we – and a keeper or two – must have wandered over every square yard of it. I like to think, too, of the amount of work I did for you and your station when both were in my charge. Good good times, and I am grateful for them. For there's one thing I know and it's this – and you may as well compose yourself and listen – a proceeding you may not be unacquainted with – it's this, I say, that whatever you may privately think about the Fates and the bitterness they can inflict upon us, still and on, and in their teeth if you like, man

has created a golden time of his own. You and I have had a share of such a time and those who were near us helped to sustain it, bless them for evermore. Unless you are feeling too tired, there will be a powerful urge of speech upon you now, and you can see me prepared to listen with all my customary patience.

I have been feeling very tired myself for a while – a sort of sheer physical exhaustion and the medicine men don't seem to do much good, with their iron injections and what not, but I'm still hanging on to the idea of setting off next week for the Canary Islands, arranged by the writer Neil Paterson (from about Banff) and under his care. Do you remember our old idea of buying a couple of donkeys in Seville and doing a loop round that southern part of Spain? It's just about the only thing we didn't bring off. Perhaps the sun will do some good. I'll be telling you. Perhaps it will make me tough enough to come over to see you on my own. Here's to hoping. All the best, bless you.

Neil

This letter is addressed to Maurice Walsh's son about his father, soon after Maurice Senior's death.

TO MAURICE WALSH JR.
DALCRAIG, KESSOCK, INVERNESS   17 MARCH '64

My dear Maurice,
I have got back from the Canaries, where I heard from Robin MacEwen of the departure of my old friend. I was touched by the appearance of Dev[2] at the Blackrock service, and by other items of news, too; though for all that and all that, I doubt if there was ever a better man came out of Ireland than the one I knew so well and so long. For there was a fundamental goodness in him that kept him whole, whatever his voice boomed in the small hours of theories and absurdities, whilk, I must confess, never failed to draw a few booms from myself. When I first entered the Service I was sent to Forres (Glenburgie) and so paid my first polite visit to your parents. We had what seemed no more than a few passages of

conversation (I rather think I was advancing the notion that man was a pianola) when sweetly from the stair-head your mother's voice floated down: "Mossie, darling, it's three o'clock in the morning." So we were sunk from the beginning. Ay, they were more than brother and sister to me, and in all our long friendship there was never a harsh word or thought or misunderstanding between us. On special occasions he would even address me with politeness and the outward appearance of deference; as when, after a considerable amount of chatter from a party in Forres House, he boomed across at me: "What do you think of God, Mr. Gunn?" It sort of interrupted the chatter! And I'm glad to think I never let him down. Sometimes he raised ordinary mortals to poetic heights, as when Michie Anderson, after we had listened to Dora playing the opening of Beethoven's Moonlight Sonata, was ordered to his feet at the supper table to interpret, and positively waxed lyrical over the way the music reminded him of a beautiful evening, shooting pheasants at Blackhillock.

You were blessed in your parents; and now you are head of the clan, I may tell you that your father had much pride in you. I know you can never hope to emulate Michie Anderson at the pheasants, though in my time I've done my best to instruct you by example. (I still think, after I had missed that last pheasant out on your shoot, with a right and a left, that I could have hit it with a stone). But pheasants are not everything – as I probably said when in my turn I got to my feet to deal with the Moonlight Sonata. But I had better stop for the very thought of him generates a warmth in the core of the spirit. It always did. And you are of the kind that was there with us.

Ex-provost Wotherspoon, Inverness, sent me newspaper cuttings, and got in touch, I believe, with Robin MacEwen.

I'm tired after travelling, but I think I'll feel a bit better when I've rested.

Give Mairin my love, and my best wishes for all of you,
Ever yours,

Neil Gunn

And thank you for your letters which came just as I was leaving.

TO FRANCIS RUSSELL HART
DALCRAIG, KESSOCK, INVERNESS   13 JULY, 1964

Dear Francis Hart,
    Your interesting packet has kept me pleasantly engaged for a
while, and silently I have answered a lot of it at great length.
But I'll have to keep the length until you come across the ocean
next year if not earlier. You must spend a few days with me
here in a pleasant garden overlooking the Beauly Firth. We
could take a trip to the West Coast in my car, for though I can't
walk very far I can drive all right. No strains or stresses here.
Though I live alone (my housekeeper comes in the morning
and leaves in the afternoon), with the nearest house about a
mile away, I manage along despite my condition of physical
exhaustion, with my doctor still taking a blood test occasionally
but really baffled, like the specialists. I have even had pleasant
moments on the verge of a groggy collapse (groggy without
grog – think of it!). The flowers have been a bit too vivid and
beautiful this summer, perhaps, but otherwise I have no
complaints. You should have written to me when you were so
taut and I might have loosened a string. I find my Eastern
reading, if I may so call it, very helpful. Words like mysticism
and transcendence never bother me. I am a simple empiricist,
accepting what I experience; but to be able to communicate the
experience is another matter. I think I explain in *The Atom*, or
try to, that an unusual experience cannot be communicated to a
person who has never had an experience of a similar kind. I
fancy I called it a "law". I remember reading some of your
novelists, whose characters were reputed to act "spontaneously"
in the Zen manner. Obviously they were almost completely
conditioned – especially by beds and bottles. It takes a Zen
master thirty years to learn to be spontaneous. (. . .)
    And now for *Gillespie*. I'm afraid my memory of *Gillespie*,
The House . . . and *Gillian*³ is too uncertain for any precise
comment from me. So many years ago since I read them. But I
retain enough to salute your effort, and my only criticism is
really of myself for in my present condition I can hardly take in
words of more than one syllable. If you find what you have
read so far lacking in cohesion it's because I can only do bits at a
time on this typewriter. The two bits which I have facetiously
marked "stunning" may indicate what I mean. Actually when I

put my head together and go over them again I find them packed and dynamic. But I think that for the ordinary reader not used to critical terms they may be a little overpowering. Your stuff is so good that it's a pity if any of it should be lost. But don't trust me these days. I put pencil marks intending perhaps to elaborate if I could, but elaboration in agreement would be mere gilding; and as I haven't a rubber, I leave them in. Let me mention two things. My pleasure at the way you introduce Gillian and "truth" gave a Hurrah. What other critic would have thought of it in the given context? And then the "town" and "provincial" contrast in novels: an old bit of criticism in Scotland tricked out to appear new. You not only handle it well, but you add something new which interests me very much. See my first pencil stroke on your p.3. My difficulty here is that I would have to write so much before I could make myself clear not to mention convincing. (...) In an instant you open up possibilities ("I'm off! I'm away!" in *The Atom*). This is exhilarating. This is what I felt like when I started, for example, *The Well at the World's End*, if I may mention a book to which you referred so touchingly and accurately in the fragment of letter which you didn't send. And if I may stick to it for a little time, let me say that I thought I would look up the book to see what I had said about Fand (which wasn't my wife's name, of course). And it began with an inscription on the first blank page: "This is Fand's own copy, from her husband, N.M.G.". So your insight was at work all right. Anyway, I began to read – and (I hardly expected this) read on. For it described right off our setting out for a spell at one of our remote places, called the "Picts' Houses" (an actual place, on the map), coming to a cottage, being directed to a well and so on, all as it actually happened. Then the vehicle that wasn't there – I still remember how desperately I looked for a passing-place. Then, having arrived, my attack on a salmon and Fand standing so awkward and gauche on the slippery stones with no boulder in her hands. ...
Last thing we did when the sun was setting was climb a near hill, see the silver sea that the sun left behind, listen in stillness to a hill bird then wander back, and while Fand made the bed (the seats folded for the purpose) I'd fetch some water from the nearest hill burn for the dram, which was a good dram, and sat quietly on the sill of the car window as the gloaming deepened.

It was at some such moment I conceived the notion of a sun-circle tour round the northern Highlands and in the process, of meeting people, and adventuring, and – and now I come to it – "going through the boundary". But I can't go on about this now. I'm merely trying to suggest the vague notion of an extra dimension. If that could be achieved – and something like it must be the next step in the long run – then . . . dicta about "town" and "country" are simply old hat and boring. But clearly I must stop. Oddly enough, a girl in Alberta University (. . .) is doing a thesis on such books of mine as she can find for her M. A. and asks me searching questions about things which at first I couldn't place in my books – until I realised they were all in the Well. . . .

Yours,

Neil Gunn

TO FRANCIS RUSSELL HART
DALCRAIG, KESSOCK, INVERNESS   11/8 (1964)

Dear Francis,

(. . .) I begin to look out when I hear even the word "idealism". In my youth I stood far left – and hopeful, later, of the Russian experiment. But the purges of '37–38 in Russia set me researching though I could find little of authentic account, even in London (I must have written *The Green Isle* in '41 at latest). It was not the political aspect that troubled me but the psychological – the applied psychology, so to speak, that could produce such extraordinary "confessions" from the Old Guard. However, all that would take too long to tell now – including a visit to Munich in '39 where I was at a fancy-dress ball in the Europa Hotel (where Hitler and Chamberlain had met) shortly before war 2 broke out. And learned a lot, from Germans who could trust me, about the ways of dictators. Anyway, you may take it that if I got interested in the "East", as we may call it, it was not all lack of knowledge about the West's more hellishly destructive subtleties but when you ask me about this "East", I just don't know how to begin – or even what to say, for the use of paradox can be irritating. However, I can say this, that when I began reading about Zen, I seemed to know a lot about it and to have used it in my writings from the beginning! In *The Atom*, for example, I described a boy (myself) sitting cracking nuts in a river and what I try to convey there is a condition of mind "on the way" to what the Japanese Zen masters call *satori*. All tensions (mental and muscular) vanish and you rise out of yourself into freedom. A long moment – an atom of delight. You don't search for it, and certainly not intellectually or metaphysically. It comes to you by chance yet you must be in a condition to receive it – i.e. not obsessed by anything in mind or body. Not trying, not acting, not doing, just being. But I know it's of no use writing like this, because it explains nothing, doesn't give anything in the mind or intellect to bite on. No logic. Just nothing. And, if I may say so, you have a beauty of an intellect. But you also have the other thing (. . .) The other thing is a byway running into Tao. It's what makes you ask me about the East. You belong on this way. I somehow know a little about it without knowing (there I go!) Anyway, I haven't read much, and that by chance (the chance that wouldn't happen unless . . .). As for books to read, I never was a scholar. You mention *Zen in Archery*, and the remarkable thing about that little book to me is the German author's simplicity. The arid acres of German metaphysics – then to arrive, after 5 years, at putting an arrow in the bull without trying. The very thought of it should relax the jaw muscles. Surely it is gay if nothing else. I bet you he learned how to bow to the target, like his master, too. I hope so.

The only Frenchman I have read on "The Supreme Doctrine" (as he calls it) is Hubert Benoit.[4] Gallic logic, exquisite subtlety, refinement upon refinement – but leave him meanwhile. Too much mind and not enough no-mind. Your countryman and authority is Alan Watts. Very good. *The* fellow, of course, is the Jap. Suzuki. But if I may make a reading suggestion it is this; get a mixture of bits and pieces and dip into it *now and then* (Aldous Huxley did something of the sort in his *Perennial Philosophy*, though not about Zen in particular). By "chance" someone, when in Los Angeles, sent me a couple of books about Zen, and one of these is a delightful anthology (I will now go up to my bedside to get the title for you). *The World of Zen (An East-West Anthology)* compiled by Nancy Wilson Ross (looks very Scottish!) I thought the publishers were American, but I see "Collins, St. James Place, London, 1962" on the title page; but it's printed in America. Should be in your library. So have a look at it when you feel like being irresponsible. It covers the whole realm, with sufficient intellectual passages – essays – to keep you going from one nothing to the next. Don't mention it to the Zen "authorities" about – enjoy it in silence. When you find yourself escaping to it for fun you are on the way.

I understand your attitude to Edwin Muir's *Scott and Scotland*.[5] I reviewed it for a magazine at length, and so dealt with his attitude to Scotland in particular that he was cut to the quick, and wrote me at once about it, for what I had to say in praise pleased him too. Muir *was* a good critic when dealing with the darlings of his time (Joyce, Lawrence, Virginia Woolf, etc.) and he was a tender-hearted fellow in himself. I remember his being perceptive about a novel of mine in *The Listener* (BBC), even if he did say that my conversational passages were obviously influenced by Hemingway (whom I didn't know and hadn't read). (. . .)

And thank you for your tempting coloured cards about your beautiful country. What sort of winter climate have you? Write soon.

Neil.

TO J. B. PICK

DALCRAIG, KESSOCK, INVERNESS   28/9/64

Dear John,

I like your aim: "I've tried to give an account of Lindsay[6] and draw out the truth within rather than argue with him." That reassures me a whole lot, especially when, if I may quote from your article: ". . . a sense of the remarkable profundity and coherence of the vision and its message", is what matters for you. This is criticism doing its high task, and to tell the truth, I was getting more than a distaste for it . . . Nothing like destruction for publicity. There's been quite a lot of it in Scotland, I'm afraid, and sometimes it's naive, too, for the critic wants to show he is no provincial but, on the contrary, a diver in the European stream.

Also you are not following the usual pattern by dealing with Eliot, Joyce, etc, but taking one who had been neglected totally and finding the light there. Nothing can be derivative; the vision must be singular, the penetration and understanding original and with – and this seems to come through your article and letter – human warmth. And life needs warmth. And the spirit, too, in the sense anyhow that those who have had it awaken in them talk of light, enlightenment, radiance. It glows. Even the official name of whisky is *Plain British Spirit*. It glows in you, too. The purely analytic doesn't glow. On the contrary. When you analyse the life cell into its elements and say that's all it is, you're wrong, because you've knocked the glow out of it. Life is missing. I wonder where it goes? At least I wonder where Lindsay thought it went. Do you think you could arrive at a fairly accurate notion of Lindsay's attitude to, or belief in, an afterlife (life after death here)? Does he believe there is such a thing, and after that, what? Is his attitude or belief something like this: I do believe we live on after physical death, but in circumstances, or states of being, to us utterly inconceivable? It would be extraordinarily interesting if you could produce some kind of clarity here. And there are a few words you'd have to be careful about; e.g., reality. You quote Maskull to Polecrab: ". . . reality and falseness are two words for the same thing." Presumably by reality Maskull means the world of the senses. But when Polecrab speaks of the "real world" *he* means something quite different, presumably. It was this kind of difficulty that made me in *The Atom* talk of a first self and a second self. By the way, Polecrab's saying that the real world lies on the other side of the *one*, etc., is interesting because I have never seen it expressed in quite that way. The One and the Many, yes. The one interpenetrating the Many; Buddha in everyone and everything, yes. I can even get now just what is meant by no-mind or the not-one. And so on. It would be more than interesting to have Lindsay's vision here, for he is a tough and original visionary, and in his visioning you can now and then get an extreme depth of feeling. His spirit has been to the place he has seen.

Altogether I am hopeful about this effort of yours – in the sense that something will come out of it that matters, but just what we cannot know yet. It might even be published!

I am not going to read "Arcturus" before I see your script. In that way I'll be better able to assess your powers of communication – and stumble on obscurities. I'll be a bit difficult to satisfy always, for I've wandered far in this realm.

I intended to send you a verse I made some moons ago in

payment for yours (which is its own self) but no, because it came too near the bone, even to make another.

I am going to Caithness on Friday morn until middle of next week, and I hope the weather will let us go up the Thurso river, so that I may get my native air and exercise my arms. About Xmas, – I fear for the road at that time and the short daylight, but that needn't interfere with your sending some script later on. I do wish I'd get a little more vitality so that I could concentrate for a short while at a time. But I do feel I'm improving, slowly perhaps, but still . . .

Give my love to Gene. I hope the boys are flourishing. And I hope my writing isn't as bad as yours.

Neil

TO IAN GRIMBLE
DALCRAIG, KESSOCK   OCT. 5 '64

Dear Ian,

Many thanks for giving me your dates, which I passed on to my doctor when he was here on Thursday, giving me some more of what he considers good for me. The Wotherspoons, Inverness, told me how very much they had appreciated your programme. I *heard* most of it fairly clearly and particularly the concluding part where the grabbing nobility are condemned. I think I once put it in writing that Scotland was cursed by the worst nobility – landowners – ever known and I could name you one or two today!

The rest of your letter about political parties leaves me a little sad. If my (what was meant to be a leg-pulling) use of naive (or naif) troubled you, let me assure you that in my time I have been more naive than you could dream of. I believed once upon a time that when a political party, or any other kind of party or individual made a promise to do something, and then went back on their promise when you had voted them the power to fulfil it, it was wrong! Anyhow, when that sort of thing happened a few times I grew less naive. But you apparently agree with the Labour Party (in this particular instance) for having gone back on their promise, and are prepared should they go back on their secret promises to you, still to think that the fault would be yours. You sure have me beaten. Then you go on to say that the "radical action" that has to be taken "has already been agreed at the top." But why in the name of little apples don't they say *precisely* what the radical action is going to be? By so doing they'd give Highlanders a chance to vote for something *real* and *specific*. Long years ago, before I left the Civil Service, the Labour leaders in Inverness arranged a private meeting between Tom Johnston and myself, and details (precise) I gave him then about Highland crofting economics became, I was subsequently told, the top of a great file. For the larger part of my life I gave time and cash in the nationalist cause. I really did study the whole complex. And I was extremely interested in the rise of the Danish co-operative movement. I spent a fortnight in Denmark; and in Jutland walked over the moors that were being reclaimed, and on my knees pulled over the surface peaty matter so that I could compare with our West and the Outer Isles. (Really, no comparison, for the whole terrain quite different.) I have read what has been, and is being done in Norway. And so forth. And then I came to our parties. . . . Well, I hope you'll have better luck, when Labour get in this time, which seems pretty certain! But please, when you are referring to Scottish Nationalism, don't wantonly indulge in expressions like "Maurice Lindsay type." Good men have worked for generations for Scotland and that, let me tell you, includes the Highlands. And your preference for London rule, rather than have Lowlanders helping to run Scotland, is most saddening of all. In our time can you mention – just to give one instance – any Highlander who has done a fraction of what Lowland Tom Johnston has done for the Highlands? And I mean *done*.

You see for me what has been *done* in the last week or two has been marvellous. I can still hardly get over the wonder of it. All the Minch and *part* of the Moray Firth closed to foreigners at last! The late Sir Tom Taylor, Aberdeen (our chairman on Crofting Commission) recalled a few years ago how by-laws prohibiting trawling in the *whole* Moray Firth by foreigners had been upheld by a bench of 12 judges in High Court of Justiciary, in an appeal by a Danish skipper in Dornoch Sherrif Court in 1905. But though we've had Tory and Labour and Liberal parliaments since then, the law of Scotland had never been enforced. (. . .)

The second thing is the signature of Michael Noble, SOS,[7]

to a new crofting scheme for a Shetland island put forward by the Crofting Commission. This kind of action is what I had worked for since I went on the Crofting Commission of Inquiry . . . Folk blame St. Andrews House. Absurd. They haven't control of cash. All your Development Boards, Advisory Boards, all the exhaustive inquiries made by Committees and Commissions with recommendations (blue-prints like the one you have, no doubt) are utterly futile *unless* you can call on cash. The ultimate and all powerful: The Treasury in London. (. . .)

You have good work to do, and are doing good work in keeping alive the remnants of an old culture which has always been very near to me. And good luck, too, to all your Labour Party efforts, which after all are efforts in our mutual fundamental cause.

Looking forward to seeing you on BBC Mod. TV.

Neil

TO GENE AND JOHN PICK

DALCRAIG, KESSOCK, INVERNESS   17 NOV.'64

Dear Gene and John,

I was glad to hear from you and learn you are busy being hospitable to all kinds of beings. It cheers me to think of it. I'm back from two very hospitable homes myself, and in Edinburgh talked to relays in small pubs. George Bruce was as usual crammed with business, so we had to step up the rate of our exchanges, and so I forgot to thank him for something. Norman McCaig was in good form for half of a Saturday, and so was Alex Reid for another half day, and Stanley Cursiter invited me to be his guest in Orkney for a week next year. Altogether it was a talkative four days. Neil Paterson is working on a short novel. I told him about you and David Lindsay and he was very pleased. The young American professor (Francis Hart) has just finished a book on Walter Scott and is coming over to see me next June. So all my friends are busy, and I'll be seeing their efforts presently. Which also cheers me. Naomi Mitchison had me to lunch yesterday and tried to inveigle *me* into writing again. Some hope! She's an incredible woman, and read me a poem in her high "county" voice in a lounge full of people of whom she was genuinely unaware. In short, I've been getting around, and am none the worse, though a heated room gets the better of me fast; and I never feel quite sure of all going well. But I'm cunning. I insisted on driving to Crieff, though from Dalwhinnie onwards it was dense fog, with lights coming up at me, and I was truly grateful for the white marking lines on mid road. I circled around the Patersons' house for about 20 minutes, before spotting a known street mark. (. . .) I've had the old face neuralgia for a few weeks, but so long as I don't touch the sensitive place (a feather touch makes me jump!) I don't feel it. And it's not spreading. I rather think I got it on way to Keith Henderson's near Spean Bridge some little time ago. It was bitterly cold. I stayed a night and saw all his pictures, and I enjoyed that and them. Keith, at 81, is tremendously busy, and in first week in Jan. they're off for 3 months to south of Spain. (. . .)

I very much enjoyed your brief note on Lindsay, *The Witch* and C. D. Broad, John, and could do with more. You haven't got Broad's book on Kant and Psychic Research? I only do little bits of reading at a time, so like it good and "difficult", if you follow. My eyes still sting if I read for any length of time, but I gather this is due to my general condition. Anyway, I have no complaints, though Daisy's absence gets the better of me whiles.

(Fri. morn.)

The postman cometh, so just a few words. Neil P. gave me a new book on "The Clearances", and asked me if I had a copy of *Butchers' Broom* to spare, as he hadn't read it. But I haven't. However, in looking over my own copy – I happen to have a copy of each and all of my books, simply because Daisy demanded one, with inscription – I started reading. It's slow on the lines of glens and hills, and remorseless and intense. Not in the modern mode exactly! But in a letter from Prof. Nakamura, he said that what held him was not the actual clearances but Dark Mairi. So I wondered – and there she is, mindless and timeless, into and out of the earth, and when I made her I hadn't even heard the word Zen. He says his students read my books because they find something they know. I mention this because it's being reprinted – as I think I told you – and if you haven't a copy I'll send you one – in the Spring.

Give my love to Gene. And I'm glad to know the boys are flourishing.

Neil.

TO J. B. PICK

DALCRAIG, KESSOCK, INVERNESS   6 JUNE 65

Dear John,

(...) I enjoyed your tit-bits of news and quotations. Here's a quote from Jacques Maritain: "The more deeply the modern novel probes human misery the more does it require superhuman virtues in the novelists." And I should say the same goes for these playwrights we were talking about (...)

Let me also give a quote from *The Key of the Chest* (which I thought I'd better have a look at to see what it's all about). Daisy (it's her copy) has 3 marked passages. But one of them is double marked, thus: And though one would need to read the previous page to get it properly, here it is: "But at least once each one turns away from a grave, and the sunlight is on the face or the soft rain, and lo! that which is buried is not buried but is the sunlight and the rain, for love knows no burial but remains everywhere."

My fond devotion to you all.

Neil

TO PROFESSOR TOKUSABURO NAKAMURA

DALCRAIG, KESSOCK, INVERNESS   26 JUNE 1965

Dear Professor Nakamura,

(...) T. S. Eliot: as it happens I never discussed Eastern philosophy with him, not that I remember. I do recollect his saying something to the effect that Indian philosophy was so subtle and intricate that he realised it would need a lifetime's study ... No, I'm afraid I never studied Bradley's work, so my "second self" could have found no origin there – nor in any French work. Any prompting influences could have come from, say, Zen Buddhism (Japanese) and some books by Ouspensky wherein he deals with the teaching of Gurdjieff – though I'm not blaming them! With such work when I came to read it I always felt immediately at home, even familiarly, because really, I suppose, any ideas I may have expressed concerning such notions as a "second self" came from personal experience, including flashes of insight and intuition, and not primarily, anyhow, from ideas and theories which have been got from others. Often when such ideas or theories coincide more or less with notions of his own the writer will happily find them acceptable; they may even help to clarify his mind; anyway he is always delighted to meet them for they are companionable. How I first – a very long time ago – experienced or had an intuition of this "second self" may perhaps be found in the brief chapter "The Nut and the Stone" in *The Atom of Delight*. In that extraordinary moment when one becomes aware of oneself, self-aware, it is exactly as if there was an over-self seeing the ordinary self, and this creates a sort of amplitude of being in which there is light and delight, and understanding. The "first self" and the "second self" (or, above, the ordinary and the over-self) are now one, the second containing the first within its circle, which can – and generally does – expand outwards with a wonderful sense of freedom, or may narrow upon the first self with an understanding that has its own clear affection; a seeing that comprehends the whole, the unity, and accepts it within a – or the – region of ultimate Reality. I know this kind of "explanation" can sound wordy and confusing – though I don't think it will to you. But generally to try to communicate such strange glimmerings to one who has never had them is inevitably fruitless – as I tried to show somewhere else in the same book. Perhaps it also explains a final emphasis on the virtue of silence by some of your master philosophers. Though in the ordinary way most of them go on talking – as we all do! And indeed, unless we do, how can we meet without meeting? However, if I use "first self" and "second self" because that's a simple way of expressing or illustrating an elusive affair, I recognise that they may be similar to the use of "self" and "Self", or allied terms, by sages of different places and times. For in this region nothing is new. Reality remains the same. And we *know* each other when we meet there.

So in my case philosophising "about it and about" stems, primarily, from experience. Which answers, I hope, part of your questions. The second part, about Celtic influence on my work – well, I suppose, that is simply an inevitable matter of tradition and environment. And it is quite real because in some measure within a common way of life and speech, one is saved the trouble of explaining many attitudes to one's fellows; there is much that can be taken for granted. However, even here there is a certain subtle or ultimate aspect as far as true creative writing is concerned, namely, that the truly creative springs from the region of Reality (already so lightly mentioned), that is, from the region that underlies it all, is common to us all – comes alive when evoked by the creator. You will get more than I do from, let us say, Basho's haiku. But what is fundamental in Basho does touch me, awakes true awareness, I feel sure. Similarly, you may not be as interested in the Highland Clearances, described in *Butcher's Broom*, as some of us here may be, but you *are* interested in Dark Mairi in a way that is profounder, more lasting, more universally meaningful, than any record of violence can be . . . Each likes his own – but it is wonderful when they meet!

May I tell you a story by way of illustration. I hope that it may at least amuse you. *Young Art and Old Hector* is about a little boy and an old man in the Celtic Highlands. I confess I patterned the little boy on a nephew of mine who at the time was a very engaging little fellow full of unexpected attitudes and sayings and questions. The old man is a composite of two or three old men whom *I* knew as a little boy. In a word, both characters are natural products of the old Celtic way of life in the Highlands. The talks between the two, or with others, were as true to life as I could make them. In a certain way, this is a difficult kind of writing, in the sense that, as more than one distinguished poet has pointed out, the most difficult of all characters to depict is a good man. I don't mean that it is difficult nowadays because in recent fiction and drama goodness has gone out of fashion and therefore embarasses the usual run of readers and spectators (*and* "clever" critics!) I mean quite simply, in the timeless or fashionless sense, that goodness runs closely parallel to sentiment, to a sentiment that *might* step over into sentimentality, a thing which true goodness never does. A difficult course or parallel to hold, but when naturally successful, how wonderful. There is also, need I add, the final difficulty of making goodness interesting, for in goodness, why, there is nothing to write about. So it really is very difficult. Then add to that that the book is about nothing at all! And where am I? James Bridie even got embarrassed about praising the book to me, so adopted his forthright and exaggerated manner, and called it "a bloody great master-piece". But then he was a lovable fellow himself, a good man. But please try to excuse this rambling preamble for I am trying to prepare you for what happened next. The Scottish writer, Naomi Mitchison, an old friend, confessed that she had not come across this kind of Young Art-Old Hector relationship in the Highlands; so she thought perhaps I had been exaggerating. Was there, in other words, something sentimental? This truly astonished me, for such relationship in my youth was as natural as the flying of birds. Then perhaps my vanity was touched! Who knows?

So my mind switched to the intellectual Leftish circles that she moved within (she has written some fine historical novels). Now I myself had been at home in such circles for a long time, so I realised how provincial, even parochial, not to mention "simple" to the point of sentimentality such a book could appear there. I didn't really mind this – obviously, presumably, or I wouldn't have written it. There was something somewhere at a deeper level. And this was tied up, I could see, with the Celtic culture out of which I had come and to which you refer (and by "Celtic culture" I finally and simply mean the background and tradition from which I came and which I cared for) I now had to ask if that old culture was in fact an anachronism? Had it no meaning for modern living? Was I recording old ways of life beyond possible human interest any more? Or – wasn't I? So the idea occurred to me to try to let the questions be answered by placing these two characters in the world of today, complete with intellectual argument on government, freedom, and all the other pet themes or theories of our time, and just what happened. So I arranged that the old man and the little boy, on an ancient hunt for the salmon (of food and wisdom) would fall through the bottom of the pool in the river and wake up in the Gaelic paradise (sometimes called The Green Isle of the Great Deep) and – to be *ultra* modern – a paradise run on authoritarian lines. This would permit every kind of dialectical attitude and action, and through the whole the old man and the little boy would adventure, carrying with them and fighting to retain the way of life that was theirs. I even did not shrink an interview with God! And what was the end of it all? that Naomi Mitchison recommended the book strongly to her intellectual and even psychiatric friends. Recently I was having lunch with her in Inverness and told her how it came about that she was the cause of the book's being written (. . .)

(Typed copy, unsigned Ed.)

TO FRANCIS RUSSELL HART
DALCRAIG, KESSOCK, INVERNESS   23 AUG, 1965

Dear Rus,
    The sun is shining this morning and if Lorena and you were here, we'd be off.[8] "I'm off! I'm away!" from which you may gather that you've compelled me to look up something in *The Atom*. But before we come to your diggings in my disreputable lit. past, let me say that I was pleased to get your letters and should have liked to hear more about the plays – or, at least, your reactions to them – in London. Not that that matters, when the sun is shining and no one has done me wrong, except by absence. I think that when I become a rich man, following Faber's enthralled interest in all I do or have ever done, I'll phone up Lorena and ask her to put the beautiful morning into song. Even if I know beforehand that she wouldn't be able to do so for laughing, I'd have a try. Maybe her laughter would be more than the song. But I'm not going to become complicated – not this side of *The Grey Coast*. For I must first thank you for *Siddhartha*, which I enjoyed reading for a few nights before switching the light off. It was companionable. It was and is where some of us belong. From the end of time I can only say that that is what literature is for, the lit. that matters. Here and there in time individuals have gone on quests, or have met in esoteric schools. They are the growing points or bud points of man's evolution. And I'd better not start on that either, for at the moment only "companionable" is in my head – and the sunny morning. And now I'd better have a look at your last letter and answer things by or on the way, so I have no fear of making sense.
    I think it was noble of you to read the book[9] on my behalf, and if it weren't for the sun I do swear I'd have tried to read it myself out of compliment to you. But not just yet, if you please. Edward Garnett wasn't so worried about "wordiness", if I remember, as about simplifying a phrase or two. But I

wanted hefty words, full of thickness and urgency, at these points, so, to my everlasting shame and loss, I didn't do nothin' about 'em. I was really full of what I was trying to do, so don't tell anyone. There are points of thickness and urgency when man's only response is to burst into song and declare to a bootless even unstockinged heaven that she done him wrong. That said, I'm prepared to defend Edward to the death. And you, too, of course, when you instance the ' "timeless silence that might be waiting on the passing of the footsteps of God", etc.' (I liked your "etc.") At such points I felt compelled to look up the text. So once in turning over the pages my eye landed on the top of p. 212 and there again in the same words were the passing of the same footsteps but now in a satiric context. So what *can* be made of a sockless writer like that. Don't ask me, for God with his socks off was bad enough. Not to mention the bus that was going to Tongue when it was going to Thurso. I can but murmur after you "and all manner of thing shall be well". The rest is Bettyhill.

The schoolmaster and Fiona.[10] If you look up the book of short stories, *The White Hour*, you'll find a schoolmaster who was treated at greater length than Moffat in the Fiona manner (*Half Light*). Remember the book was written about 40 years ago, when Yeats and the Celtic Twilight and so on ("so on" meaning the Scottish Renaissance, and so forth) were exercising minds further afield than Balriach – I'm referring to *The Grey Coast*, and the short story must have been written just before or after. So a new writer, who knew his Celtic lands, would make an effort to break through the Twilight. You ask about Balriach, which to you is so like Dunbeath. But it is difficult for a writer to use any specific country place by name (I never do it), for the time or period being known, then also would be known the name of the schoolmaster, the doctor, the minister, or whom have you. That you get odd unusual characters, including schoolmasters, in remote places is simple fact. You sometimes refer to *The Other Landscape*. Well, the somewhat destructive army major in the book is drawn from the life, but it was in an hotel in a small Hebridean island that I met him. And even if he did not set the hotel on fire, he did light all those candles, and I remember going to sleep with a smile for the thought of the place going up in flames and the hope that I might wake up in time if it did. No, Moffat is not so much the academic as simply in doubt about a beloved poetic mode, and already has wee devils gnawing at the Fiona rhythms. When he looks at what appears to him to be reality (Ivor) in this way of *real* life, he gets no help. (. . .)

You were especially interested you say by the wording on p. 202. Your penetrating remarks that follow interest me very much. I suppose I may have introduced the teacher as a member of the community at the educational source, and may have used him a little deliberately to comment on Fiona and literary problems of the time, though after all they were the lit. problems for that area at that time. And it would be very natural for such as the schoolmaster to pose the Lake Isle to Ivor to see what happened. The problem worried Yeats himself, when he got past what critics call his first phase, as you well know. And in every small community there is the odd one – and maybe not so odd – who understands and feels, even if he doesn't speak much. And clearly Siddhartha thought they were all like that, if only he could get to them. Really when as a writer (a writer like me anyway) you come to grips with the simplicities they can become inconceivably complex. I think I must have suffered specially from this when doing *The Grey Coast*. And perhaps one of the reasons for my reluctance to re-read, is the intensity and complexity which are split open and seem too much now, if not then. It is not easy for me to read it over easily or lightly. As if there is a too muchness that embarrasses. Yet when I have started to re-read another book, and keep on reading until I am back in the past, and the old creative mood, then once again I am as I was. I suppose that would happen with the *Grey Coast*. You quote "There could be the crying of desire, of the soul's longings – even in this grey land of hunger and lean soil." And then you comment: "The book celebrates the triumph of a little life over such forces, the triumph of the redemptive dream and of the possibility of renewal." It seems I take simple country characters, with no particular "plot", no particular happenings beyond those of everyday, no central violence even as you note, and then proceed to get busy in violent and explosive depths that hardly show in a flicker of the face. Almost perverse, until you're caught there. Here are at once the forces and the dream, perhaps, as you suggest. And yet I haven't said what needs saying about this. I shall sometime because it's central. It's the first self and the second self. It's my hunt. Or quest. And it's yours. And that's what matters. Prof. Nakamura has also been writing about *The Grey Coast*. And he quotes what I once wrote somewhere about Sesshu's pictures. He finds his own angle of approach, from his own background. And we are all really concerned about the same thing. And this is companionable. And who does what, is neither here nor there. Anonymous and intensely second-personal and so on and so forth and, all the same, she done me wrong. As simple as Siddhartha. But never forget the atom of delight, over and above all. (. . .)

Yours

Neil

DAIRMID GUNN, second son of John Gunn, Neil's younger brother, was born in 1933, and in 1949 entered the Royal Naval College, Dartmouth. He served in a variety of warships, then from 1965–67 was Assistant Naval Attache in Moscow and Helsinki; and from 1969–71 on the staff of Commander, Far East Fleet, based in Singapore.

TO DAIRMID GUNN
DALCRAIG, KESSOCK, INVERNESS   23 MAR. '66.

Dear Dairmid,
        Thank you for your picture card of the beehives of the industrious and the universal. Here we still have the old bee-skeps, secreting the delicious heather honey of the ancient vintage. And we don't feel backward besides. Perhaps I should have said distillation instead of vintage, but we are not long back from Majorca where we consumed a considerable number of bottles of wine, with a thick Spanish body and very good at its best. Your father lost his somewhat worn or greyish look, put on weight, and assumed a genuine tan before the end. But of course he came back to bundles of exam. papers and, today, snow. I have been trying to knock sense into him about doing arduous and responsible work out of the goodness of his heart – unpaid, at that! But he's coming round by degrees, and when his desk is empty he'll be coming up here for a spell and a

few jaunts to Caithness where, I gather, a few salmon are knocking about, poor fellows.

Glad to hear you are all in good fettle. I manage to stagger around in the same old way, but I do believe Majorca saved me from going under.

Love to all,

Neil

TO PROFESSOR TOKUSABURO NAKAMURA

DALCRAIG, KESSOCK, INVERNESS   28-3-66

Dear Professor Nakamura,

(. . .) Also I feel somewhat embarrassed by your claims for myself and may appear too often to interfere with your personal judgements of what I have done. This, and other aspects of your work here, have set me think (sic) for some time.[11] I discussed the whole matter with Ian Grimble when he was last here and we wondered whether your work might be enriched if you first wrote it in Japanese and then got some suitable English writer (native) who knows Japanese very well to translate it into English. This is the way all great translations have been done. My writing friend in Majorca[12] (who values my work highly), a Scot, talks Spanish fluently, and writes it, too, of course, and he says that when he writes or talks in Spanish he becomes in some measure a different personality. Don't you feel something of that when you write in English? I am thinking particularly of the passages where you deal with subtle psychological distinctions, inward spiritual matters, exquisite responses to backgrounds, all those attitudes indeed where the Japanese excel possibly all other writers. You have a marvellous tradition here, and writing in another language must, it seems to me, impede its expression. . . . For there is an ultimate way in which you and I are concerned with values that go beyond us both and which will be enriched by the genius of *both* tongues in expression.

Yours sincerely,

Neil M. Gunn

ALONE

TO FRANCIS RUSSELL HART
DALCRAIG, KESSOCK, INVERNESS, SCOTLAND   29-3-66.

Dear Rus,
    Cheers for the Guggenheim chance of Something. My severely factual statement[13] suffered, I felt, from compression, and there's no doubt that it was Lorena's incomparable typing that did it, for it opened up the mess and let air in to activate the Guggenheim understanding. Q.E.D. So let's bow to Her Grace.
    I gave the "Mayor of Inverness" your observations. No, I never saw Nessie, though, of course, many of my friends have. I really mean that there's no doubt but that the Monster is there humps an' all, and such illustrations as you may have seen on the TV screen would be genuine enough. So we'll do a tour of the loch without bursting into song, if that's possible, when you come over next year, all otherwise well and, I should like to think, more than well. If I won't go the length of saying that Majorca lifted me up at least I feel satisfied that it saved me from going under just then. We – brother John and I – had marvellous weather, the best winter in Majorca for 60 years it was said. The second week I shed some clothes and the third week we actually dipped in the sea and then sat on the sand in the sun. Once or twice I heard a voice murmuring "This is divine". It was mine own. The cafes too were attractive and one in particular made a wonderful champagne cocktail which became a daily rite. We didn't go anywhere much except roam about – though that brings to mind one day of extensive travelling in a car driven by Douglas Day, an associate of yours. Fortunately we did the island sunwise, so we had the inside berth on the road that twisted and reared and dive-bombed in hairpins so I hadn't to look over the unguarded edge to infinity. Talking of hairpins, there was a young lady, named Elizabeth, who was so devoted to Douglas that I could gaze at the sunbaked earth and the old suntanned houses in the remoter mountains and commune silently with them, though Alastair Reid sparked off flights of wit now and then and altogether it was for me a memorable day, with its visions of more ancient days, the rocks like solidified sunlight, and the houses, tiles and all. Which sentence seems to have dribbled out of that day. But I know you won't mind, and when you

don't mind nothing a sense of freedom steals over you and peace, deep peace, with the sunbaked. And when you return to a land of snow – it's white for miles – well, there's snow too. But I don't like the cold, and had I known I might have seriously thought of taking off through Hercules' Pillars, as you did suggest in your letter, for your invigorating spring april. By the way (that's my address, but don't mention it) while sitting on the sunbaked sand (paler than the rocks) brother John and I one day began talking about you, for a memory came out of me about your saying some very odd thing about the possibility of my getting my expenses paid (travelling, that is) if I'd do a stint of talk on Scotch – Scots literature, that is – though, indeed, why not Scotch its very self? And as my mind stirred, out flew the suggestion that he, John, might get a fare paid, too, for Rus's university will no doubt have some sort of department of Education and you (sic), being a retired H.M. Chief Inspector of Schools, could talk as an authority particularly on Scottish education and its remarkable history, an expert who could answer every conceivable kind of question – and so on – until he actually stirred and said he would be delighted. So I hastily retracted, saying I couldn't lecture; but then, the day being divine, as I have indicated, I heard my voice murmur that even a miracle might happen if Lorena opened the classroom proceedings with song. So at least we were thinking of you both in that place and time (and even my typing seems pretty good to me, if slow, brother, slow). Now where am I? Yes, let me not forget to thank you for the wonderful picture cards. The Roualt is bloodier in tone even than the headlands of Majorcan rock in the sunset, and when I turned it over and read the title "Afterglow, Galilee" I got the shock. In comparison the Cezanne is light and pleasant and positively friendly, bless it for that moreover. And all the time I realise I must say something about something and stop being the evasive Highlander. And it's about that you sound as if you had it in mind to do more writing about my stuff if not even me and that leaves my head both bloody and bowed. I gathered too from the valorous Grimble that he might be behind you in your scheme. His is the word, as you intuitively apprehend. And I daren't ask you to think again, for you can think so ferociously at once both of you that your second thoughts might be worse than your first. Meanwhile let us be calm and answer your questions. What you would like to do meanwhile is to re-read *The Atom* and ask me to elucidate some factual matter, and this I shall be very pleased to do. At severe factual statements I am good. Though I cannot be sure beforehand that I myself will understand what I have written. Which reminds me of once upon a time being in a beautiful Georgian house in Dublin and the man who owned it played the fiddle, for after having been a landed proprietor somewhere in Ireland he retired to Dublin to pursue his fiddling and composing, and one of his tasks was to compose for some of W. B. Yeats's pomes. I rather think they did recitals on tour. Anyhow, the composer once stuck on two lines in the middle of a poem for a long time and could make neither head nor tail of them, "So I decided to ask Willie himself, and Willie looked at them for a long time and he said he could not understand what they were about at all". I have a curious first self and second self memory – a visual memory – which I recorded in one of my novels long ago, and recently I decided to look it up, and did, and there was no visual memory at all. I still can't understand this, and no one reading the words could understand them, including myself if I hadn't the memory. But I'll do my best (. . .)

Yes, I have been keeping an eye on what has been going on in Scotland but not taking any part – apart from the question of a new University in Inverness. Behind the scenes I did a lot for that in the way of preparing memoranda for submission to the University Grants Commission and so on. But when the final decision was made we lost it to Stirling, though we were everywhere tipped to win. It remains an incredible decision to most knowledgeable folk. But we are keeping the idea in being over against the future. (. . .)

A good lot of snow has melted since I started typing this, but oh it's cold, cold. All the same Majorca saved the situation, and if Virginia had followed I wouldn't know myself, which would be a very pleasant change.

My devotion to Leonara, from whom I'll expect a few words of praise for my typing.

Yours,

Neil

Dear Rus,
   I had a forgotten experience a few days ago: I saw your letter
on my desk and after looking over some of your questions I
suddenly had the feeling that I'd like to answer it and tell Rus
all about magic. Now the feeling was like that which I used to
get sometimes when I was writing a book, long long ago – an
eager pleasant feeling, at a little distance (and yet of the inner
essence) in a magical light, but which I had completely
forgotten, so that I suddenly realised: yes, that's what made me
engage in this queer writing traffic; that's how I felt, that's how
I was magically charmed to go ahead. (At odd moments, I need
not add.) But don't let me overdo it, particularly as the labour
of doing the actual writing has to follow, and nowadays a
drowsy numbness . . . as of hemlock . . . and lethewards . . . or
thereby supervenes, yet when this does happen, I can still hear
the nightingale, in that charmed light, at a little listening
distance. And if this sounds a little strange, I can quote from
your own letter where you are so moreover, as when you write
of Finn's climb *The Silver Darlings* . . . struck me at once as one
of the most tremendous chapters I ever non-read in my life
(non-reading without Reading) . . . In fact it reminded me of
the last poem I wrote long ago (came across it in a pencil
scribble the other day):

   Not to be able to read further because the eyes sting:
   Then to go on reading the finest wordless stuff
 ' that has ever been not-written.

And I'm sure that after reading that you'll smile at once. No
need to explain. To think on't: rather peculiar that the page of
your book vanished as subject and object became one. Only
because of some such experience does one get a hint of what the
Eastern wise man feels when saying simply that subject and
object can become one or even are one. From which you'll
gather that I am not preparing to deliver myself on magic, but
only, at first, to hint at "intimations" of it (. . .)
   Having got so far with Rus, my dear Lorena, I went into the
garden for fresh air. Your two swans draw near now and then,
but they are not nesting around here. For the most part they are

distant, remote, close together, and telling a silent story about long ago now. It's an old story but you tell it now. Perhaps you have heard of it before now? I wouldn't put it past you. The shell duck in white and a saffron band are numerous – or nearly. Then I started gardening with a hoe and shears and a barrow, broke my back in two places, mended the breaks, and cooked my supper. And now the evening blue is on the water, and a pigeon has just looped up and clapped its wings. I wonder what it's been up to? The number of up-tos and goings-on are many, but they do pause to sing, just to show that the up-tos were delicious and the goings-on exciting. In other words no morals, so I switch to Rus and his questions. Though why we bother with questions and morals, heaven knows . . . especially one of them. Is the second self amoral, you ask. In the moments of experiencing the second self there are no morals, no good or bad. Consider the seconds of silence that follow the completion of a superb piece of music, and in such a silence look at the fellow who asks you if music is good or bad. You sigh and come back to the first self and begin to put on your intellectual skates. Wordsworth had his moments of tranced enlightenment, his intimations, but then he resumed his first self, but a first self affected by the rare enlightenment, so that it quickens and spells fear with a capital F. The real problem about Wordsworth to me (. . .) is how after his fruitful period with the "intimations", he then lost them entirely. I remember being troubled about this long long ago, and remember reading somewhere that Ruskin had such "intimations" up until he was seventeen-eighteen, and then they vanished from him too. Let me put it this way. In the enlightenment attained by the Eastern there is neither good nor evil. It is a condition of mind beyond them. Simply a state of being, a wholeness in which opposites are fused. How long this state of being can be held, or hold itself, will vary according to the individual and his disciplined experiences. But that's enough and more for the nonce. If you would like me to continue it sometime please say so, and I'll answer before breaking my back. But perhaps I should add that though this state of being is beyond good and evil as I have tried to suggest, that is far from implying any superior attitude. On the contrary, it is only after such an experience that you see good and evil clearly, see them with understanding and compassion.

And the great and the good come back to help. That's the sort of way I read the riddle. And you'll come on quite a lengthy bit about Fear later on in *The Atom*. But in books like *The Well*, *The Atom*, *The Other Landscape*, there is traffic with this sort of Light or Delight, I find. Perhaps in the others, too? But I'd have to read them, and that needs courage. Has this Light been playing a game with me all along? (. . .)
Yours,

Neil

TO FRANCIS RUSSELL HART
DALCRAIG, KESSOCK, INVERNESS   3 OCT. 1966

Dear Rus,
    You had a jolly narrow squeak in the matter of becoming a VIP or manager, as you say, of the academic Green Isle. It must have been for the sheer hell of it, as the phrase goes. But now you can sit back among ordinary mortals like me and Old Hector and Young Art (now married with two young daughters) and sic like, meaning the rest of us, who have a small untaxed (so far) share in the sunlight and the colours (still pretty rich before me in the rockery as I write) and in the sounds that birds make in the distance at night. Being a VIPer means in some measure a loss of freedom, I suspect. Can you have freedom if you are of Importance? I mean, have you time for it? Can you burst into song? Can you turn back and go off the other way? How would you get to Thurso by bus? On the campus at jolly Jolla you could have created in thought and then built ideally, and if I have any small regret about it, it's that no one less could have done it so well, but yet and on you would have been conditioned by your doings, whereas now that you are not who can say what you may do, including going what looked like the wrong way to Thurso, and yet getting there, where they have fast breeder reactors, if I may coin a literary phrase. Certainly you could never have written like *this*. And that's something, if you follow. And you do follow, and you may not be a fast breeder literary creator *yet*. At which point, (if not long before) the Zen master says: Stop it! So I stop, though if Lorena were here, I'd start all over again with her.
    Yes, Alastair Reid and his painter friend Schuler[14] (and

daughter) were here, and the painter told me how once he was at quite a dinner in your house, where an odd thing happened, so you see you were both in our words and thoughts. (How I should have enjoyed being at dinner too!) The artist has fallen for Scotland – the Highlands – in a deep way. In fact, he's looking for some old place in the West that he could convert into a studio. The mountains, the sea, the light . . . Perhaps he started from Turner. He talks clearly and well and might have been offered an administrative constructionalist job on some jolly old campus instead of being in a wrestling booth with old Turner and the like. His future, like yours, is now unpredictable somewhat.

A lady came the other day to interview me on my approaching birthday in the *Glasgow Herald*. That knocked me stiff. But I said that she must not mention my age, that I hadn't written for ten years, no prospect of writing – for, dear heaven, how could I tell her why? However, I gave her stuff about Highland writers (Jane Duncan among 'em, though I haven't read any novels for years and can only remember one of hers – well done). So I gave her my copy of SSL, with your article in it on me, in order to try to deflect her from the personal (which is what her editor wants no doubt). I have never met Jane[15] though I gather from the lady interviewer that she would like to meet me. Jane D. was talking to an Inverness Writers' Club, and I was invited, but I don't care about going to places alone. Perhaps I'll write Jane and attempt to make my introduction interesting by quoting what you said to The Grimble about her (. . .) and adding that I should make a point of doing myself the honour of introducing you to her next year; assuming the faeries attend to their own affairs meanwhile. (I suspect an old thorn tree as a haunt of theirs – about a mile away). (. . .)

Well come along. Your foot is on your own campus, and you can now ask all the questions you like and so help keep me alive.[16] I enjoy your letters.

My devotion to Lorena as always,

Neil

TO FRANCIS RUSSELL HART
DALCRAIG, KESSOCK, INVERNESS   (1966)

Dear Rus

(. . .) *The Serpent,* like *The Shadow,* is one of my own
peculiar ones about which I'd say nowt – having forgotten
most of it anyhow. It did absorb me when writing it and I can
remember odd moments of what I can only call clairvoyance,
with no memory of violence need I add (I never was one for
violence, but I know you won't let that interfere with your
appreciation of certain dramatic moments). Of course I have
no clear memory of how or why I wrote it, but let me try to
reconstruct a possibility. Many books about the Highlands
because many aspects, and possibly I had a vague notion of
dealing with most. Let me start then by saying that when I was
a boy there was a man who had gone to Glasgow to work, then
returned, opened a cycle shop, hired cycles, did many kinds of
repairs *and* was a freethinker. A quiet but persistent man, with
a sense of humour. Sporadic talks about most things, including
socialism and no doubt religion, though I was too young to be
more than vague about it. He is not Tom of the book, though
the seed of the conception may have been there. But I should
say that in most communities in the Highlands there would
have been then one sceptic at least. Now I was a teenager in
both London and Edinburgh (15 to 20, or thereby) and know
all the arguments (Huxley, Darwin, Haeckel and what have
you – wasn't it Haeckel[17] who wrote *The Riddle of the
Universe?*) Anyway, that kind of atmosphere. And though my
reading was very limited, basic statements of doctrine, etc.,
were whizzing around among us, or a good few of us. (. . .) So I
know just the kind of life Tom spent in Glasgow, for he was an
intelligent chap like me (offered as proof). Well, where am I?
Yes. Next, the place is not Caithness but, as you surmise,
Ross-shire. But the place is "arranged a bit" though the hill
behind the glen, that Tom climbed, is very like the hill and
moor where Daisy and I spent wandering days when we stayed
in that part of Ross-shire. I fished in the small Skiach burn,
while she hunted wild flowers or bathed in a pool. Blessed
days. (. . .) If standing stones are mentioned, see my stones on
p. 22 of *Highland Pack* and read what I say about them. We
went normally and naturally to our moor and burn. So did the

Philosopher. So perhaps went the wise men of the East, if all they had was a desert! Keith Henderson also gives a drawing in H. Pack of the moor country. I like his drawings even better now than then. I can remember holding an umbrella over his head as he did the stones. . . . But to come back to *The Serpent* and attempt to answer your "what came *first* in the conception of such a story." I don't know, but I suspect that it was the notion of the freethinker in a Highland community; then I would make up the community, using the pattern of the place where we lived so long, and gather the ingredients necessary for a rounded whole. Vaguely – the principal character would think of a walk up the hillside where the wild roses and heather and grouse and of course the wild flowers that Daisy knew all about, and other familiar things, grew and shone and felt the wind, the wind, too, that came from the back of time, the Philosopher's own time with its past and reflections and wonders, if you follow me. You see, I never worked out the moves ahead in a book. In this case I probably got the character going in a first paragraph, and then simply went on, for I never found any difficulty with invention, never had to wonder where next to go or what was to happen, for I was "told", if you can follow. And often the telling astonished me. If I had known exactly what was going to happen in a book of mine from the beginning I think I would have been too bored to write it. There would have been no surprises on the way. And often it's "the way" (dear old Tao) that holds the lot, and certainly the unexpected insights. Sometimes I was bothered a bit about these insights, because I had a liking for them (like having a drink, a tot, on the way), but the internal thing that did the "telling" would stand no nonsense. It kept a continuous rein as it were on my *way*wardness, in the interest of what I could see it believed in as balance. Sometimes when I got an insight (let the word pass) that might run to two sentences, the "balance" frowned on what it obviously considered was self-indulgence if not worse (like vanity or whatever). But if I had done a fair amount of straight action, I might have my own way for a whole small paragraph. It was sometimes amusing to look on at this happening. On the whole "balance" of course would stand no nonsense, but I got my dig home now and then. Heaven knows what this reads like (this is "balance" having *its* dig, I suppose) but I let myself off by thinking of

Lorena. . . . And reverting to the Serpent pome in H.P.[18] – to deviate for a moment, and for the first time – I there say, to my astonishment, that I couldn't remember the actual serpent that came through the heather runts, when at this very moment I remember perfectly clearly. I was a very small boy with an elder brother and two others when we saw a serpent (as we called the adder) pouring through a clump of heather. I think that was the first one I had ever seen. Next (Balance is almost giving me up) about what you deem is some sort of intrusion into the novel – Janet, her mother, Donald and that side of Tom's life: all that is really made up. But blame Mr. Balance, who got the notion that a man like Tom, who was a full man in his fashion, must have had his instinctive or passionate side, and I have little doubt but that Mr. B. (serves him right to give him just an initial) linked up this side with the other (freethinking-intellectual) by making Donald a son of the manse. Oh the old B is very cunning, and yet detached, positively objective. So what can a poor author do? However, I secretively enjoyed the balancing, I reckon; and when I read the other night a translation of an ancient Indian MS[19] (over 4,000 years old) on balancing (and so in time on Zen) boy was I amused! At home, anyway. Tom's relation to his father: not unnatural, in the context, and without going all Freudian; even if I personally had no such parental experience. But not another page of such gabble, so farewell. . . . But more again. Indeed you sometimes make me feel that I might go into things after where *Atom* leaves off. In letters. And Balance can boil his old head.

Neil

TO FRANCIS RUSSELL HART

2 NOV. 66

Dear Rus,

I was pleased to send Alastair Reid a flimsy about the reactions of virgins who fled to their Southern Mammies from an inscrutable combination of good looks and innocence as I hadn't written to him for a long time and accordingly tried to be as interesting as possible forthwith. I may not hear from him now for a long time. But I fancy I almost overheard some remarks about wizards in Black Isles. Elizabeth there, too –

and do you mean to suggest that she actually remembered me? Her attention was so directed elsewhere that, as I think I told you, I did not require to open my mouth, and so could leave my eyes wide open to the old sun and the old red tiles, at least half as old as time, and I did not realise that when Douglas and Elizabeth[20] absented themselves for awhile it was to visit and inspect an old sun-red house where once upon a time Chopin and George Sand had habited together, bless them – did not realise it I do declare until this moment, if I can trust my memory, which I sometimes can't. Not that I know what it is I cannot realise. But I do know that it would be wonderful to fly to Virginia when you'll all be together again in March, and I salute your offer of escort from New York, but if I'm back from the Balearics then I'll be happy to look forward to seeing you here, for I haven't all that amount of pith. Meanwhile I read about Yoga and breathing exercises and then forget the exercises because of the fascinating distinctions between all the variations in Yogas and Yogis and so am where I was. Except that I know now (perhaps) something about the actual exercise of meditation; and anyway had a wonderful one about you and me, a philosophic difficulty, and a rowan tree. Now I'm going to deal with it as evocatively as I can and earnestly request your close attention for a brief (I hope) space. Ready?

Have you ever been able to understand, or intuitively apprehend, a final unity of subject and object, of the knower and the thing known, the seer and the seen? Have you ever even for a moment tried to experience it, to enter into the unity? If you think for a few searching moments will you then, like the rest of us, confess you haven't? Do give it a try now. Because I don't want to be done out of the delight of astonishing you. Behold the wizard and his magic in one!

In an affaire with the rowan tree. You quote from p. 224 of *The Silver Bough*: "The rowan tree was a more solemn riot, full of convolutions of itself and high bursts of abandon, but sticking to its own root at all the odds". And then you continue: "Fess up now: you know it was you in the rowan tree". And so you caught me at my magical antics and you were delighted. Even if you don't say you were delighted. I know. And I do confess up (not down) that (hold it, brother) myself and the rowan tree *were* one. Subject and object in unity. And if you don't care much for unity, because of its grey philosophic connotation, then delete "in unity" and insert "in high bursts of abandon". Subject and object united in a high burst of abandon. Isn't it wonderful? For that's what happens always at such a conjunction at such a moment. The branch-arms thrust at the sky whence the light comes..And "abandon" is a magical word for it entered on its own. Light and delight. And the pure exhilaration of freedom.

And next a very odd thing happens, for it doesn't come into any Eastern statement about resolving subject and object into one, duality into unity, that I have heard tell of or seen writ, and it's *your* oddity in *your* happening; for it's very clear for me to see that you not only observed this remarkable rowan tree – me magic, but observed it so inwardly that you too became involved if not indeed part of. So where are you – and me and the rowan tree – now? Very astonishing. Let me try to draw our totem pole:

> Thee,
> Me,
> Rowan tree,
> Three in
> Unity.

If I had elongated it with double spacing it would have looked better, but what can a fellow do with one typing finger who taps to his thinks as he goes along?

At which point I went out for a walk. Golden red trees among others and the evening light on the water all the way inland to the mountains, and spots of very cold rain in the brightness. Where was I? Oh yes, up the pole. So let's swing back to the *Silver Bough*, same page ... "The grass was greener, fresher ... the grasses flattened themselves, wiggled, in a green mirth that held on ...". The rowan. The cat. The blackbird ... You can see the landscape, I know . . . or is it the other landscape you see ... sort of new magical aspect, the aspect that does not die with the seasons . . . ? Please don't analyse or intellectualise ... hold to the light, the mirth, the brightness ... for it's as real as anything you ever saw, or realer, for your own words tell me so.

Have I made you do your own magic, or at the very least made you give yourself an "intimation" of it? Have I spent so many words – not enigmatic ones I feel sure – because I think they carry somewhere inside them something valuable? I have. But first, what actually happened when you saw the rowan and me and called it my "portrait"? You had a sudden *insight*. (There may be a better word, but if so I don't know it). But how potent the insight, how charged, how transforming! It is as if with this kind of insight you go from the passing into the permanent.

But let me look at it in one more way and then I'm done (and I'll do my best to remain done). As you may know, Zen students have hurdles to surmount like things called *koans*. On the face of them they are plain absurdities, not decent respectable paradoxes even. Meaningless nonsense that drive students to exhaustion. Now wild geese are passing over here every day – the firth outside must be a landmark of sorts for them – and they brought one of these koans to mind today. The student or young monk after his Master and himself had seen some of them flying over and away, said "The wild geese are gone." As the geese had in fact disappeared the student had to say that "they have flown away." But more emphatically than before the Master said that they had not flown away. And before the mystified student could repeat what he had said already the Master gave a strong tweak to his nose. And, says the record, at that moment the student achieved enlightenment or, as it is called, *satori*. Wonder apparently brought the sweat out on him. (I should have said that to the student's first observation the Master replied "They have not gone".) No wonder I got muddled even telling you about it. Can you make head or tail of it? I certainly couldn't; and of course if you try to reason it out you'll never understand it. It's got to be the flash, the insight, or nothing. The application of logic is fatal. (Again: "What's the true path?" asked the student. The Master: "Everyday life is the true path." Student: "How do I study?" Master: "If you try to study you get far away from it.") Well, now, let's think. Does your experience with me and the rowan help? If you told your story and someone said in answer that all that was long ago and the landscape was gone, rowan and all, now, what would you reply? Would you say, "But the landscape has not gone."? And if he insisted that it was, would you feel like giving a real good tweak to his nose? Do you see how you are leading me up the garden with your magical rowans?

A frightful count of words to suggest something of what "Other" may mean in *The Other Landscape*. Better than nothing? You can tell me. As I say, I looked up p. 224 of the SB[21] and found myself reading on until I finished the short chapter. A distinct scent of otherness about the whole thing, even the conversational passages and actions. So I stopped.

But let me give you a delicate insight of your own. It happened when the lady brought the article about me[22] before she submitted same. She actually said nothing about my age nor about my not-writing for years, so the sub-editor will put it in headlines, if put it he does anywhere. She was wearing pink svelt knee-boots that toned perfectly with her lipstick and carried her article and the copy of SSL[23] with your article in't. (A brief snapshot to amuse Lorena in case you have the brutality to ask her to read all this). I made tea for her and me and we had a pleasant session, but she did not refer to your article, and I did not ask. Perhaps a trifle formidable for her. So when she left, I looked at it myself – and finally landed on: "Brotherhood is a matter of the most delicate tact or instinct, which acts as its brother's keeper without violating the individual wholeness of its brother." Apart from Thee or Me, its light warmed my heart and I felt life was good. Insight. (...)

Pray present, with high abandon, my respectful regards to Lorena.

Yours,

Neil

Thought I'd add a note about *The Other Landscape* that might interest you. When I went to fetch Daisy's copy (she *made* me give her a personal copy of each of my books as it appeared, thinking no doubt among other things that otherwise a time might come when we wouldn't have a copy. She knew me.) there fell out of it a letter from a scientist and an advance copy of an Address by Sir George Thomson, FRS to the British Assocation, August 1960. Says the scientist in his letter "I fear that I must record that, to my cost, it has only been within recent days that I have read your most excellent book *The Other Landscape*. Shortly after reading I received a pre-print of Sir George Thomson's Presidential Address ... and what he says about "atomicity" so closely follows your own words (about p. 300 of *The Other Landscape*) that I am

taking the liberty of sending it . . . A one-time scientist myself
(now turned science writer and editor) my own feeling is that
the ultimate solving of the "secrets" of the atom will come
about via philosophy or intuition of a religious or semi-
religious nature, although it is always possible that experimen-
tation – the hard way – may produce a result, but I doubt it."

TO J. B. PICK
DALCRAIG, KESSOCK   16/11/66

Dear John,
   You have caught the shape and spirit of the true haiku in "the
chemistry of Highland light". A man, who was head of some
shipping concern in Japan, has sent me an additional two books
of haiku (Blyth), and I dip into them now and then. Often one
haiku is enough to be going on with. In the middle of last night
I awoke and began thinking of the koan about Joshu's "Mu"
and got into some rare regions of light, where the light not only
lightened but enlightened, never precisely, logically or in such
nonsensicalwise, but expanding into freedom, formless as
being itself, which has its own form, before it goes beyond it.
At which point one laughs with delight, atoms of it sparking
off and out and away until the whole universe – but I pull up.
For, as you say, we've got to start at the beginning, if we're
going to deal with committees, planners, authoritarians,
VIPers. And I'll tell you my beginning: the body and the mind,
the material and the psychic. We've got to be clear about it and
accept it; the two things are distinguishable and each has its
own characteristic evolutionary trend. But the heavy words are
beginning! so I shan't start to go through the thicket and dance
out on the other side. Think of me trying to dance anyhow!
Without thinking I did a step or two to a Highland reel on the
radio the other night while my bacon was sizzling – and had to
sit down. (The body – that the gay psyche had forgotten.) To
have some sort of immortal body to match an immortal soul:
what a dance would be there! To shout hooch! once in paradise
would be something. The word "squeeze", beloved of financial vipers, had a different connotation when I was *young*. It
sure had. A lady phoned me last night, from the Glasgow
region I think (phone indistinct) introducing herself as Miss or
Mrs. Yum-yums, asking me if I would act as judge, at some sort

of *old* folks' gathering, in a clothes or dress competition (I rather gathered, at third repetition) embracing Scotland (I feel sure), and when I again asked for her name she said Mrs. Yum-yums, though it may have been Williams, or thereby. I told her I was exhausted and couldn't, anyhow. She was *so* sorry, because . . . *so* much appreciated my books. . . . It was Isobel[24] who solved the riddle of this, saying: "It's that photograph of you in the *Glasgow Herald*, over the article about your birthday." In this photo I stand poised, or posed, one hand grasping a branch of a flowering viburnum and the other disposing of a walking stick which supported me aft in an elegant manner, thus exhibiting to advantage a well-tailored suiting and a new rather small modish hat. "You look young," added Isobel (ref. to photo). "No wonder they asked you to judge." And she was definitely disappointed at my refusal. By the way, the Press photographer happening to see my shotgun which brother John had been inspecting, begged me to carry it, but I was firm and so we compromised on the walking stick. What a world I inhabit! I thought it would steady down when I at last became a permanent Hermit. Then Isobel threw a tantrum this morning and told me I should have to get somebody else. (She suffers from an anxiety neurosis.) She says that between me and Sammy (the crofter whose house etc. she runs and whom she brought up) she'll land in Craig Dunain (previously known as the Asylum). Now all this may seem so much chit chat to you, but to me it's a profound race with achieving sufficient Zen enlightenment so that I may hold my balance in the teeth of circumstance. One koan in a paperback begins: "What is the path?" Master: "Everyday life is the path." You see what I mean? It's no laughing matter. At least not until 3 a.m. when I awake farther and farther away in the universe. But even then everyday life whispers that I'll never get a housekeeper to stay in this lonely spot. The path is the Now, alas! And I thought that being a hermit would be freedom from worldly cares. Do you know of a Zennish monastery anywhere? And all the while, Gene, your beautiful Birthday Card smiles down at me from the mantelpiece. So I smile back and know that you are, and remember, and likewise John. And I'd have written earlier had an editor not asked me to do 800 words on any subject I like for 25 guineas. So I may do 2, and then, after deducting taxes, I'll have enough over to buy a case of 10 year old Glen Grant for the New Year. But for fleeting moments I did catch again the writing moods of ancient mornings. Would have been quite magical if someone hadn't been missing.

Having mentioned Haiku, I enclose a letter from the shipping man, whom I've just told reincarnation is one thing of which I have no inkling. You? Love to all,

Neil

TO PROFESSOR G. ROSS ROY, EDITOR *Studies in Scottish Literature*
DALCRAIG, KESSOCK, INVERNESS, SCOTLAND   9 APRIL 1967

Dear Professor Ross Roy,

I have been abroad, trying to get the sun to give health a fillip, and correspondence has accumulated, but I now hasten to acknowledge your letter of March 27 asking me for a review of Hugh MacDiarmid's *The Company I've Kept*. It is with the utmost regret that I cannot do this for SSL. I have read the book, thought about it, and had to decide that I am not the person to undertake this particular task. It would be difficult for me to make this decision appear reasonable in a brief space – even embarrassing, because in the nature of past events there would inevitably intrude the kind of "personal" element that I dislike and in the end could not use. Yet I appreciate the honour of your invitation so much, and the pages of SSL have contained such distinguished criticism of my work (by Professor Hart), that perhaps I should try to indicate at least one instance of my difficulty.

Primarily, in writing, I am a novelist and as such would have to refer critically to anything MacDiarmid has said about the novel and his attitude to it, and to me, as he does on pp. 19 and 72: "... I have known or want to know few novelists ... Neil Gunn, one of my earliest and closest associates in the Scottish Literary Movement ... I can read little of his works. Against the strong vigour of Scottish life almost all our novels of this century are flimsy constructions of cardboard ..." (p. 19). For me to avoid referring to such remarks would imply that I was afraid to meet his challenge or that I agreed with it. If I do accept then I should have to take one of my own novels and test its texture for cardboard or anti-cardboard, even if it sickened the gorge. Still it could be done. Perhaps like this:

"In a recent issue of *The Listener*, Bernard Bergonzi writes: 'No one would doubt that the novel is the central literary form of our culture . . . and apart from excesses of commercial promotion we may still feel that Lawrence was right when he said that the novel was "the one bright book of life", and the self-respecting novelist might well echo Lawrence's magnificent apologia for his craft: "Being a novelist, I consider myself superior to the saint, the scientist, the philosopher and the poet, who are all great masters of different bits of man alive, but never get the whole hog."'" From which one might deduce that the novel is not exactly the negligible literary form that MacDiarmid suggests or implies!

But, being up to date, critic Bergonzi goes on to consider some criticisms of the novel as a traditional form in recent years until he lands in France and the writings of Robbe-Grillet, from whom he quotes: ". . . the unconditional adoption of chronological development, linear plots, a regular graph of the emotions . . . etcetera . . ." of the traditional form portray a stable universe that does not exist. And so on. But you'll know it all.

At which point I should have to introduce one of my novels, so let it be an early one, published over 30 years ago (as Prof. Hart dealt with the later novels, which on the whole he preferred) – *Highland River*. Well, Highland River has no "unconditional adoption of chronological development", it lives in the past *and* the present, going from one to the other as naturally, (I hope) as the mind does; it has no "linear plot", indeed it had no plot at all; and as for a "regular graph of the emotions", I cannot find one. And if we may respectfully leave Robbe-Grillet to look at what has now come to be called the controversy of "the two cultures" (Snow v. Leavis) I find that I had discussed some aspects of this as a natural ingredient in the latter part of this 30-year old effort. But let me ignore other items to seek any measure of attainment. So I would have to mention that it was awarded the James Tait Black Memorial Prize as the best novel in English of its year (on the recommendation of the Professor of Eng. Lit. in Edinburgh University – on this occasion Prof. Dover Wilson, the distinguished Shakespearean scholar). Finally, how could I refrain from adding that Kurt Wittig, who is on your board, mentioned in a personal letter (I have never met him) that it was as a consequence of reading *Highland River* in the Continental Tauchnitz edition with the aim of reviewing it for a German periodical that he was prompted to make a study of Scottish literature on its native heath and thus produce his brilliant and penetrating book, *The Scottish Tradition in Literature*. Edwin Muir and Hugh MacDiarmid, whose works he criticised, both praise it; indeed Muir thought it the best we have on its subject; and so do I. Now if you look up the last page of this book you will find that K. Wittig thinks of modern Scottish novels and why. The word "cardboard" doesn't arise.

But really I feel ashamed of being forced to write stuff like this, and the more so because I am aware that it is so much verbiage used to conceal my real difficulty: the "personal" element which in recent years he has increasingly employed by way of denigration, too often of a non-literary kind. Consider the ruthless way in which he pursued Edwin Muir over many years. Or even take the simple instance of a short paragraph on p. 24 wherein he accuses Sir William MacTaggart, the President of the Royal Scottish Academy of "social climbing". I have known Sir William for a great many years, and I cannot readily think of any artist who is by nature so genuinely modest and unassuming.

To avoid any wrong impression I must add that in MacD.'s remarks on our all-night sittings he is completely right. I remember those old days with great pleasure, and all the greater because he was then producing his splendid poetry in Scots. And even if his particular concern for the Lallans did not in practice affect writers like Edwin Muir or myself, still it was invigorating to be engaged in the common national effort.

But I hope we shall be able to talk about such affairs when you come over in '68. In this letter my concern is that you may understand why I'd rather not write for SSL unless I could do so whole-heartedly and without cavilling.

Yours sincerely,

Neil M. Gunn

STEWART CONN was born in Glasgow in 1936. He joined the BBC in 1958 and first met Gunn three years later. When he became a producer of radio drama he was responsible for the programme,

The Boy and the Salmon (an extract from *Highland River*), for John Keir Cross's dramatisation of *The Green Isle of the Great Deep* and for Alexander Reid's version of *The Well at the World's End*. In 1985 his own adaptation of *Bloodhunt* was shown on Television. Stewart Conn is a poet and a playwright.

TO STEWART CONN
DALCRAIG, KESSOCK, INVERNESS   15 MAY 1967

Dear Stewart,
   How delighted I was to find the review of a play of yours in today's *Scotsman*! I live outside the pale – the lit. one anyhow – and did not know of your dramatic powers, though I distinctly remember having an intuition thereof when I first read a poem of yours and both saw and heard a powerful draught-horse knocking sparks off causey-stones.[25] You can give a poem a physical embodiment, and that's quite something these days of intellectual finesse and abstraction. However, what has really delighted me and prompted me to write this straight away was one of the critic's opening remarks: "But both plays end with anguished cries from the heart – protests against pain and destruction". All at once it meant to me a turning point – a turning away, anyhow, from plays of destruction, of negative emotions like jealousy, hatred, violence and so on through black humour, sadism, cruelty to nihilism and destruction of life itself, self destruction. Clearly from whatever materials your play may be made, its core is *positive*. And that's what I have been waiting for. "Targets are provided for those who would like to sneer . . .". Of course! We know them in Scotland, inflated egotisms and all. I still get my share of them. Ignore them; they are of no significance. I now have two positive points in Alex Reid and yourself. With the life warmth out of which everything that matters grows. Hold to it . . . (. . .)
   But I confess to feeling more than a bit spent at the moment, but the talk was positive!
   Greetings to Judy,
   Yours,

Neil M. Gunn

ALONE

TO FRANCIS RUSSELL HART

DALCRAIG, KESSOCK, INVERNESS   23 JULY, 1968

Dear Rus,

I'm feeling worse than you when you wrote about 90° and humidity. I have just phoned the bank saying they gave me too much cash the other day and they say they haven't. The manager also blamed the weather. So don't expect coherence. However let me begin with the first things first.

How is Lorena? Also under the weather? Answer responsibly. You cannot expect me to think of going to Virginia in October if Lorena isn't doing acrobatic feats with an umbrella on stone walls. Not, I mean, that I'm going. But when John hauled me in to his travelling agent's den in Edinburgh last week to learn about banana boats to the Canaries in the winter time, somehow or other we were suddenly discussing flights to America besides. You know how the wind bloweth where it listeth. And you know how strong we are all going to be – tomorrow. And John said that if he saw me onto the plane at Prestwick, I would only have one change at the small burgh of New York. And John Pick said it would be an ADVENTURE. But I don't really listen to such romantics. So answer my leading question, please.

2nd point: my delight at your winning that distinguished award.[26] Pity you couldn't get the cash *and* the semester away from teaching. Which is not the kind of thought that would occur to a responsible person, for whom the honour is justly all. True, indeed. But I was brought up on thoroughly irresponsible people like Fitzgerald Omar to take the cash and let the credit go. So never expect anything above a cash motive.

And now let me say that I haven't factual stuff with which to attempt to answer the many questions you ask, so look upon this as an interim report. Indeed you shook me a bit when you wrote about John MacCormick's book *The Flag in the Wind*. Surely I must at least have read it, and if I had read it I would possess it. But I don't remember reading it and his remarks about Larachan seem new. Do you think the humidity has gone to the brain and submerged the memory? However, I've asked a friend in Inverness to get it for me. Meanwhile you can rely on him and what he says. It was he who got the Glasgow students – as a student he led them – to vote for Compton Mackenzie and make him Lord Rector. In all these early years he did more than anyone else for Nationalism in the political field, not to mention other fields, and when fellows like Grieve and Mackenzie try to make it appear 'twas they, those of us who know may momentarily smile. I remember the trouble Duncan McNeill and myself had when MacCormick stood as parliamentary candidate for the Inverness constituency over Mackenzie's statement to a R. Catholic body in the Lowlands that he did not believe in putting up candidates for Parliament (Nationalist candidates, i.e.) *The Inverness Courier* came out with a headline about Nationalism's Two Voices. The *Courier* mocked us bitterly, for it was rabidly anti, and here we were fighting strongly to save £150 deposit which we hadn't got. McNeill tried to contact Mack at his home near Beauly, but his secretary always put him off, saying he wasn't available and so forth. McN. was MacCormick's official agent and a lawyer, so meanwhile he concocted a plackard referring to lying statements in the *Courier* and engaged sandwich men to parade the streets with a plackard fore and aft (...). Then we wrote to Cunninghame Graham who lived on the Clyde and that gallant warrior at once agreed to come and speak for us. D. McN. thought he ought to write to Compton and tell him C.G. was coming. I disagreed with him there; however, he was the agent and should do what he liked. So McN. and I arranged a dinner at the Station Hotel and McK. came and was one of the platform personelle (sic) behind the speaker that evening (...). We had some anxious but also many amusing times. As a civil servant I shouldn't of course have had any public dealings in politics. And when Wendy Wood, whom you ask about, came to help on pre-election night, bringing some cash from H.Q. to complete the £150 required as deposit, she was amused to learn that I had written a blank cheque which McNeill was to fill in and cash if she hadn't turned up. Which is neither here nor there – but when she went south again she addressed a *public* meeting and mentioned what I had done! (...)

You ask, in particular, about the break-up of the Party in 1942 and if I was at the meeting. I wasn't, and I doubt if the split would have taken place had I been there, because here once more the ugly head of schism rose up and did its work (...)

My fond devotion to all.

Yours,

Neil

ALONE

TO ALEXANDER REID

DALCRAIG, KESSOCK, INVERNESS   10 SEPT. 1968

Dear Alex,

I have been strangely moved by your poems and found myself re-reading them with the detachment that is completely engaged, a sort of wonder at their being there, so technically simple, so profound. The first one of 8 lines about the "owner of this place" who "perhaps lives elsewhere", creates the "Second Self" (as I once called him) before my eyes. The human tenement, the stairs, the grimy windows. And though that second self always lives inside, for most of us he lives elsewhere. So I read it again, and dwell with it. And realise at last, at long long last, that I am reading poetry as I once read it long ago. . . .

Which is pretty high praise, perhaps aroused in part by the contrast between your voluminous even drowning explicatory arguments, and the quiet words of the poems, words that themselves fade away as they do their work of revealing the invisible: with one notable exception, when Li Po addresses the moon! (Not Li Pu, as your typist spells him). Why not try about 3 of them at a time to the only two papers I get – *Scotsman* and *Listener*? Anyway write more of them. But I'll say no more because I'm a bit tired – caught shocking cold on the way home, no worse for over 3 days, antibiotics, and so on – I merely wanted to send a word of salute. Before you submit 'em anywhere, check for misspellings, of which a good few.

My love to Genevieve,

Neil

TO FRANCIS RUSSELL HART

DALCRAIG, KESSOCK, INVERNESS   3 OCT. 68

Dear Rus,

Anent your two glooms xxxxx (these crosses of affection indicate that my typewriter's joints had with long oblivion gone dry) (so I've stood 'em a drink) two glooms, there was once upon a time a small isle in the inner Hebrides with a little school and a schoolmaster, and on a gloomy day it was his custom to greet his pupils with the remark: "My curse on gloom!" whereupon he took out his fiddle and played to them, and there are some real sprightly measures in the Gaelic repertoire. Of the same island (I think it was Canna) it is also recorded that when someone called from a neighbouring island upon friends and stayed with them a week if he was in a great hurry to reach the mainland – or longer if he wasn't – their parting words to him were: "Isn't it the great pity that you are going instead of coming!"

Now that schoolmaster was a Teacher, the highest of all human occupations. (. . .) Of course you have your peculiarities, even your blind spots. E.g. you did not foresee the absurdity of thinking that Scots literature could be anything but a waste of time for young wallahs with an eye on the main chance. Or for any wallahs, as London critics make clear. You are a hopeless adventurer. I remember the shock I got when you told me, after you'd done it, that you'd addressed a most learned assembly on *The Green Isle*. You are an individual, a marvellous independent, and proclaim merit when you see it. You are of the same build as Walter Scott, large and all-embracing (odd term as it may seem), wanting to tell glad tidings. And you have the real tidings. You are that rarest of all things, a Teacher. So go ahead you must, and without your knowing it what you'll have to say about Queen Victoria and her prose will yet contain the essence of you and this, quite unknown to the Phders, and to yourself, will come through and be remembered as rare, like a scent one can't remember the name of. Already hasn't it won you what is called a tangible reward, on the strength of which you may come and see me – with Lorena, of course, so that when I was overawed by your learning, she might sing me a Gaelic song and so And so the sheet fell out of the typewriter in protest at such personal meanderings, but I can tell the sheet – and you too – that I was only beginning, and in a future letter may go on – and on, for there is a haunting central something. . . . Meantime you are perhaps lucky that you are not the victim of such goings-on straight from the horse's mouth, as would have been the case had I reached the Virginia of my desires. And I hated having to give in. I did, and it wasn't a beautiful morning. And I got landed with a bad cold for three weeks by way of punishment, and with three injections from my doctor, and with my Caithness brother[27] and his wife who have been very kind to me. Now they have gone north again, leaving me with you and Lorena. So now you will say you understand my meanderings.

But really I am feeling pretty good – physically, of course – and may go back with you when you've come over next year. Perhaps I should add ha-ha, but I won't. Mentally I'm not all that bad either and did some of the usual intellectual tricks with John Pick who travelled over-night from Leicester to hold converse with me. I can even remember one spark of insight, and that's a fact, but as you may not believe it, let me proceed. We were discussing the "haunting" thing already mentioned by way of threat to you, when Wordsworth dropped in. He was welcomed, especially lines:

> A primrose by a river's brim
> A yellow primrose was to him
> And it was nothing more,

got quoted, and I said that once in my youth I had liked them in my fashion, but not too well; and now that I didn't like them because the primrose faded away into the mists of the aforesaid Orthodoxy, itself vague as the mist. Anyway, to think of a primrose being nothing more than itself – well! So I promptly soared East and came down among Basho and haiku and heard myself making an undersized haiku on the spot, thus:

> By the river's brim –
> Look! a primrose.

I can even hear Lorena's voice crying the words in wonder and delight (not at the words, but at the primrose). So I am warning you not to try any mental tricks on me lest you be hit by an unexpected haiku. I'm a tough guy still.

One of your American writing chaps – was it Thoreau? – said: "Give me health and a day and I will make the pomp of emperors ridiculous". In youthful days I thought them pretty good, but now – ah me! Health, brother. You have it, and also you have the vision of the haiku, the breakthrough to the second self (I'm off . . .) enough to put the rifts of ore into Victorian prose, and so encourage the only counter to the fellah who may press the button and vapourise us all. It's a responsibility upon you. But my typing is getting uncertain so I shan't write a letter this time. Meanwhile my fond devotion in a certain direction plus. I do hope her health is wonderful too. The page is slipping again.

Neil

Dear John,

Many thanks for the *Points*.[28] Shall pay for 'em in due course (short of ready cash, and going to Bank in Inverness is a considerable adventure).

Less morning crystals in your Insights and more of "dark" thought (nuclear) this time; so your scope widens. Live with it and keep your notebook handy. Let me say again that the light from a breakthrough comes suddenly. And in any case, as G. says (so you'll guess I have read my own contribution): "*Doing* is magic". He certainly could hit the nail. The breakthrough is a vision of all the insights in a whole. Possibly in a pattern you never foresaw.

Sorry to have to say that I am somewhat disappointed by Idries Shah contribution. Rather schoolmasterly; and somehow his science parallels *seem* a trifle forced. And he does not give an instance of personal experience or commitment – (which I have laboured to do in order to get beyond theorising. I did not like doing it; but it's meant to be beyond the ever varying "I", as you know.) He refers often to the "higher level", but does not show its nature and reactions . . . I thought he was going to do it with the elephant-in-the-dark story, but he doesn't.

I like the Doctor's surgery very much. I am going to present my own doctor with *Point* when he comes again on Tuesday. Indeed he comes every Tuesday afternoon for a couple of hours, tea, and a dram or so. The only thing we forget to mention is our states of health, for he has fallen for our Zennish thought and talk gets very varied and pleasant. Somewhere (probably *The Atom* . . .) I have suggested that there are far more people who have had moments with their Second Self than we (blokes like you and me) wot of. I sometimes use my evasive Highland technique to find 'em. And so. So – carry on with the good work.

Rereading W. S. Robertson, I was once again completely interested. It had the forthrightness-and-no-humbug of your doctor (is Peter Llewellyn his real name? I don't expect so). And it is extremely pertinent at this point in human affairs. The early communists I knew were genuine idealists in whom

communism had simply taken the place of religion. For them
it worked. But now, what with, first, Hungary and then
Czechoslovakia, there's a vacuum, and no "religion" of any
kind to put into it. But they must have something, so they hang
on to Revolution itself. "Perpetual Revolution – for the Hell of
it", as one leader has it. But you know all about that. I am
merely trying to suggest how timely and apt and realistic and
responsible an article of faith like Robertson's is, dealing as it
does with an actual situation.

After that your friend Perlès. He got his moment of
breakthrough in *retrospection*. Really doesn't matter how it
comes so it comes. A personal experience, too. Then the short
story or parable. Very good, too. Suspect it's yours.

And then dear old Nakamura with his 3,000 insights at one
moment instead of that Zennish Nothingness. I enjoyed it, and
you kept his idiom just right. And I'll enjoy telling him that he
is unjust to Zen, which will probably produce a lengthy reply.
Extraordinary the arabesques the intellect can weave about a
moment of illumination. I can imagine some of the old Masters
saying "Have your moment and shut up." Wallop. I confess I
was at first contact rather repelled by the walloping stuff,
having grown beyond the wallopings we got at school from the
three-fingered strap. I'm not so sure about growing beyond
now! Possibly because we got what we knew we truly
deserved. . . . But enough of that. No idealism and false
sentiment no more. That's the ticket.

At which point Kate[29] came in to cook my Sunday lunch. Isa
and Kate spoil me a bit. At least that's the impression brother
John, his Wing-Commander son Alasdair, his wife and
daughter, who flew over from Singapore to spend a few days
with John and me, think. They left on Friday, so I am now
finding time to look at unacknowledged correspondence. My
hand o' write is bad, I know, and none the better because I'm
sitting in my armchair with an empty Van Huesen shirt box for
desk on my knee. The sun glitters on the western mountains. I
was going to *prove* an attitude just as Kate came in and to quote
you out of your own mouth: "In one sense 'mystical'
experience is normal experience lived by a man who is fully
awake." But I'll spare you. (Of course I like the quotation
muchly).

I hope to go north in 2 or 3 days time to Caithness to

celebrate my birthday. As for my health it's no worse than it's been, if not better, slightly. I touch wood.

Anyhow, your adventure with *Point* was real and remarkable. Amid your busy life – this is your witness. Cheers for you.

How is my dear Gene? And the boys?

Yours,

Neil

TO LORENA HART

MAY 1 1969

Dear Lorena,

My doctor calls once a week so I kept the gorgeosity until last night, when we opened proceedings with a solemn salute to an ancient malt, followed by tea in the appropriate manner, with attractive sandwiches, and then – the cake! It really was wonderful the way the malt came through and finally married the cake. And – well – you can't *explain* wonder, though we did our best. As the cake melted and caressed the palate the doctor rather thought it had its own malt though my palate suggested the grape (without the beaded bubbles and the winking, of course). I mean, this was a divinely serious matter. And if I used the word "married" above it was in a purely technical sense, for that is the word distillers use when referring to the way the elements in a cask of malt behave during the maturing process. And if you can't explain that wonder, no more can you explain the wonder of marriage. The one thing hangs as it were on the other and they get intoxicated simultaneously. But I shall not try to evoke our final conclusions, for they were very subtle indeed and got beyond all words, for true wonder leads to silence – or at least to "one more, just a small one", so that once again the malt may be sampled and the cake chewed, that delicious morsel. Besides the doctor had brought with him the English paper which his 15/16 daughter had got in an examination set by the Scottish Education Dept. the day before: four printed pages of it, and the first was taken up with a long quotation from a book called *Morning Tide* by Neil Gunn and the second page consisted of a list of questions, each of which carried a certain number of marks, about the matter in page one. Was it old Omar who wanted still another drink to "drown the memory of that impertinence"? Your husband may know, for I assume he is still "in it" (as they say in the Gaelic), though for all I hear of him he mightn't. We got beautiful weather in Malta and now brother John is fixing a fortnight in October (from 11th) with a lagoon, few or no bikinis, and a castle with a drawbridge and huge rooms which a Portuguese aristo has converted and turned into guest rooms. However, it's the cake that is still with me. And my doctor instructed me not to open it until he comes again. But he forgot to ask about my health.

Neil

TO STEWART CONN
DALCRAIG, KESSOCK, INVERNESS   1 FEBRUARY 1970

Dear Stewart,

I read parts 2 and 3 with great interest, after reading your letter which was a tonic, better than the doctor's, I may say (I'm recovering from a neuralgic bout). But first let me salute the scripts, the series of chords which comprise the production, as you so well put it. Indeed I certainly was – to express it another way – after my reading of the lot left with a feeling that all the varied incidents had been orchestrated into a unity. And that's what I had hardly hoped for. Altogether a remarkable piece of construction, sustained, unconsciously, by some spiritual reality which underlies the emotions, as you suggest. Indeed your letter is charged with searching suggestions of the sort, so much so that I'd better not begin on them; but I am delighted to see them, and from now on I shall take them for granted. And apart from Alex Reid I know no other in our country of whom I can say that. So when you say you are in doubt about this "deeper implication" being conveyed let me talk about it for a minute. (And do forgive the typing and a vagueness that signify the state of my rather dithery psychomatic condition – of no account). And that long word recalls my doctor who visits me regularly, for after some years he has told me that on reading a book of mine a second time he realises what he completely missed in the first reading. I'm afraid the dreadful truth is that all my books are permeated with this "thing", but when I was writing I ignored it and concentrated on the "story", doing my best to get that across. In other words – let me warn you – when this "thing" becomes part of your essence, it will in one way or another come through your writing. So don't try to bring it through, for then you'll ruin it or at least become vaguely boring to your reader. Accordingly when you say you are "in doubt" about having conveyed – you have succeeded from my viewpoint. Now I know that these apparently enigmatic remarks will be quite clear to you. Let me refer to a letter from Prof. F. R. Hart which came in yesterday. He is writing a lengthy book on Scottish novelists, their novels, and has, I'm afraid, a highly exaggerated idea of my novels. Did you meet him in Edinburgh a couple of years ago? From Virginia University. Anyhow, he writes "I have triumphed, I think, over a final obstacle in the Highland chapter – i.e., what I should say about a final group of three novels that I simply have never come to terms with, and have always been critically confused about (a healthy condition I know, but one that needn't last for ever). The novels *The Silver Bough*, *Well at the World's End* and *The Other Landscape*. I feel that they belong together, that they represent a kind of final development, that they have certain crucial things in common, that they represent a dissatisfaction with narrative, with story as such. The last of the three – the final novel – has always puzzled me more than any of the others, and I think I finally see why, and so now I am free to appreciate it: analysis as you know can liberate." And then he quotes me: "Man must forever move, like a liberator, through his own unconscious". In view of what *you* have found in *The Well* I thought that might interest you. For about all Enlightenment (in the Eastern sense) there is an ingredient called Delight. However, to return to the Professor. When I answer his letter I'll comment on his dissatisfaction with narrative, with story, and I may quote from your letter when you take an uncertain header into *The Well*. Let me mention again your "series of chords" or my orchestration of incidents, and wonder whether what you may be pulling off is a new kind of narrative or story as "such" on a higher or deeper level. Something for you to ponder, when, say, you are staring at the waves on a rainy Sabbath and thinking of another kind, or similar, *Off in a Boat* adventure. Anyway, the cuts, being in narrative, are all to the good in the sense that they keep the "story" going on the entertaining or physical level.

By the way, it may interest you to know that *The Well* was

produced in a library edition about a year ago by (wait for it if you are as nationalist as I) the London and Home Counties Branch of the Library Association! The actual publishers are Cedric Chivers Ltd. Portway, Bath, who are pleased with the results, they tell me, and are now informing all their libraries of the forthcoming radio dramatisation. So I was glad to get your interpretation of the Transmission note on the front of the script.[30] He (the manager) wants me to confirm that they'll get the programme in the south. The publishers don't deal through the trade commercially, but anyone can buy copies by applying direct.

One or two other remarks in your letter – but my replies will keep. They are all good anyhow, including the clarity of Neil Brown's voice. The light in the Spanish garden; the early morning clarity.

I'm very glad, in particular, to have your remarks about Alex Reid. I can see he has pulled through the dark wood. Now I'll write to him again.

Yes, we've a lot to talk about when you come.

Yours,

N.M.G.

TO STEWART CONN
DALCRAIG, KESSOCK, INVERNESS   2 MARCH, 1970

Dear Stewart,

I have tried these last two evenings to get in touch with you by telephone (using number given to me by Alex Reid) but failed, for I wanted to tell you how much impressed I was by your production of *The Well* and by the way all the characters played their parts. I have had a few telephone calls from people whose critical attitudes I respect and they are all highly pleased (. . .)

And now in *The Scotsman* I have just read a drily damning criticism by one Ian G. Ball, of whom I have never heard and know less, and I do hope you will not be unduly affected by it. Surely the primary duty of a critic is to tell you what the play is about, its inner meaning or intention. He admits a "quest theme"; but a quest for what? Plainly he hasn't a clue. How, then, can he assess Duncan McIntyre's performance? No wonder it appears "leisurely" to him, even "slack". This is pretty dreadful. For Duncan McIntyre *is* the storyteller, and being a Highlander concerned with a Highland story he talks with the pace of a Highlander. What the blazes did this Ball expect – someone to gabble on at a frantic pace? And when he at the beginning talks of the rare distinction of a full page in *The Radio Times*, the major effort of Stewart Conn, etc., surely that should have prepared him to expect at least something out of the ordinary, and try to pin it down, and *then* set about trying to destroy it, if that was what he felt like (. . .). I'm not going to say more about it. And I wouldn't even have said that (for I've never answered critics) were it not for my annoyance at any discouraging effect it might have on you in your valiant attempt to do something new. I can assure you it got over to the people that matter, as we say, and to the ordinary run of us it had a "something" that vaguely attracts, and they'll want to hear more.

I'm writing hurriedly to catch the post; but I did want to tell you that I was cheered on by you and your players, and some day I may go into details of the whole production. Meanwhile the best to you all.

Yours,

Neil

TO NAN SHEPHERD
DALCRAIG, KESSOCK, INVERNESS   24/3/70

My dear Nan,

(. . .). I have done a fair amount of reading on the "revelations" that follow a dose of certain drugs (Aldous Huxley was quite interesting about his experiences): not to mention other means of inducing a "transcendental" state; but they all remind me of the remark that a Hindu scholar-philosopher made (more years ago than I care to remember) in a weighty tome about achieving "samadhi" (revelation) to the effect that such drugs etc. induced what he described as "*false* samadhi*", which remark he relegated to a footnote; or take another way of looking at it: the more you experience the genuine light or enlightenment the more profoundly it irradiates even the flesh; whereas the more drugs the more diseased the flesh (and mind) becomes.

As to your remark about "the sheer shock of joy" that true

moments of revelation induce get fewer with age – that is more difficult, though I would venture this: that if you have cultivated the habit of enjoying the light, the light will be there in the dark moments. (. . .)
Yours,

Neil

TO NAN SHEPHERD
DALCRAIG, KESSOCK, INVERNESS   (1970)

Dear Nan,
Give that chap Simpson[31] what he wants. I've striven against publicity but it's no use. He kept after me about letters and only last night I found some old ones praising *me*, and I've just sent them off – too late I imagine – or hope.

After they'd studied my trigeminal facial neuralgia they daren't operate so I am back with nerves intact but feeling weaker than ever. So pills and capsules for me. "They" means the experts in Edinburgh Western Hospital. But I'll write you when I'm surer of the meaning of simple words.

In my search I came across some of your old letters. Marvellous – and you prove it by quotes. You're like a lovely day on the hills.
Yours,

Neil

TO LORENA HART
                                                      20/1/71

Dear Lorena,
I was feeling so weak that I couldn't bite my thumb – when in came your cake at afternoon tea-time and was bitten with ease, and re-bitten, until it swam around with delicious ease, bathed and caressed the uvula, and finally sank divinely on a breath of blessing. And I had been worrying because I hadn't heard from *him* over the season of goodwill! As if he mattered! Well, well. It's more sense I should and will be after having. He's probably got snared by litry succles (sic) or similar groups of worldly weasels. Once a weasel, after a dismissive glance of spitting disdain, popped into a hole in a drystone dyke, and haha thought I, as I gripped my walking stick and silently

approached the narrow orifice. But did he appear? He did – at another hole. Compared with the verbosity of an intellectual, even his glance was sharp as a needle and his teeth sharper. Can you tell me what I'm talking about, writing this on my knees, or should it be knee? This cold damp windless weather doesn't suit me at all, and I'm envious of the old boy (82) sailing his little yacht from England to the Bahamas – as you may have seen in your newspapers. Would you recommend a house on a Bahama island for me? If I don't get some such sunny climb (sic) I'll soon not be in it, I feel. If you can't translate "in it" ask your husband, to whom, should you happen to run into him, convey my regards. And the younger members of your household, I hope they are well and recovering happily from studentities.

My only other lady in foreign (or any other) parts who remembered me as you did was Akiko Nakamura, the charming daughter of a Japanese professor, who is at present doing something so fantastic and incredible in connection with my writings that I would hesitate even to mention it. Indeed it makes me laugh every time I think of it.

Gretta and Alec have been here. John will be coming soon. I rather think they have conspired to keep an eye on me! Joke! (. . .)

Love Neil
And thanks again.

TO STEWART CONN

31/8/71

Dear Stewart,
I have always been hoping to be well enough to acknowledge your letters, for I must say, at low intervals, they do cheer me on. I have been suffering for weeks from trigeminal facial neuralgia and from the physical dope one takes to kill the pain – or help kill it. No energy left. So all I can do is tell you about it and await your next interesting letter.

However, I can at least mention small points you raise.[32] *Fand*: I have always liked the name, and her shape and hair have often evoked my wife, particularly at some of those "rare moments" you mention. Peter, simply the name of a man with whom I've often spent late nights.[33] Yes, not just heightened perception, those "rare moments", but a "oneness" with things. What a pity you didn't manage along to Kessock. It is so much easier for me to talk from a comfortable chair. And I see you are one who does matter. Sometime I'll tell you just why. Just as I'll tell you the answer to your four questions on Fand: "is she passive, or demanding, or creative energy or merely rewarding?" She's all four.

But I mustn's begin because your searching questions go so deep. In them you open yourself. So write to me again and maybe the present medical treatment may help me – though I haven't great hope of that.

Thank you meanwhile for trying to cheer me on, by saying that at last the buzzing bees are Discovering me. Professor Hart (I hope you met him: another sane man) says much the same. But in the new copy of *Scottish International*[34] which has just come in, with its restricted news of literary events, present and future, there ain't no mention of the existence of such a bloke even on the lowest level. What do you think of this publication, supported by so much public cash? I must say I think it pretty dull.

However, it's of no real interest. There are the few individuals in our country who do matter and you're one of them.

Cheers,

Neil M.G.

TO NAOMI MITCHISON
DALCRAIG, KESSOCK, INVERNESS   18/12/71

Dear Naomi,
How pleasant to get your distinguished card, and inevitably to come on two lines that sum me up:

> Do not care, do not be anxious,
> Life goes as it must.

For they completely sum me up. I was in hospital in Edinburgh with a ferocious attack of facial neuralgia, but they did not operate, so back I came with some drugs. . . . Anyway, all that may explain why I cannot go across the water to buy some Xmas cards and send you the best one.

Also I must confess I told a critic who is doing an essay

on me for a book to be published next year[35] sometime, the story of your finding *Young Art and Old Hector* a trifle sentimental and how I duly decided to send them to a place called "The Green Isle". At that time you and I were about equally Leftish so it seemed a fair joke. I hope you still think so.

I send you my very warm greetings,

Neil

TO DAIRMID GUNN

DALCRAIG, KESSOCK, INVERNESS   12/6/72

My dear Dairmid,

I was interested in your letter about *The Scottish International* and Gifford's general attitude to my books[36] – and particularly in your assessment of his views on *The Silver Darlings*. When one gets a bit too intellectual, the stuff of story-telling and all that goes with it are lost. However, I am pleased with his general understanding and penetration. It's a long time since any Scots critic reached his standard and his generous reactions. Indeed it's the first time that my name ever appeared in that particular magazine – by which I'm afraid I have rarely been impressed.

But I have just had word of another kind of international appraisal of Scottish writing. I expect details may be in the press in a week or so. It appears the Scottish Arts Council have been diligently building up an International Fellowship from a Scottish viewpoint: namely, select the outstanding European or American novelist and confer the Fellowship upon him, with the gift of £1,000 and much looking after by Edinburgh University. But I need not go into details, apart from its title, "The Neil Gunn International Fellowship". To be repeated every 2 years.

I have agreed to accept this, but have now definitely turned down the Stirling University request to confer upon me an honorary degree. My health is just too uncertain for me to appear in public. My love to June.

Neil

This letter is included to show that even at the end of his life, when he had given up writing novels, an idea for one could still occur to Neil, and if the energy had been there he might well have pursued that idea despite his feeling that his kind of writing was no longer wanted. D. H. McNeill is the Duncan McNeill who was a close assosicate of Gunn in the SNP

TO D. H. MCNEILL
DALCRAIG   17/6/72

Dear Duncan,

There is a clarity of mind behind a clarity of exposition that reminds me of old days, and the pleasant times we had together. Alas, I have been suffering for a long time from a state of exhaustion, and my correspondence grows ever more uncertain; but I know you'll forgive me. Anyway, here you've done it again and I feel assured that one day your works will become a fountain head for those who have a natural liking for their old land.[37] This quality of work is never wasted. It endures. Indeed lately I had a sudden vision of a novel that started with the Picts up around my old home at Dunbeath, came down to King Brude's Court at Inverness, followed the Great Glen to the Western Sea and Iona, and from there to Europe, missing out, I'm afraid, whatever may have been going on in and around the London area!

But I'll never have the energy to start a book, I'm afraid . . .

My warm regards to all of you

Yours,

Neil

TO FRANCIS RUSSELL HART

(1972)

Seems you have forgotten me, but not I you, for your poems follow me about, turning up now in a precious drawer and again among stocks and shares, and even under a blotting pad, which suggests a writing intention. Its rhythms affect my writing as you may see. But enough. The simple truth is that I have long wanted to tell you about them, a greatness of attitude and elements of a listening distinction they generate in me. Indeed I had a clear mind about you going to your own country and finding time there, and at last producing wonders, and not always returning to your timid valley, but now and then taking off one-footed. For it's in you. John has spent much time with me, and Alex and Gretta are here for a few weeks now. They don't like the idea apparently of my being alone in an empty house, especially at night! Absurd, isn't it? Enough . . .

Neil

TO FRANCIS RUSSELL HART
DALCRAIG, KESSOCK, INVERNESS   14 SEPTEMBER 1972

Dear Rus,
  (. . .) But enough. On your part you might help understanding if you got your secretary to pick out "O" and "P" on your typewriter! And how is the Witch[38] herself? Speachless (sic) I watch her in her speachless ways. Dear me, that I should have to be silent. Fare thee both well. Neil.

Neil Gunn died on 15th January 1973.

NOTES

One: The Beginning Writer, 1925 to 1937

1   The date of this letter suggests that the book referred to was *While Rivers Run*. The remark about "percentage" was not persiflage; this was accepted as reward for supplying plot and advice.

2   The "poaching novel" must be *The Poaching at Grianaan*, serialised in *The Scots Magazine*, but never issued in book form. Gunn transformed it into a play, *The Ancient Fire*, produced in Glasgow during 1929.

3   *The Poaching at Grianaan*.

4   *The Ancient Fire*. Neil was right – it didn't "do them any good". The production was badly received.

5   *Under the Sun* was the provisional title for the novel published as *Morning Tide*.

6   First published in 1920, reissued in 1931.

7   The two-year-old book was *The Quarry Wood* (1928) – reissued by Canongate in 1987. Nan's second novel, *The Weatherhouse*, appeared in 1930.

8   Neil was right in his forebodings. Grieve was buying into a printing firm, and the "good thing" proved not to be a good thing at all.

9   In fact the reviews were not uniformly bad. Those in *The Spectator*, *The New Statesman* and *The Times Literary Supplement* were a mixture of praise and doubt, and as Gunn admitted in a letter to Grieve dated 16/6/32, "Hugh l'a Fausset was extraordinarily generous in *The Yorkshire Post* seeing right to the heart of what I was seeking for."

10   *The Albannach*, published in the same year as *The Lost Glen*.

11   The first paragraph of this letter sought Grieve's support for Pittendrigh Macgillivray in the Rectorial election at Edinburgh University.

12   By A. J. Cronin.

13   *The Scots Independent*, a monthly Nationalist paper issued by R. E. Muirhead's "Scottish Secretariat". In 1939 it became the official publication of the SNP.

14   *The Lost Glen*.

15 Gunn had defended Grieve when he was attacked in this journal, which disapproved of them both in consequence.

16 John Macnair Reid was an old friend of Neil's. Grieve wrote to both Gunn and Reid dissociating himself from the publisher's attack.

17 In support of Pittendrigh Macgillivray as Rectorial candidate. Macgillivray, then seventy-six years old, was a sculptor and poet, standing with Nationalist support.

18 An opposing candidate, Sir Ian Colquhoun.

19 Compton Mackenzie.

20 This refers to a resolution, passed at a Party Council meeting, which embodied the material later referred to as "the Four Points".

21 Robin MacEwen, born 1907, the eldest son of Sir Alexander and Lady MacEwen. He joined the National Party when he returned to Inverness from legal studies.

22 Angus Clarke was Chairman, Ian Gillies Hon. Secretary, and Dugald MacColl a Committee member of the National Party's London branch.

23 John W. M. Gunn, born in 1897, who became an Inspector of Schools.

24 Carl Brandt, of Brandt and Brandt, New York literary agents, had written Maurice asking for short stories for *The Saturday Evening Post*.

25 *Saturday Evening Post*, the highest paying journal of its day.

26 Jammet's was a famous Dublin restaurant, now vanished.

27 *Whisky and Scotland*, Routledge, 1935.

28 Toshon was Maurice's wife.

29 Nan's book of poems, published in 1934.

30 J. Keran McDowell had been a prominent member of the Scottish Party; he did not remain long in the SNP.

31 *Scots Quair: Sunset Song, Cloud Howe, Grey Granite.*

32 Published as *Whisky and Scotland*, Routledge, 1935.

33 Gunn was at the time employed by H.M. Customs and Excise, as officer attached to the Glen Mohr distillery, Inverness.

34 Carl Brandt.

35 *And No Quarter.*

36 Maurice's description, in *And No Quarter*, of Montrose's defeat of the army of the Covenant at the battle of Tippermuir (1644).

37 Gunn damaged an eye in an accident. This is the only mention of it that I know, in writing or in conversation.

38 Their Honours were not persuaded and Neil received no pension.

Two: The Full-Time Writer, 1937 to 1956

1 *Off in a Boat.*

2 Douglas Muhr.

3 I don't think this question was ironic.

NOTES

4   Margaret does not remember who wrote *American Testament* and I can't trace it.

5   Dr. Peter John Macleod and his wife Ena; John Macnair Reid and his wife Josephine.

6   *Son of Apple*, Chambers, 1947, the re-telling of an Irish Legend.

7   *Second Sight.*

8   Dr. Peter John Macleod had recently been appointed Medical Superintendent of the Miners' Rehabilitation Centre, Gleneagles. The "opus" was his initial report on the establishment.

9   *The Arts and Future of Scotland*, Saltire Society, 1942.

10   James Loch: *An Account of the Improvements on the Estate of Sutherland*, London, 1810.

11   This was Douglas Young's account of his resistance to war-time conscription, on the grounds that under the terms of the Treaty of Union no Government of the United Kingdom had a right to impose it on Scotland. He fought his case through a Conscientious Objectors' Tribunal, the Sheriff Court and the High Court.

12   John MacCormack writes in *The Flag in the Wind*, Gollancz, 1955: "I had no rancour against Douglas Young whom they had just elected and who, I was certain, would as deeply regret any personal attack on William Power as I did myself. But, in his election, decisions had been taken on matters of principle which far transcended personalities and, in effect, the party had gone back on its former resolution to give full support to the war effort. Although I was nominated as National Secretary, and, indeed, had been the only person nominated ever since 1929, I now felt I had no alternative but to decline the office and intimate my resignation from the Party . . ."

13   This refers to the filming of *The Silver Darlings*, by Karl Grüne.

14   Carradale is Naomi Mitchison's home in Argyll.

15   Tom, the main character in *The Serpent*, is also referred to as "the Philosopher."

16   Scottish Convention, a devolutionist movement set up by some of those who left the SNP with John MacCormick.

17   *The Green Isle of the Great Deep.*

18   It's worth comparing this account of the genesis of *The Green Isle* with the contrasting one given in letters to Alexander Reid (17 April, 1958) and Professor Nakamura (26 June, 1965).

19   The radical Labour politician Tom Johnston was an inspired choice for Secretary of State for Scotland in 1941. Gunn wrote to Ian Grimble in 1964: "In our time can you mention . . . any Highlander who has done a fraction of what Lowland Tom Johnston has done for the Highlands? I mean *done*."

20   A play sent by Douglas Muhr to Neil for comment.

21   Naomi was distressed about local poachers taking salmon from her river.

22 Bridie took Gunn to a meeting called to discuss the formation of a "Scottish Academy".

23 William Maclellan, Glasgow publisher.

24 J. D. Fergusson (1874–1961).

25 *The Drinking Well.*

26 Andrew Taylor Elder, whose brother Clarence Elder wrote the screenplay for *The Silver Darlings.*

27 About the typescript of *The Shadow.*

28 The name "Gene" took some getting used to.

29 *The Living Mountain* – not published until 1977.

30 The author referred to was James Barke.

31 *The Shadow.*

32 The film was never made.

33 Andrew Taylor Elder.

34 "Plastic Scots" and "Synthetic Scots" were terms used to describe the dense, literary Scots employed by MacDiarmid and others in their poetry, words being drawn from every age and dialect.

35 This refers to an article "Neil M. Gunn" written anonymously for *The Scots Review* by David MacEwen in February, 1948.

36 Published as *The Lost Chart.*

37 Gunn wrote an article for *Jabberwock* in compensation for refusing to stand as Rectorial candidate.

38 This letter refers to the typescript of a novel published as *Out of the Pit*, Faber, 1950.

39 A reference to the first page of Graham Greene's *The Heart of the Matter.*

40 Dr E. B. Strauss of Wimpole Street, who wrote to Gunn about *The Green Isle* and *The Shadow.*

41 *The Well at the World's End.*

42 Dr E. B. Strauss.

43 In *The Well at the World's End*, to which this whole letter refers.

44 The main character in *The Well*, after nearly drowning, has a "timeless" experience in a hotel in Zarauz, Spain.

45 Robin MacEwen.

46 This concerns a passage in *Bloodhunt* about Sandy's experiences in Italy, which is unexplained and for which there is no clear provenance.

47 Daisy's niece. Jean Robertson wrote a children's book, *Little Nickum.*

48 A reference to *Zen in the Art of Archery* by Eugen Herrigel.

49 The new book was *180 Games for One Player*, Phoenix House, 1954, and the game was "Teams": "Imagine you are selecting a football team of composers to play a football team of generals, or . . ."

50 Neil had entered the Northern Infirmary, Inverness, for investigations into possible causes of his low blood count.

51 *The Other Landscape.*

52 The two "new" magazines were *The London Magazine* (edited by John Lehmann) and *Encounter* (edited by Stephen Spender and Irving Kristol).
53 *A Strange Woman's Daughter*, Chambers, 1954.
54 Daisy had asked me to suggest a book for Neil to write. A tentative approach about "wise insights" eventually led to *The Atom of Delight*.
55 *Holiday*.
56 The short story was *Half-Light*, which appeared in *Hidden Doors*, 1929, and again in *The White Hour*, 1950.
57 John Raymond, a reviewer in, I think, *The New Statesman and Nation*.
58 P. D. Ouspensky published in 1950 (Routledge) his account of the teaching of G. I. Gurdjieff, *In Search of the Miraculous*.
59 *The Other Landscape*.

Three: After Literature, 1957 to 1963

1 *The Atom of Delight*.
2 Gunn and Maurice Walsh had become involved in a film project: a story about whisky. Gunn invented the plot and wrote an outline script. Maurice was to produce a novel based on the story. The film was never made, the novel was never written.
3 The Picks moved from Wester Ross to London in October 1956, and were there for a year.
4 "1957" was probably a typing error for "1959", but I have placed it where Neil's date places it. The book referred to must be *The Zen Teaching of Huang Po*, translated by John Blofeld, published by Rider in 1958. See Note 6 for confirmation.
5 This refers to a series of articles Neil contributed to *The Saltire Review* while Reid was editor, beginning with "The Heron's Legs", No. 15, Summer 1958.
6 By Richard Rumbold, *Encounter*, January 1959.
7 Lord Bracken.
8 *Five Men and a Swan*, London, 1957.
9 "The Theme is Man" *Scotland's Magazine*, July, 1958.
10 *Anarchy*, published by Freedom Press, Whitechapel, of which Prince Peter Kropotkin was a founder.
11 Arco, 1959. Published in U.S.A. (and filmed) as *The Last Valley*.
12 *Room at the Top*, for which Neil Paterson wrote the screenplay.
13 Gunn acted in an advisory capacity regarding choice of site for the Tormore Distillery.
14 Norman MacCaig.
15 Forsyth Hardy, of "Films of Scotland".
16 This refers to an unpublished play, *The Waters of Truth*, originally intended for radio, then withdrawn and rewritten.

17 A novella, *Thomas Warren's Profession*. It was never published.
18 "The Hunter and the Circle: Neil Gunn's Fiction of Violence", *Studies in Scottish Literature*, 1 (1963–4).
19 The operations were for prostate trouble.
20 Nan is the protagonist in *The Shadow*. The first part of the book takes the form of letters from Nan to her lover Ranald.
21 The title was in fact *The Narrow Place*, Faber, 1943.
22 It was favourite delusion of Neil's that he did not keep letters.
23 This refers to a dinner held in Edinburgh to celebrate Neil's 70th birthday. It was organised by Neil Paterson and George Bruce.
24 A historical adventure novel, *The Strange Forest*: written, rewritten, scrapped.
25 In 1962 P. H. Butter published a short critical study of Muir in the Oliver & Boyd "Writers and Critics" Series. His biography of Muir followed in 1966 and the Selected Letters in 1974. Neil wrote to Butter enclosing a Muir letter in 1962, yet in 1963 says he hasn't "looked properly" for them. The fact is, he found one letter in a copy of *The Silver Bough*, and only much later felt the obligation to search further.
26 Rob Donn Mackay's wry references to his wife Janet are applied humorously to Daisy.
27 G. I. Gurdjieff. "Ousp." later in this letter refers to P. D. Ouspensky.
28 Chrystine Frew in fact had a job. Neil never fully appreciated the inconvenience caused to Chrystine by being always "on call".
29 The second of Herrigel's "small books" was *The Method of Zen*, Routledge, 1960.
30 He is referring to David Craig, who wrote an adverse review of *The Atom of Delight* in *The Cambridge Review*, February 23, 1957.

Four: Alone, 1963 to 1973

1 *Studies in Scottish Literature*, January 1964: "The Work of David Lindsay". Lindsay was the author of *A Voyage to Arcturus* (1920).
2 Eamon de Valera.
3 Hart had referred in his letter to:
Gillespie. J. McDougall Hay (1881–1919). 1914.
The House With The Green Shutters. George Douglas Brown (1869–1902). 1901.
Gillian the Dreamer. Neil Munro (1864–1930). 1899.
4 *The Supreme Doctrine*. Hubert Benoit. Routledge, 1955.
5 *Scott and Scotland*. Edwin Muir. Routledge, 1936.
6 I was preparing a book on David Lindsay, much of the material eventually being used in *The Strange Genius of David Lindsay*, John Baker, 1970.
7 Secretary of State for Scotland.

NOTES

8 Rus and Lorena Hart paid their first visit to Kessock in Summer, 1965.

9 *The Grey Coast.*

10 The schoolmaster in *The Grey Coast* was deep in inner struggle with the atmospheric melancholy of "Fiona Macleod" (the pen-name of William Sharp, 1855–1905). So, at one time, was Neil himself.

11 Nakamura had sent for comment the English text of a book he was writing on Gunn's work.

12 Alastair Reid, born 1921, poet and translator, correspondent for *The New Yorker.*

13 Neil had written to further Hart's application for a Guggenheim Fellowship.

14 Jon Schueler, born 1916 in Milwaukee, lived and painted in Mallaig from 1970 to 1975, and between 1975 and '81 divided his time between Scotland and New York.

15 Jane Duncan, the novelist, lived only a few miles from Neil. They did meet, on Hart's next visit.

16 This is no more than the truth.

17 Ernest Haeckel (1834–1919). *Die Welträtsel* was translated into English as *The Riddle of the Universe.* Haeckel was convinced he had proved there was no God, no immortality, and no free will.

18 *Highland Pack*, Faber, 1949.

19 "Centreing", in *Zen Flesh, Zen Bones*, Ed. Paul Reps, Tuttle, 1957.

20 Neil went for a sightseeing trip in Majorca with the poet Alastair Reid. Douglas Day and Elizabeth were friends of Reid's and known to Francis Hart.

21 *The Silver Bough.*

22 An article which appeared in *Radio Times.*

23 "The Hunter and the Circle: Neil Gunn's Fiction of Violence", *Studies in Scottish Literature*, 1 (1963–4).

24 The loyal lady who cycled several miles each day to keep house for Neil.

25 The poem was "Strange Seraph", later included in *Stoats in the Sunlight*, Hutchinson, 1968.

26 Guggenheim Award.

27 Alex, youngest of the Gunn family, headmaster of Castletown School, Caithness, and his wife Gretta.

28 *Point* was a little review produced during 1968–9. Neil contributed to two issues. His comments here refer to articles in No. 4: Idries Shah on "The Teaching Story"; a look at the state of the medical profession by "Peter Llewellyn"; W. S. Robertson on "The Future of Man in a Technological World"; Alfred Perlès "In Retrospect"; and Professor Nakamura about Neil's article "Light" which had appeared in the third issue. Gunn's piece in No. 4 dealt with Gurdjieff's teaching.

29 Kate Sharpe had looked after the Gunn's garden. When Isobel could no longer carry on as housekeeper, Kate took her place. No one could have been kinder or more attentive.

30   The Transmission Note meant that *The Well at the World's End*, adapted by Alexander Reid and produced by Stewart Conn, would be heard throughout the United Kingdom.

31   Stanley Simpson, Assistant Keeper of Manuscripts in the National Library of Scotland, was preparing a Neil Gunn Exhibition to mark the 8oth birthday.

32   About *The Well at the World's End*.

33   Dr. Peter John Macleod.

34   *Scottish International Review*, edited by Robert Tait. Note 36 shows that this journal was not so indifferent to the work of Neil Gunn as he imagined.

35   F. R. Hart's essay in *Neil M. Gunn: The Man and the Writer*, Blackwoods, 1973. Edited by Alexander Scott and Douglas Gifford.

36   Douglas Gifford, at that time Lecturer in English at the University of Strathclyde, wrote on "Neil M. Gunn's Fiction of Delight" in *Scottish International Review* for May 1972.

37   Duncan McNeill's book was *The Historical Scottish Constitution*, Edinburgh, 1971.

38   "The Witch" was Neil's nickname for Lorena Hart.

INDEX

Indexing is confined to the main text and does not cover
Introduction and Notes.

INDEX

WORKS BY NEIL GUNN